THE
URSULA FRANKLIN
READER

PACIFISM AS A MAP

URSULA M. FRANKLIN

INTRODUCTION BY
MICHELLE SWENARCHUK

BETWEEN THE LINES
TORONTO

The Ursula Franklin Reader

© 2006 by Ursula M. Franklin
First published in 2006 by
Between the Lines
720 Bathurst Street, Suite #404
Toronto, Ontario M5S 2R4 Canada
1-800-718-7201

Additional relevant papers, articles, and talks by Ursula Franklin, as well as more comprehensive biographies and publication lists, will be made available on the Internet. Please visit the publisher's website at **www.btlbooks.com** for further details on the Franklin Web Collection.

Library and Archives Canada Cataloguing in Publication

Franklin, Ursula M., 1921–
The Ursula Franklin reader : pacifism as a map / Ursula Franklin ; with an introduction by Michelle Swenarchuk.

Includes bibliographical references.
ISBN 1-897071-18-3

1. Peace. 2. Technology—Social aspects. 3. Social justice. 4. Feminism. I. Title.

JZ5538.F72 2006   303.6'6   C2006-904617-4

Cover and text design by Jennifer Tiberio
Author photo: courtesy of Ursula M. Franklin
Printed in Canada
Second Printing December 2006
Between the Lines gratefully acknowledges assistance for its publishing activities from the Canada Council for the Arts, the Ontario Arts Council, the Government of Ontario through the Ontario Book Publishers Tax Credit program and through the Ontario Book Initiative, and the Government of Canada through the Book Publishing Industry Development Program.

To Fred Franklin, my husband, friend, and companion for more than half a century

CONTENTS

ACKNOWLEDGEMENTS

IT IS AN IMPOSSIBLE task for me to acknowledge fully the individual help, support, and stimulation that enabled me to carry out the work assembled in this *Reader*. Each talk or essay represents my response to a specific situation, and I am forever indebted to all who were part of providing context and occasion: those who have agreed, and—even more so—those who have disagreed with my thoughts.

Yet, without the ongoing love and support of my family, my religious community, and my sisters of the women's movement, I would not have had the strength and endurance to engage in this work for so long.

The actual creation of this *Reader* could not have taken place without my friendship with and the co-operation of Michelle Swenarchuk. Our wide-ranging conversations, our discussions and examinations of individual papers, and our decisions on their selection and ordering shaped this book. Michelle's refusal to be acknowledged as a co-author should not distract from her central role in the development of this collection. To her go my profound thanks.

The massive undertaking of turning a stack of reprints into an editorially and technically defensible manuscript was flawlessly accomplished by my friend Ruth Pincoe. I cannot think of anyone who could have brought the same degree of professional skill and personal empathy to the task, and I am most grateful for her help and advice.

Kathy Chung, on whose assistance and computer savvy I have depended for many years, became an integral part of the project and contributed much to it.

The Three Guineas Foundation provided financial help for the preparation of the electronic manuscript, which we acknowledge gratefully.

And then there is Massey College. Its hospitality and openness continue to sustain me, and the generosity and friendship of Master John Fraser and Elizabeth MacCallum have made my work both possible and enjoyable. The publication of this *Reader* is an expression of my indebtedness to the ideals of Massey College.

INTRODUCTION
BY MICHELLE SWENARCHUK

U RSULA FRANKLIN'S words and actions have long been an inspiration to me, and several years ago I began to urge her to publish a collection of her non-scientific social writings. I believe they contain a wealth of knowledge and a loving perspective on the human and natural condition of our time. Our collaboration on this project, an honour and joy for me, has included many wide-ranging discussions of interlinked themes: peace, Quaker faith practice, women's equality, nature, government, citizen's activism, and education.

Early in our discussions Ursula identified the basis of her perspective—her pacifism and her belief that only a commitment to ethical means and non-violence in all human actions can address the problems of society and lead to a peaceful, just, and egalitarian world. From her I learned of the Quaker focus on the importance of individual conscience-based decision-making, not only when it comes to the choices of daily living, but also in acting on the most momentous national and global issues. Quakers do not apply dogmatic instruction to life's questions. Rather, they use a collective process of prayer, study, and discernment to guide their decisions.

In current political discourse the idea of pacifism tends to be either dismissed as naïve and unrealistic or disparaged as connoting appeasement and passivity in the face of force. There is no reflection in mainstream political thinking of the Quaker idea that commitment to a moral means of problem-solving provides a creative impetus to resourceful, non-violent, and humane political policy, even though, as Ursula makes plain, the dysfunctionality of violence as a means of problem-solving stares us in the face.

When Ursula asked me to provide an introduction to the articles "to make the argument for the practice of pacifism," I came to realize that her viewpoint has a second foundation—her feminism, born of her life experience as a woman and as a scientist, engineer, university professor, mother, and member of an embracing women's community. In all of these spheres she has asked questions that are different than those asked by her male colleagues, and she has provided different answers using language and imagery from women's experience.

Ursula considers that her pacifism provides an alternative map to view the world, illuminating the present and past in a different light. My role here is to highlight the salient features of her map: particular aspects of the human and natural world that become visible when viewed from this perspective. I believe that on this map and with her words and actions we can recognize a creative pathway towards a more hopeful world.

PACIFISM

For members of the Religious Society of Friends (Quakers), pacifism is not a prescription for "passive-ism."★

Given that they reject participation in war and the use of violence for any cause, Quakers are committed to an active engagement in the pursuit of peace and justice. They consider that non-violent means provide "a positive witness to the better way."

Friends have made important contributions to scholarship regarding war, the causes of war, and approaches to peacemaking. Over time their refusal to participate in war helped lead to the modern right of conscientious objection to military service. More recently they have attempted to extend the principle of conscien-

---

★ For a brief overview of pacifist and Quaker belief and action, see p. 36.

tious objection to the "conscription" of tax revenues for military preparations in times of peace. Quakers are committed to acting in the world, believing that "wherever life places us, there will be needs and openings for our witness, and what is required of each of us is to be present where we are." Friends believe they have an obligation to refuse to co-operate with laws that violate God's laws and to do so openly. Such actions may encourage others to follow their convictions and support them in their struggles. Friends are advised to "live adventurously."

Ursula Franklin's pacifism is grounded in her experience of war, her Quakerism, and her life experience as a woman.

Ursula was born in Germany and spent time as a prisoner in the Nazi concentration camps, where she lost members of her family. She experienced the bombing of Berlin and later the Soviet occupation. She became convinced of the "dysfunctionality" of war, that "war doesn't work, even for the winner." Ever since, she has been engaged in the pursuit of peace and justice, contributing to Quaker thought and practice on war and peacemaking, and on the understanding of violence.

Ursula has described the benefits she gains from her membership in the Religious Society of Friends, including her joy in attending the Meetings for Worship, when the collective silence is "enormously powerful." Someone may rise and speak "about something that had just entered *your* mind. It's an uncanny thing, but the strength of collective silence is probably one of the most powerful spiritual forces." She describes Quaker thought as "a theology of peace that focuses primarily on discernment of means— a discernment that is equally valid for decisions on small and on large issues. In such a theology of peace one would find the practical manifestation of the prophetic voice; such focus on means would expose the common roots of many issues that are now addressed separately."

She has asked, "If I were accused of being a Quaker, would there be enough evidence to convict me?" and in response emphasizes that the only evidence of her Quaker faith is the testimony of daily decisions and personal conduct. Applying these standards in everyday life in the modern technological world is "really very, very difficult."

The goal of Ursula Franklin's practice of pacifism is to contribute to building a society of peace, justice, and equality for all, "step by bloody small step."

To Ursula, peace "is not so much the absence of war but the presence of justice. Peace is the absence of fear," whether it is a fear of "the knock on the door at night," a fear of hunger, unemployment, or danger to our children, or a lack of "a public sphere in which the issues of peace and justice will have priority over the issues of profit." Peace is "a commitment to the future," and it is a necessity for an equal society in which people have control over much of their own lives.

Peace requires justice, the "hinge of a civilized society," and can only be achieved through "the persistent application of social truth and justice and the strong and intelligent application of love." Both peace and justice are indivisible. They must be equally attainable for one's loved ones and allies and for "all the people you can't stand." The unconstrained practice of justice is the price of peace. "If you want peace, work for justice." Ursula envisions a peaceful world in which society would work somewhat like a potluck supper, where everyone can contribute their work and care and in turn receive nourishment and friendship. For a successful potluck supper, a diversity of offerings is essential.

Throughout her lifetime, in keeping with the Quaker practice to "be present where you are," Ursula Franklin has been engaged in scholarship and activism to build peace.

Ursula Franklin's writings reflect her continuous reassessment of changes in the world from the Second World War through the Cold War and post–Cold War periods to the aftermath of September 11, 2001. She has addressed the arms race, the potential for global destruction from nuclear war, and the borderless threat of nuclear fallout. Working with the Voice of Women, she made proposals to Parliament regarding Canadian foreign policy. She worked to bridge the gap between East and West during the Cold War through delegations to meet women of the Soviet Union and North Vietnam. She participated in Friends' successful efforts to send medical supplies to all parts of Vietnam during the war there. She also contributed to Friends' unsuccessful attempts to persuade the Government of Canada to permit the redirection of the military portion of personal income tax to non-military uses. As a physicist she refused to participate in classified research and all work that could be adapted to warfare. Sharing her scientific knowledge with non-specialists, Ursula helped them to become "citizen scientists" engaged in public policy discussions. Later she identified the dangers of a new form of oppression—globalized economics and privatization—and in recent years has addressed the world of terrorist attacks and the U.S. military response.

We live in a world of violence and war, in which governments and corporations use fear and threats as a "universal management tool," and the protection of citizens is used as a false rationale for war and arms production.

It is important to be clear on how we got here: we live in a mess created by men who did not listen. Their push for winning, meanness, and leanness led to the current strife-torn, degraded world; the means were wrong. In the long run the immoral does not work.

Although the "dysfunctionality" of systems of war and threat stares us in the face, we continue to live in a world dominated by violence. There was no peace dividend at the end of the Cold War, the legacies of which include a world awash in arms, senseless divisions between peoples, too few non-military perspectives on problem-solving, and the financing of costly high-technology military projects in lieu of productive public spending for human needs. Changes to military technology have resulted in wars that are endless and borderless, and are financed by a permanent conscription of public revenues.

As a physicist, Ursula Franklin has been acutely aware of the devastating potential of nuclear war, "the ultimate threat." She has illustrated the irrational destructiveness of the arms race by comparing it to neighbours who deal with conflict by acquiring dogs for protection, eventually destroying their peaceful neighbourhood through vicious dogs and "the accumulation of dog shit."

Ursula contends that violence is not a normal human reaction; rather, it represents an unacceptable response to change. To understand the prevalence of violence in our time, she reflects on atmospheric weather patterns, picturing two massive fronts moving towards each other, creating a zone of turbulence. What is occurring at this time is social change of immense proportions, with a transition from the Old Order, the hierarchical society of "institutionalized dominance," to a new non-hierarchical world of equality for all, where women will be free to choose their own paths, and diversity is normal and cherished. We are living in the turbulent zone between these two historical fronts.

There is no way to peace; peace is the way. Effective citizen initiatives to build peace and justice must be based on non-violence and must emphasize ethical means in order to reconcile conflicting claims and needs and achieve society's goals.

Non-violence is both a kind of power and a response to power. For citizen peace-builders to speak truth to power, our lives must speak truth through what we do and what we refuse to do. We need to focus on the means of private and public activity: "to not be overly impressed with grandiose schemes and big promises, but rather to fathom the ways and means in which such promises and projects are to be realized." To make the moral dimensions of political decisions more evident, we must ask who may suffer or bear the burden of a decision, and who will benefit.

Prescriptions for non-violent solutions to problems are more difficult than are prescriptions for violence because non-violent responses arise out of a specific context. In our technologically prescriptive world, there is structural resistance to allowing people to use their judgment to find creative solutions. However, there can be "a vast variety of acceptable, appropriate [non-violent] means" to solve problems.

In considering how religious people can contribute to peace-building, Ursula urges them to recognize that the modern world is very different from the Galilee of biblical times. In the nuclear age we need to hear relevant arguments regarding the futility of war and the inappropriateness of threat as national policy.

There is a need to transcend the imperial approach to world problems and apply a co-operative, tolerant, confederated model.

Women can inspire movement in this direction through their feminist, non-hierarchical practices: co-operation, respect, and "horizontal solidarity." These practices cross all boundaries and are based essentially on an understanding of means, and on the conviction that some means, including violence, are not acceptable.

The U.S. response to the attacks of September 11—identifying an enemy, increasing violence, and failing to look for the root causes of the attacks— cannot provide security; security can only come from understanding and discernment, leading to changes that ensure justice for all peoples.

Abhorring the violence of the September 11 attacks, Ursula suggests that an alternative approach in considering these events is to see them as a "social earthquake." Such an interpretation would have led to a search for the root causes of the events, and for actions to address them, rather than to a "war on terror." We need to get rid of the notion of "the enemy," because the notion of the enemy prevents us from understanding the cause of a social earthquake, much like the belief in "angry gods" once blocked an understanding of natural earthquakes. The notion of the enemy makes constructive learning almost impossible. Ursula questions whether those involved in violent attacks would have chosen other ways of acting on their convictions if they had seen real prospects for peace and justice in their countries.

A Canadian response to war and terrorism must be legal, peace-building, open, and reciprocal, based on a recognition that security can come only from justice and that there needs to be justice for all. Canada must pay attention to the means of its response, recognizing the dysfunctionality of the threat system. The South African liberation strategy, in which the oppressed themselves made requests for economic sanctions, is an important model.

A time of quiet can help encourage people to think. Or a day of mourning can offer an opportunity for us to shut out the trivia and look at our resources, remembering that children are more important than faster airplanes, and that most religions hold that all people matter equally.

WOMEN AND FEMINISM

As a pacifist, Ursula believes that the struggles for women's rights and against all forms of militarism are two sides of the same coin: the promise of a livable future.

Early feminists understood the relationship between militarism and the oppression of women. Many were pacifists. As well, men who opposed war often supported the struggle for women's rights. Militarism is "the prototype of structures of threat and violence," an "internally consistent system of attitudes, perceptions, and actions which, when stripped of all its extraneous verbiage, simply says 'Do what I tell you—or else.'" This system requires both military and political branches, and "operates with our money and without our consent." Women who want a "why not?" world of respect and diversity should object to this threat system.

Women's achievement of full equality with men is a necessity for the just and peaceful society that pacifists seek.

As a friend and colleague, scientist, teacher and mentor, supporter of women students, concerned citizen, and advisor to women in many spheres, Ursula Franklin has contributed to the advancement of women. She finds in feminist thought and practice a pathway to a peaceful, egalitarian society.

Feminism is a movement to fundamentally change the relations between people to a more caring, egalitarian, and non-hierarchical pattern. It is not a mere employment agency for women.

Feminism promotes a social and human environment that is fundamentally different from that of patriarchy. It promotes a different way for people to live together; it is not merely patriarchy "delivered by lady patriarchs." The values and potentials of non-hierarchical structures hold the key to equality and peace.

In contrast to patriarchy, a feminist, egalitarian society would be peaceful, non-hierarchical, focused on co-operation and community-building, and equally caring towards all people.

Peace is the "absolute necessity for an equal society" in which people can live without fear and have substantial control of their lives. All human beings would matter equally, so that the well-being of "fat cats and small people" would receive equal weight in decision-making. In contrast, in today's world the greatest equality across the earth is "the equality of destruction," in which everyone becomes a victim.

A feminist society would be non-hierarchical, unlike a church, army, or university, in which people are ranked in relation to each other and rank is equated with competence "in spite of the obvious practical experience to the contrary." The prevalence of rank is a relic of hierarchical societies. Ursula believes that rank and competition in male hierarchies is one of the reasons that men tend to have so few close friendships compared to women. Feminists favour a co-operative, non-competitive approach to tasks because women's traditional realm—the family, farm, school—teaches that rank is pointless in dealing with many problems, such as the distress of a sick child.

The nurturing of community is essential to an equal society.

Ursula assures women moving into traditionally male work environments that it is not wrong to be kind, and to want to overcome loneliness, as community can do. Solidarity in the workplace among all women (scientists, engineers, librarians, secretaries, cleaners), regardless of their tasks, contributes to friendships and security. Women need to remember and stress the positive aspects of women's culture, achievements, and resourcefulness to create "a non-judgmental, non-pressured support of all women by all women," preventing assimilation of women into traditional male structures and mentalities.

The evolution of society from patriarchy to a non-violent egalitarian society is a long process, like the Reformation, and is catalyzed by ideas.

The long process of breaking down the medieval Old Order was inspired by new ideas of justice, equity, and human worth, and the belief that knowledge and competence can be accessible to all. The Old Order rests on a restriction of knowledge, and women's struggle for access to education is part of the struggle against the Old Order.

   If we practise equality by judging people as human beings, without labelling them, we will be able to achieve an equality of caring long before achieving political or material equality. We must particularly avoid the label of "enemy," because the presence of an enemy means that government will divert resources from social spending to building armies and prisons. We may deeply disagree with people, but must not assume that these people are unchangeable.

To achieve a peaceful egalitarian society, women in power need to retain feminist values and not act like lady patriarchs. Women's achievements must come about through means that ensure that others do not suffer from the success of women in power.

The conduct of women in power must be guided and informed by the collective experience of women when they were powerless and experiencing exclusion and discrimination. There is nothing inherently wrong with women and their values, including values that may make professional advancement difficult. There is nothing wrong with caring, with not being aggressive and pushy, and expressing the hurt of being treated unjustly. It is insensitivity and lack of justice and respect, not women's response to them, that are wrong. Women moving into senior positions must not to be hypnotized by rank, but rather continue to extend care and friendship to all women, both those who are promoted and those who are not.

Women have particular contributions to make to scholarship, science, and technology, beginning with their choice of questions to study. What matters most in research is the initial question.

Feminists have underlined that research is a social process of study and experimentation. It is evaluated through discourse and leads to knowledge and understanding, which are usually accepted by society as fact. To Ursula, scholarly activities are like a sandbox controlled by boys, who occasionally allow girls to participate and use the boys' toys (or tools). For women to ask different questions and to want the opportunity to study these questions is to assert, "We want to use our own tools. Maybe we want to make our own facts. Maybe we even want to have our own sandbox." This challenge to legitimize different methodologies and vetting processes can be threatening to established hierarchies.

Feminist inquiries have done much to identify the limitations of the scientific method and its reductionism. Reductionist inquiries produce information that cannot simply be transferred to a broader context.

Researchers using the scientific method rely on experimentation to discover laws of nature. This process entails the separation of knowledge from experience, neglecting context and emphasizing abstraction. Feminists have identified the dual myth of the objectivity and neutrality of science. Any experimental design that reduces the number of variables being studied requires a priori selections based on the researchers' views of the nature of the question. It is here that social and political biases enter the supposedly objective research designs. Most "scientific experiments" are insufficient for the study of complex problems, such as ecological pollution and the pursuit of international peace.

Women's attention to context in problem-solving will provide the basis for important contributions to many fields.

Ursula Franklin agrees with psychologist, educator, and writer Carol Gilligan that context is more important to women than to men in developing problem-solving strategies. Women prefer to look at a problem from a broad perspective. They prefer to consider the context and arrive at a strategy that is appropriate rather than universal, whether in small daily situations or large research designs. Ursula considers that this is "the seedbed from which women, through their historical and collective experience, will make major contributions to many fields."

Building on the work of other feminists, including Margaret Benston, Ursula Franklin proposes that women should develop new scientific methodologies and study questions that have been ignored.

Chemist and activist Margaret Lowe Benston advocated moving towards a "different science," keeping in mind the limitations of reductionism. We need different approaches to study complex systems that can't be broken up for study without changing their nature. Ursula proposes that women pursue new methodologies in the study of environmental assessments, the social impacts of technologies, and "machine demography," and she calls for a much-needed feminist critique of technology, with guidelines for the design of non-hierarchical systems.

The creative scholarship of feminists is often constrained by funding systems.

Few scholars in Canada can decide on research projects on their own terms, because funding is dependent on granting agencies or the priorities of the private sector. The process for funding may eliminate many of the most creative ideas. When good ideas, particularly from the young, are stifled because of a concern that they won't be funded, the system constitutes a "mortgage on the imagination." Ursula Franklin imagines an annual conference on unfundable research, "an invitation to imagine," to dream about the kinds of ideas that are now abandoned as unfundable.

For women in the engineering profession and in the universities there must be change, since "What doesn't work for women, doesn't work. Period."

Observing the reluctance of some women engineering students to oppose the "filthy, sexist, and racist rag" published by the engineering society during her time as faculty member, Ursula realized how difficult it is for women to retain their values when entering the professions. They are like immigrants to a new country, people who work hard to establish themselves in a new milieu, and tend not to vote against the government that admitted them. But also like immigrants, women may feel a malaise caused by breaking ties with their natural community. One should not expect these women to lead demands for change, but change may be fostered by clarity, by building a feminist understanding of the nature of power and technology, and through community-building.

Ursula does not want to see women engineers become work-hardened, losing their "acute sensitivity" to discrimination or injustice. Changes needed for both women and men come most often through women's efforts. For years, if women left a meeting because of their child-care responsibilities, the chairman would groan; men now do the same and receive approval, without appreciating how much struggle was required to gain that privilege.

Improving the status of women in universities requires long-term vigilance; salary gaps have recurred when new women have been hired at the low end of the scale and new men at the top. Ursula proposes that a multifaceted index of the well-being of women on campus be developed to evaluate their status and ensure long-term equality.

Ursula Franklin understands the hesitation that some young women feel about entering the environment of science and engineering.

The life and work of Margaret Benston illustrate that it is possible to seamlessly integrate scholarship, feminism, union support, and environmental concern. Young women need to understand the feminist critique of scientific methodologies and the political and social structures of science and technology.

Students may want to choose supervisors for their human qualities, consider studying neglected fields, and remember the joy of science. Women need to keep their feminist perspective—an important layer of the coat of inner security for protection from the chilly climate—and ally with other women.

Finally, Ursula suggests that when the male science world is tough and "you find yourself surrounded by jerks, take an anthropological approach." Record the experience by taking field notes like an explorer who's come upon a strange tribe. "Observe the tribe's customs and attitudes with keen detachment and consider publishing your field observations.... I know from experience that the exercise works."

Recognizing the prevalence of violence in the world, Ursula Franklin considers that Marc Lepine's murder of fourteen women engineering students in Montreal in 1989 must be understood in light of how his action was related to the broader world.

In her statement of commemoration for the young women murdered by Marc Lepine, Ursula asserts that this terrible event cannot simply be treated as the action of a madman. Rather, we need to understand what contributed to Lepine's state of mind, and also face the painful fact that the murdered women were abandoned by the male students. We need to examine what it takes in our society for individuals or groups to be abandoned, and what constitutes the opposite, solidarity. Who is your sister, what does it take to abandon her—a shot, a joke? We need to look at how Lepine's action is related to the social climate around us, since "*how* people get mad, *how* that escalation from prejudice to hate, to violence, occurs, what and who is hated, and how it is expressed, are not unrelated to the world around us." We need to consider the availability of weapons, the prevalence of prejudices, the effects of jokes and harassment, and the necessity of respecting others (here, women in an engineering faculty); we need to consider their right to be there on their own terms, not just on sufferance, not just as if they were silently fulfilling requirements.

The massacre led to a quantum leap in reality recognition regarding the situation of women in engineering faculties across Canada, the recognition that "it could have happened at *our* university, in *my* class." The tragedy provided the first opportunity to name what was going on in engineering faculties by speaking about the chilly climate, bias, sexism, misogyny, and patriarchy. For Ursula Franklin the solution lies not in changing women to harden them, but in achieving systemic change in the profession, involving "the elders of the engineering tribes" and other male engineers. Some progress was made in the five years after Lepine's murders, but much remained to be done to make engineering fit for women, and not women fit for engineering.

TECHNOLOGY

Ursula Franklin's pacifist perspective on technology begins by asking different questions and promoting different values.

She answers the very first question—what is technology?—by defining it as practice or "how things are done around here," a definition grounded not in technical considerations but in the commonality of human activities. Recognizing that "every tool shapes the task," Ursula asks very basic questions of modern technology: what does it do, what does it prevent us from doing, what don't we do anymore because of it? Flying is now common; home-made meals and clothes are not. Her focus on human impacts leads her to identify the underside of technological change as well as its helpfulness.

Pointing out that technologies are value-laden, Ursula does not examine them according to the usual orthodoxy of how machines influence speed and efficiency. Rather, she asks how machines affect the well-being of all people and the pursuit of peace and social justice. Her point of departure is that the central priority of technology should be respect and love for people, but she perceives that most modern industrial practices are "anti-people."

Ursula's religious belief leads her to examine how technologies restructure time, space, and society over periods of time longer than a human lifetime. She believes we have long-term obligations as stewards of nature and of human society.

The religious viewpoint, with a sense of history and time greater than a human lifetime, recognizes the enormous scope of change brought about by modern technologies.

Modern technologies are creating momentous structural changes in society, of a depth and magnitude comparable to that of the Reformation. Many of these changes are irreversible. The ability to separate message from messenger (telephone, e-mail, fax), sound from its source (recordings), and images from objects, together with the speed with which information is transferred, has created a new reality. The manipulation of space and time has been one of the driving forces behind new and complex ways of doing things. Modern practices increasingly interpose things between people, and with new electronic technologies has come a blurring of concepts of space and local community. There is a loss of synchronicity in some of humanity's most long-standing actions, a resulting "great longing for meaning and fellowship out there."

Ursula Franklin identifies the prescriptive, controlling quality of modern industrial technologies.

Ursula's pacifism led her to ask what could be learned about the political and social structure of a society from the nature of its technology. Her experimental observation that the capacity to cast very large bronzes in early China depended on a highly structured, centrally controlled production process led to her theoretical distinction between "prescriptive" and "holistic" technologies.

Holistic technologies are artisanal. They are used by workers who know each step of the production process and can exercise judgment, experiment, and constantly gain in knowledge.

In contrast, prescriptive technologies are externally planned, organized, and controlled. Such systems divide the production process into tightly specified parts. The work and the workers are regimented, with no room for judgment or experimentation. Prescriptive technologies have proliferated since the Industrial Revolution, ranging from the mass production of manufactured goods to nuclear projects, surveillance, and machine-based warfare. They are now so widespread that we are all "enmeshed" in technology-based systems of dominance and control.

Modern technologies have transformed warfare. Relying heavily on technical support, professional and permanent armed forces can be maintained merely through conscription of citizens' taxes.

Technologies have changed the nature of war, both as an activity and as a social institution. Mechanized and automated systems now constitute the core of standing armies, requiring not conscription of people but rather national conscription of people's resources through taxation. Military technologies and their development are capital-intensive, so governments must maintain the phantom of an external enemy, one that is cunning and threatening. They require "truly ingenious and heroic technologies" to justify the long-term high level of military spending. This creation of "the enemy" seriously impedes conflict resolution and reconciliation. War is no longer set apart in time, territory, and participants. Rather, the boundary between military and civilian activities has disappeared. Civilians are targets in war, and nuclear fallout presents a danger to everyone, everywhere.

Technologies provide the means for "war transposed into another key": economic oppression.

At the end of the Cold War, war preparations were not dismantled. Instead of initiating a peace dividend, governments utilized the technologies of control and conquest for global competition on the "battlefields" of the faceless markets of electronic transactions. This war includes the familiar characteristics of propaganda, loss of lives, displaced peoples, and environmental destruction. The newly designated enemy consists of ordinary people—all those who build community and believe that people and nature are sources of meaning, and not merely commodities. This is a "market-driven war on the common good."

The use of modern technological systems often means that people are involuntarily included or excluded from their uses and impacts, with no right to choose.

Technologies are a means not only for achieving certain goals, but also for preventing other goals from being reached. People are involuntarily included in the effects of war and pollution, and are involuntarily excluded from many significant decisions about the design of projects. Entry into buildings can be denied by electronic barriers, and modern, technological workplaces can deny satisfying, holistic work experience. Someone who needs a hug gets an answering machine instead.

Modern planning, a prerequisite for the deployment of modern technologies, including war and other megaprojects, often involves an unethical and undemocratic process.

Modern planning approaches evolved during the Industrial Revolution, and they now entail planners' increasing control of social processes. Such planning locks people ("the plannees"), usually without their consent, into "schemes of power and dominance that do not work for any length of time, not even for the powerful. Yet these long-term directions are difficult to change. The goal of industrial planning is the maximization of profit. Its practitioners treat society as a mechanism. However, society is not a mechanism, but an organism in which all parts exist by and for each other, and interact.

A more ethical planning mode would recognize that the means used to achieve a goal are as important as the goal itself. It would look for consensus on what means—such as killing people, whether by force, oppression, or deprivation—are unacceptable. Such planning, which would serve not to maximize gain, but to minimize disaster, requires the consent of the plannees.

The world is increasingly mediated by technologies that affect all social institutions, government processes, law-making, work, schools, universities, and scientific research, creating new threats to human rights.

Prescriptive administrative, legal, and social control techniques are as important as prescriptive production in the technological world. Together they form a global system in which changes in one part affect other parts of the system. The expansion of mechanisms of control and surveillance over workers and citizens poses a challenge to human rights and to law, whose purpose is the expansion of liberty. Bar codes and the Internet allow many possibilities for surveillance, because users can be flagged. While technological innovations seldom eliminate poverty and oppression, they may change who is subjected to oppression and poverty. Prescriptive innovations seldom bring new freedoms, but frequently introduce more constraints.

Fewer people can now see the consequences of their work in order to take responsibility for it, because some technologies impede or disguise the opportunity for individual decision-making. For example, no one will admit responsibility for the construction of nuclear weapons; although each weapon is planned and built deliberately, what we have is the apparent "virgin birth" of nuclear weapons.

Women's equality, values, abilities, and contributions to society are often undercut by modern technologies.

A feminist critical perspective on technology is based on a common commitment to the values of a feminist non-hierarchical society. Today's technological structures were grafted onto the existing patriarchal control patterns and have extended them. Feminists need to understand prescriptive technologies to recognize their effects on feminist goals, but we still lack a systematic feminist view of technology.

In the technological domain, tasks are prescribed by hierarchical command structures and are fragmented, scheduled, and carried out regardless of context. This milieu values efficiency, innovation, and maximum gain, but has little use for experience, loyalty, or continuity. In contrast, in the domain of women tasks arise from a specific context; they are flexible, unpredictable, integrated, and full of the unexpected. This milieu employs and values loyalty, community, experience, inventiveness, and a diversity of skills to achieve its primary goal of minimizing disaster.

Because most modern technologies are prescriptive and make things predictable, they cut out women's strengths—building on experience, listening, mediating, coping—strengths that women as an underclass have used together with mutual reliance and a sharing of feelings and knowledge. Women tend to get their strength not from power, but from people.

Having concluded that most technologies are designed to be anti-people, Ursula Franklin identifies strategies for surviving in and coping with the technological world.

First, in the tradition of the Quaker emphasis on clarity, she calls for a greater depth of scholarship on technology.

Society lacks an in-depth study and understanding of technology; there is a "stunning discrepancy" between the depth of scholarship regarding language (what people say) and technologies (what people do and how they do it). We need "an anatomy of technology"—its syntax, structure, signs, and symbolic components—and, given the "machine population explosion," a machine demography. If we don't have adequate analytic tools to understand and foresee the impacts of a technology, we are less able to make good public decisions. There is also a pressing need to have an ecological understanding of technological societies.

Second, citizens need to be engaged in the systems design phase of technologies.

Complex technological systems are difficult to change once they are implemented. It is essential then, that systems be designed not only for what they can do, but also for what they should not do. For example, data banks must be designed to exclude access to personal data. More information about the feelings and preferences of the users should go into the design. Valuable parts of some technologies can be decoupled from negative parts.

We are stuck with some technologies because "we don't question enough." An obvious example is nuclear reactors—"a hare-brained way of producing electricity, an afterthought, an attempt to redeem an unredeemable military technology never designed to be a source of electricity." Corporations must bear (not share) the costs when deploying a new technology, providing not mere verbal assurances but substantial monetary deposits to compensate for possible harms, because "moral deposits go bankrupt before the financial deposit."

Third, women need to retain their values.

Women, the underclass of history, survive through their relationships to other people, not through power, and even in the technological world women need to retain these values. Women need non-competitive teaching and learning opportunities; if given such openings, they freely give and receive knowledge and experience, and "break the stranglehold of exclusion and power" of science and technology. Women can become citizen-scientists and guardians who ensure that technologies are not misused.

Fourth, when we examine science and technology we need to focus on the means proposed for achieving society's goals.

Society's means must be based on conscience and must be ethically robust. Rather than focusing on grandiose technological schemes and big promises, we need to pay attention to how the schemes will be realized, who will suffer and bear the costs, and who will benefit. Outcomes are often not controllable or predictable, but a focus on means would facilitate negotiations between planners and plannees. It would return to principles of life and community and would honour religious perspectives that acknowledge "a moral obligation towards 'the other.'"

NATURE AND ECOLOGY

Nature, an ever-present and independent reality, has a veto that must be respected.

The concept of "environment" has become increasingly techno-centred and ego-centred, focused on the man-made milieu, and has deflected human awareness away from nature. Similarly, the term "sustainable development" as currently used seems to imply that with just a little tinkering, "making things a little less lethal," we can continue to ignore our abuse of nature.

The inordinate sense of power that humans have gained from technology leads modern societies to assume wrongly that everything on the planet is just infrastructure that can be rearranged. This misjudgment ignores the reality that nature, "that powerful partner in whose house we all live," is an independent force, more powerful than humans, which will retaliate when abused. Our governments should be as concerned with the power of nature as they are with powerful nation-states, such as the United States, and should recognize that nature, like the United States, can retaliate.

Given that nature's diversity is vast, and all parts interlink, reductionist studies—investigating a small number of variables at a time—have limited value in advancing our understanding of nature. Scientists need to utilize additional sources of knowledge, including evidence from faith communities and peoples who live close to nature (First Nations, farmers, fishers). There is a "pressing need to reach an ecological understanding of societies, particularly technological societies," and to "study human societies as part of nature—subject to the same laws and considerations, governed by the same ultimate dependence of one on all."

Chinese cosmology emphasizes nature's processes of time and change, and encompasses human and non-human dynamics in an "ecology of all things."

Unlike Western thought, Chinese cosmology lacks the concept of a moment of creation of the universe, or of movement towards a permanent, unchanging state of paradise. Rather, it is centred on a belief in cyclical rhythm changes in which the universe, heaven, and earth are one unit moving through phases of change. Human affairs, individual and collective, are also subject to such cycles; to arrive at a right way of doing things (the Confucian idea of "li") we need to understand how various cycles fit together, while respecting the dynamics of cyclical change.

Even monarchs were seen as part of nature, and their conduct was required to be especially correct, grounded in right processes of governing. Citizens had an obligation to respond when this standard was not met, and dynasties were overthrown periodically because of inappropriate conduct, which was seen not as personal sin but as failure to work in harmony with the cosmos.

These ideas of harmony and balance are also reflected in many sectors of Chinese life, including medicine. A physician would seek to balance the functions of body and mind, the dark and light (yin and yang), to restore health.

This idea of an "ecology of all things," of the need to blend human actions with processes of nature, stands as an elucidating contrast to the Western compulsion to exploit nature for advantage and gain, a pattern that has resulted in a host of environmental problems.

Energy is "the technological society's currency" and should be managed like money: "Don't waste it. Spend it intelligently. Don't fall for schemes of con men. Don't buy on credit if you don't know what you are doing. Don't leave bad debts."

Having chaired the Science Council of Canada report *Canada as a Conserver Society*, Ursula Franklin observed that although citizens and professional bodies (architects, builders, engineers) implemented many of the Council's recommendations for conservation, institutions that should have changed their regulations, spending, and research priorities were "totally immovable." The failure to change tax and price structures to provide incentives to conservation means that in many circumstances wasteful consumption is still financially rewarded. In contrast, a green energy policy would recognize the significant atmospheric pollution from radioactive contaminants, and would reject nuclear plants, megaprojects, and export-oriented energy developments that result in social and environmental damage, like the ones affecting Native peoples in James Bay. It would consider who gains from, and who pays the costs of, energy proposals.

Most important is to bring people back into the picture—not just as consumers, but as participants, as experimenters and monitors of energy use, reversing the usual policy assumption that people are the source of problems and technologies the answer. The underlying barrier to a green energy policy is the nature of contemporary government, which no longer mediates power for the benefit of all.

Our environment includes the soundscape, which is increasingly polluted and appropriated for profit, eliminating silence—an invaluable wellspring of human spontaneity and spiritual strength.

The soundscape has been profoundly changed by modern technologies that permit the separation of sound from its source, so that what was once ephemeral and time-limited can now be permanent (the sound recording). The soundscape is part of the commons, but it is increasingly manipulated and appropriated for private purposes, whether through the imposition of unnecessary announcements or background sounds (Muzak in elevators; the "athletic equivalent of the Hallelujah chorus" when a goal is scored in a sports arena.)

Silence is not merely the absence of sound, but an enabling condition that allows "unprogrammed and unprogrammable events" to occur, including contemplation, meditation, and worship. As Quakers have long known, collective silence is a powerful spiritual force: "Allowing openness to the unplannable, to the unplanned, is the core of the strength of silence and the core of our sanity, not only individually, but collectively." However, silence is increasingly "taken out of common availability without much fuss and civic bother." We should insist on a human right to silence, and reintroduce that right by providing spaces for silence in buildings and moments of silence before and after meetings and common meals.

CITIZENS AND GOVERNMENT

There is no substitute for good government.

This insight, expressed in concise and deceptively simple language, is profound in its implications and its contrast to prevailing government ideology. While Canadian governments are progressively ceding decision-making to private corporations and promoting unregulated commerce, Ursula reiterates that many human and societal needs can only be met by governmental action placing a priority on serving citizens' needs for peace, equality, justice, and protection of nature. Profit-oriented corporations cannot be expected to fulfil the function of government—making decisions for the benefit of all citizens.

In keeping with the Quaker precept to "be present where you are," Ursula has been a leader in citizens' advocacy for good government locally and nationally. She has participated as a member of a religious community, as a woman with the Voice of Women, and as a Toronto citizen and scientist regarding urban development and local government.

The Canadian government no longer governs from a distinctly Canadian standpoint. Rather, we have a government that uses its administrative tools to promote globalization and profit-making.

With this change in standpoint, Canadians have lost the institution of government. Canadians are not governed but are administered on behalf of powers that do not have a Canadian standpoint and are not concerned about the well-being of Canadians. In the service of corporate profit-making, enforceable laws are replaced by "frameworks," and citizens (who have rights) are simply termed "stakeholders." Government consultations with citizens are not genuine exercises to gather wisdom; rather, officials "get ear plugs and danger pay" and are sent out to listen to citizens for two days. Government has become a kind of colonial administration.

Far from having good government, we have puppet governments that function like those of the Nazi-occupied countries of Europe, serving the Empire of the Marketeers.

With no peace dividend after the end of the Cold War, and no end to global conflicts, the mechanism of war was "transposed into another key," from a military conflict to a commercial conflict, an economic war for economic dominance. In this war the enemy is "us," those people and organizations that oppose the corporate takeover of global institutions. The goal of the new war is control of "the commons," and its strategy is called "privatization," dismantling the public sphere and occupying its territory, opening up for profit all those activities previously thought of as commons—culture, health care, and education.

We are occupied by the marketeers, as Nazi-dominated European countries were occupied during World War II; and like these countries we have a puppet government in place to run the country for the benefit of the occupiers. We need to respond by protecting our families and communities, and seeking strategies of resistance to this occupation. We need to work for global justice "not because it gives us a competitive edge, but because it is right."

Ursula Franklin envisions the world as a circular cake, with wedge-shaped pieces representing countries— "the local." Horizontal movements—travel and new electronic technologies—have increased to such an extent that local and national identities and liberties are crumbling.

Every person lives in a particular locality, which includes language, schools, Members of Parliament, and law courts. These are the "vertical slices" of the global cake, which allow social mobility within the slice, and proximity for contact and exchange. Horizontal movements—exchange and interaction beyond the local, vertical slice, including trade, travel, and modern science and technologies, are like horizontal slices into the wedge. The application of modern science-based technologies has led to a quantum leap in horizontal versus vertical activities, causing the vertical slices to begin to crumble.

National entities have been unable or unwilling to regulate the intrusion of the horizontal into the vertical, causing fragmentation of work and production. While law and liberty are embedded in the vertical slice, the most crucial social and political activities are now taking place along horizontal segments. In every country, rulers are divided between verticalists (closer to the interests of a particular slice) and horizontalists (closer to the interests of a layer that cuts across slices). Globally, governments have divested themselves of the powers to regulate new activities through international trade agreements, and have dismantled laws controlling corporate activities.

This is the central problem of developing a contemporary approach to liberty, technology, and hope. Technologies exist that could address impediments to liberty, but these same technologies also disempower society, at times quite intentionally.

Citizens have legitimate expectations of good government.

In law there is a principle of procedure called the Doctrine of Legitimate Expectations, which holds that when two parties enter into an agreement there is a legitimate expectation that each party will act in accordance with the agreement, not contrary to it. While the principle does not confer substantive legal rights, it is a norm that also applies in political practice.

Citizens are entitled to have legitimate expectations of government, including reciprocity between those who govern and those who are governed. In return for complying with law, citizens are entitled to "peace, order, and good government," which means having a government that does not harm the many for the benefit of the few.

We need to articulate our expectations, including the need for action to be taken against lawlessness at the top of society, not just at the bottom. Further, an insistence on clarity and on access to information other than the irrelevant content of most newspapers will show us how many problems are rooted in the denial of any standpoint other than profit. This realization fosters solidarity, the recognition that many problems are not private or individual; nor can solutions be. A demand for integrity in politics, meaning both honesty and undivided wholeness, will ensure that we move forward towards government that does not sacrifice the welfare of the country and earth for the benefit of the few.

Citizen politics, unlike party politics, does not seek to change government, but to improve it by watchfulness, oversight, and advice.

Ursula Franklin has participated in local and national citizens' activist groups throughout her life. For her, a city is both a habitat for people and a resource base for business. For citizen politics the central need is good government; there is a premise that governance and a public sphere are legitimate and necessary, and that citizens have a right to be heard. Ursula has noted that too often citizens can only agitate regarding the details of government, while it is the very principle of government that is in question.

The task for the future is to build knowledge and understanding among and between citizens and scientists to the extent that the distinction between the two groups vanishes and both become citizen-scientists.

The modern scientific method has allowed an accelerated expansion of knowledge and the formulation of laws of general application. This process has emphasized abstract thought, the separation of knowledge from experience, and a lack of attention to specific context. The unquestioning trust in scientific findings has resulted in lessening people's confidence in their own senses while enhancing the status of the scientific "expert."

In the modern technological society, where citizen interventions frequently involve scientific and technical issues, citizen participation in political decisions has been impeded by the separation of knowledge from experience, and a reliance on "insider" expertise.

However, Ursula has frequently worked with citizen groups regarding problems of pollution, energy, the arms race, and research priorities. She has found that given a non-competitive atmosphere, her neighbours, mostly women, had no difficulty understanding complex scientific subjects, sharing knowledge, and utilizing it. What is needed to foster citizen-scientists is their own strong motivation, confidence in their common sense, and a non-competitive atmosphere that ensures that all participants are both teachers and learners. In Ursula's experience, this is not difficult to achieve.

EDUCATION

Good public schools are the price of peace in the community.

Historically, schools are social institutions whose purpose is to acculturate the young into their community and prepare them for life, so that they become "personally happy and publicly useful." This important role leads to constant "political and social pushing and pulling around schools," reflecting conflicts in society regarding what skills are necessary and who should have the opportunity to acquire them. Today's schools also function as the hub of community, so that good public schools are essential to the evolution of Canada's complex multicultural and multiracial society. This is where "Mr. Chang and Mrs. Fitzgibbon" and parents and students from many cultures meet, learn from each other, and learn to co-operate. We need to thoroughly understand and appreciate the role of public education in community well-being.

Diversity of social institutions is essential for a viable society.

"A school is not a business, a bank is not a church, and a church is not an entertainment centre." To be part of a diverse social ecology, schools need to retain their identity as places that support a balanced interplay between information and understanding, and that foster critical thought rather than "monocultures of the mind." They must not become like business enterprises.

Education involves a subversive element: teaching students critical thought, historical perspectives, and solid reasoning.

What constitutes a proper educational process has long been contested. The debates are actually about two approaches. The first approach, drawn from the collective wisdom of agricultural societies, is a growth model that sees students as seedlings requiring nurturing, with attention paid to the particular needs of each. This model recognizes that different plants (and peoples) have particular ways of growth and maturation.

The second approach, now much in vogue, regards education as a production process, "schools as sausage factories" producing "marketable outputs"—students with skills in demand by business. Such a system emphasizes elements of quality control, testing, evaluation, and market research.

There are two basic reasons to oppose the business model: first, for its underlying assumptions—education should be a sound process rather than product-generating—and, second, because a production model places economic values of efficiency and outcome above all other values.

Students need adult teachers with integrity, people they can trust. The expanded use of computers in classrooms has greatly changed teaching and learning, and entails diverse costs.

The purpose of the classroom is to convey not only spelling and calculation but also the less visible social skills and attitudes developed in classroom learning. Mechanical teaching aids, especially computerized teaching, may deprive students of both facets. While using computers to take care of repetitive tasks such as square roots and division can free time, teachers may be robbing students of the satisfaction of showing public mastery of a skill, an innovative approach, or an elegant solution "achieved with a minimum of fuss and maximum of ingenuity—elegant in its frugality, approach, architecture." Students may also experience less of the social learning of a classroom: working in groups, co-operative learning, listening, and developing tolerance, anger management, and inventiveness. Teaching methods must ensure the continuance of opportunities for social learning.

Education in science, mathematics, and technology is incomplete unless it includes discussion of context, because knowledge is not objective or value-free.

Scientists are regarded as "socially sanctioned fact makers" (Ruth Hubbard), and they have been predominantly male, white, and schooled in a common way. In contrast, the knowledge gained by women who cook and nurse and garden has not achieved "the status of fact." Citizens need to know the context of science to understand why some problems are of interest and therefore fundable at a particular time.

Citizens need to be competent enough to understand technology well, and they need to "read between the lines," understanding the social and polit-

ical context of present technologies, in order to write different texts for the future.

We don't yet have "technological literacy," public knowledge of math, science, and technology beyond the "gee-whiz" level. Following the example of media literacy, we need to ask how to bring such technological literacy to students using texts and primers without imposing undisclosed values that may be detrimental to the students' own cultures and values. The textbooks and technical aids they use may have results beyond the conveying of technical information. Accepting a gift of computers for educational institutions reminds us of how Bibles were once used to teach literacy. They were used to teach more than reading, and at times resulted in the loss of indigenous cultures. We need to clarify the social assumptions embedded in the design of teaching, and reaffirm the primacy of young people's needs to ensure that the joy of learning is not stifled by the efficiency of teaching.

Ursula Franklin deeply values the great enterprise of universities, the quest for knowledge and understanding.

The university is where, throughout history, society's ruling classes have transferred to youth the attitudes, skills, and knowledge necessary for their futures and for the improvement of their communities. One of the important advances of the twentieth century was the increase in accessible public post-secondary education. Universities became major national resources pursuing knowledge as a common good.

Today we can no longer assume that Canadian universities will continue to operate in the public interest, given changes in research activities and funding.

Wartime showed governments the potential of focused research for achieving national objectives. Research came to dominate the nature and functions of universities, and their economic and political roles. Meanwhile, a gradual shift to reliance on research for funding occurred. This trend has influenced hiring, promotion, teaching, and curriculum, which in turn has affected what research topics are fundable. In the 1970s, with a shift from operating grants based on a scholar's merit to strategic or thematic grants, the subject matter of research became a factor in funding. Increasingly, decisions about research choices were made not by scholarly peers, but by funders.

This development has changed not only the questions being researched, but also the beneficiaries of scientific findings. Now it is commonly the funders themselves who benefit, or the concerns of interest to them. Many important subjects, such as peace and social justice, remain unexamined. While business schools have proliferated, peace research has not. Investments in higher education have created industrial-scale production sites, assembly plants for economically useful knowledge, and training facilities for skilled practitioners. They are profitable plants, but they are not universities or colleges. Institutional decision-making has been removed from those who are concerned with teaching and research stewardship for the future.

To maintain the universities' role in the public sphere requires clarity about these changes, and solidarity with the many other public institutions similarly affected. Further, public engagement at the political level is needed to protect the boundaries between the private and public domains.

The prevalence of teachings about equity and environmental protection in universities and schools has its roots in the scholarship and activism of feminist teachers.

In Canada the activism of women and women's organizations for equity, protection of nature, and peace have been interlinked historically. Beginning in the 1960s, the Voice of Women challenged barriers to women's equality while simultaneously identifying the health effects of radioactive fallout, the problems of nuclear waste storage, and the staggering costs and unreliability of nuclear power. Ursula Franklin, Rosalie Bertell, and Helen Caldicott brought this knowledge to Canadian women, who then became teachers in their own communities. Although their insights were belittled by nuclear proponents, the women were proven right, both politically and scientifically. Their teachings identify the need for a different ordering of social and political priorities based on the fundamental tenet that all living things in the biosphere are entitled to equal care and concern.

THE SIGNPOSTS ON URSULA FRANKLIN'S PACIFIST MAP OF THE WORLD

In Ursula Franklin's practice of pacifism, compassion is a central value, augmented by respect for the human need for friendship and community. A bedrock feature is the inescapable obligation of both individuals and nations to seek to do what is right, not only in setting goals but also in choosing the means to achieve those goals, while rejecting the use of force and the creation of inequalities.

Ursula spotlights the need for honesty and clarity in considering the actual reality of people's lives—including the most disadvantaged—and in identifying how public policy, technologies, and the accelerating speed of social change impact upon them. Her own clarity flows from the melding of her intellectual breadth and her deep humanitarian concerns.

Ursula's map does not include borders separating thought from action; a seamless connection characterizes her practice of pacifism. She has actively participated in the many different spheres to which she could make a contribution as advisor, mentor, and friend. Her life exemplifies Friends' dictum to "live adventurously."

A BRIEF OVERVIEW OF PACIFIST AND QUAKER BELIEF AND ACTION

PACIFIST BELIEFS have roots in several millennia of teachings on the rejection of violence, beginning with the Buddhist and Jaina religions in ancient India, twenty-five hundred years ago, and the beliefs of Christian communities of the first century CE. The commandment to love one another and the Sermon on the Mount have inspired numerous strands of Christian pacifist attitudes from medieval times to the present, including the communities of Waldenses in twelfth-century France and Taborites in fifteenth-century Bohemia. Pacifist communities founded in the sixteenth century include the Anabaptists of Zurich, the Hutterites in Moravia, and the Mennonites in northern Holland. Opposition to war, the rejection of the use of force, and the refusal to participate in military service have been central tenets for all these groups and communities.

The Religious Society of Friends (commonly referred to as either Quakers or Friends) arose in northern England in the 1650s, and spread from the Midlands through the British Isles and then across to the British colonies in America and the West Indies. Rejecting the pomp and authoritarianism of the Church of England, Quaker faith is founded on a belief in the Inner Light of individual conscience, which allows each person to understand God and to achieve redemption without priestly intervention. The Quaker Peace Testimony, formulated and first published in 1660, states that war and violence, and participation in these pursuits, conflict with the teachings of Christ. "Christ bids us love our enemies, government bids us kill them." For this reason, early Friends refused to participate in all aspects of war and war preparations.

Through the following three centuries, rather than relying on a dogma of unvarying rules of conduct, Friends have concentrated on discerning the appropriate and faith-based responses to the present conditions they encounter in each epoch and country. Recurrent themes in Quaker history include distinguishing between militarism and the use of constraint for maintenance of civil order, deciding which forms of alternative service are acceptable to pacifists in times of war, and complying with taxation obligations while declining to pay the portion of taxes assigned to war and armaments. They have described military training as "a flagrant wrong to the young." Many Quakers have endured heavy fines, imprisonment, and physical injury for their refusal to participate in war and military service.

The commitment of Friends to peace has been accompanied by active engagement in peace-building and the pursuit of social justice on both local and international levels. Important milestones in the history of Quaker belief and political involvement include the founding of the state of Pennsylvania in 1682 and the governing of that state for seventy years; the refusal to participate in the American Revolutionary War; the development of nineteenth-century British peace societies; antislavery and penal reform activities; opposition to the colonial campaigns of the Victorian era; advocacy for creative dispute settlement in order to prevent war; and citizen diplomacy, which continues to this time. In 1947 the American Friends Service Committee and the British Friends Service Council were awarded the Nobel Peace Prize for their relief work accomplished during and after the First and Second World Wars.

PRELUDE

THE IDEA OF organizing my papers and talks for publication
has been difficult for me, in spite of the urging and tangible
help of friends and colleagues.

The basic difficulty arose from my resistance to a thematic
grouping or ordering of the papers, which would separate, say,
women's issues from peace issues, questions of teaching and learning from considerations of equality, the need to care for the environment from citizens' responsibility or the advancement of
human rights.

I have had to ask myself if there is a common thread connect-
ing my different activities. Do my various explorations have
something tangible in common, even if I did not articulate this
thread clearly?

Certainly, at the root of most of my activities has been my life-
long interest in structures, in the arrangement and interplay of the
parts within a whole. Yet, while structural preoccupations might
have influenced my approach to issues, it is only in retrospect, on
looking back over almost four decades, that I can see how I have
tried to wrestle with just one fundamental question: "How can
one live and work as a pacifist in the here and now and help to
structure a society in which oppression, violence, and wars would
diminish and co-operation, equality, and justice would rise?"

It is this realization of the common root of much of my work
that eventually informed my conversations, my friendship, and my

collaboration with Michelle Swenarchuk and led to the present ordering of the papers in this collection and the book's subtitle, "Pacifism as a Map."

Maps have fascinated me for a long time, and they have helped me in various ways. Maps are fruits of the mind, grown in a soil that contains observations and imagination, things known and figments of sometimes fanciful extrapolations. Maps represent purposeful endeavours: they are meant to be useful, to assist the traveller and bridge the gap between the known and the as yet unknown; they are testaments of collective knowledge and insight.

Maps are a unique way of translating the three-dimensional reality of "the world" into symbolic, two-dimensional tracings of particular features of this reality. Mapmakers select the features to be mapped, keeping in mind the needs of the traveller and the available information. However, mapmakers make yet another, often far more fundamental, choice. They have to select their method of projection.

Representing three-dimensional features on a two-dimensional plane inevitably involves visual distortions, regardless of the conventions of plotting and reading a map. Each method of projection literally represents a different point of view, and there is more involved here than spherical geometry and its techniques of representation.

Maps help the mind to order information and impressions. The type of projection, the choice of representation, can heighten or hide the recognition of structural relationships among the features depicted on a map.

At school, children are frequently instructed using maps that show their native land in the centre of the page. Other students may come "from away"—the impression of how far away appears to depend a great deal on the customary maps and their particular method of projection.

I will never forget the feeling of intense joy I experienced as a child when I saw for the first time a polar projection of the Northern Hemisphere. To help me, my father took a globe from the bookshelf, unscrewed the mounting bracket, and showed me how I could look down on the world as if I were standing on top of the North Pole. The funny-looking polar map suddenly made sense, and the world looked quite different from what I had seen when twirling the mounted globe around its axis.

Today I recognize that the joy I felt then reflected the sense of a new freedom. I had seen that I could choose how to look at things, explore differences, benefit from different perspectives, use different maps to understand more, and gain greater comprehension.

Increasingly I found the maps of conventional wisdom inadequate for my travels. The social maps of gain and success were unhelpful for charting co-operation, compassion, and friendship; the peaks of understanding, the fault lines of historical misdeeds, the short distances between "them" and "us," and our vast common ground required a different representation.

Knowing that respect and reciprocity, understanding and common care are part of real life, practised by real people in the here and now, I became unwilling and unable to orient my life according to national maps depicting the realms of "them" and "us," of good guys and bad guys, of winning, defeating, and being defeated; in short, all those maps drawn up for travel towards private gain and personal advancement.

It was the maps of pacifism and feminism, which were not drawn up using the projections of dominance, that allowed me to come to an understanding of the real world, not only in the past and present tenses, but also in possible future tenses.

Today these maps are not popular, and I often feel very lonely trying to use them to navigate this violent and disoriented world; yet they depict an undeniable reality. I am more convinced than ever that nothing but the practice of pacifism—the individual and collective conduct by means of care and respect—offers a path into a constructive and creative future.

PART ONE

THE PURSUIT OF PEACE:
PACIFISM AS A MAP

To make the case for the practice of pacifism, I must first of all introduce the reader to the core of my view of life and living: the Quaker vision of the world.

The first writings in this part are unpublished notes that I hope illustrate the centrality of conscience and discernment in Quaker faith. They were originally compiled as part of the background for a legal team that was preparing an appeal to the Supreme Court of Canada to test the interpretation of the Freedom of Religion provisions of the Canadian Charter of Rights and Freedoms.

The specific issue to be tested was that of conscientious objection to paying taxes for military expenditures in peacetime. Quakers and others had argued that because modern wars were being largely conducted by technological means, the modern nation-state was in effect conscripting the money, rather than the physical activities, of its citizens in its preparations for war (or "defence" by military means). Just as pacifists could claim conscientious objection to physical conscription and accept alternative service, guarantees of freedom of religion should permit conscientious objectors to redirect to peaceful purposes that portion of their personal income tax used for war preparation.

Accordingly, a number of Canadian pacifists had placed the war portion of their personal income tax—corresponding to the percentage of revenue allotted to the Department of National

Defence—into a collective trust account before paying the remainder of their taxes. The trust account, in the care of an organization created for this purpose, would be available to the Government of Canada at any time for all but military uses.

The government did not accept this Charter argument, and those who chose this path were charged with tax offences. Once in court they were tried under the Income Tax Act. Even on appeal, they were unable to make the case that they were not *refusing* to pay taxes, but were attempting to redirect the use of their taxes to non-military purposes. They had no chance to show that their action was the compelling consequence of their religious belief, and that therefore such redirection should be allowed under the Freedom of Religion provisions of the Charter. They hoped to test this interpretation of the Charter provisions in an appeal to the Supreme Court of Canada. Regrettably, leave to appeal was not granted and the factum, into which my discussion was to be incorporated, was not put forward.

However, my notes here may serve as an introduction to the Religious Society of Friends (Quakers) and to the centrality of conscience and discernment in the practice of their faith.

The next papers in this part were intended to illuminate peace perspectives on daily life, first for an audience of Quakers and then for those within the broader religious community. The unpublished "Reflections on Theology and Peace" was written at the same time as the background for the factum on taxes for war or peace. It was presented in 1987 at an interfaith seminar. The gathering was occasioned, or at least catalyzed by, the—at times negative—responses from within church communities to a brief by the Canadian Council of Churches on Canada's foreign policy. The brief had been presented to a parliamentary hearing in 1985. In my contribution I tried to clarify the forms and concepts that define differing stances of concerned citizens vis-à-vis the policies of their country, without specifying explicitly the practice of pacifism.

The remainder of this part contains papers and lectures in more or less chronological order, and these are intended to show the centrality of peace to the approach to so many issues of the day. In all of them, peace is looked upon as the prerequisite of a civilized and just society, as the foundation for constructive work and collaboration in the great tasks of finding ways for people to live together. Peace is not, in and of itself, the goal or end of our political struggle, but the enabling start of a different social order. Many of the talks in this part were addressed to audiences under the shadow of the Cold War; it was the Soviet Threat, "The West vs. the Eastern Bloc," and the danger of Communism that coloured the political discourse, carrying with them the spectre of nuclear war. Yet it was the threat system itself, embodied in patriarchal structures—well known to women—and also part of the rationale of the arms race, that was of interest to me.

The Dove Memorial Lecture reflects on the change that the collapse of the Soviet Union in 1989 brought to the political landscape, without, I contended, advancing peace. The threat system, as an instrument of power and control, appeared to be immune to the loss of its official enemy, its stated raison d'être of the Cold War. Indeed, the threat system per se remained and grew at the end of the Cold War. The enemy's identity morphed, but wars and threats of war and violence continued without ever advancing peace.

Peace remained the ongoing issue; the events of September 11, 2001, and my response to them inform the final papers in this section. Never had I been more convinced than after this date that pacifism provides the only possible map into a livable future, a livable future for the earth and the human family. It seemed so self-evident just how dysfunctional the threat system, as a response to violence, had become. This realization left me quite desperate.

I asked myself: Doesn't the world see the need for clarity and the inescapable necessity of dealing with the causes of war? Why is it so difficult to turn away from images of the enemy as the root of nations' problems and as the obstacles to peace? Why is it so difficult for the powerful to understand that peace is the presence of justice and that justice and peace are indivisible? And I keep asking myself: Why has 9/11 and its aftermath not made it abundantly clear that the means of violence are no help to anyone, not even to those who claim every moral right to use them.

THE NATURE OF CONSCIENCE AND THE NATURE OF WAR

Unpublished manuscript, August 1987.

To APPRECIATE THE centrality of conscience in the lives of individual Quakers it is perhaps best to begin with a few general and historical remarks. It may be helpful to know what Quakers do not do in order to better see the significance of what they actually do. It should, however, be understood that what follows is a rough sketch, intended as an aerial survey locating Quakerism in terms of larger historical and societal processes.

Belief Systems and Reality

All religions and all belief systems reconstitute the world for their followers, giving a culturally acceptable interpretation of what life and death entail, both individually and collectively, explaining what the world *is* in contrast with what it ought to be or what it could be, and defining what stands in the way of transcending the "is" to the "ought." Troubles arise among groups of believers when serious contradictions occur between the publicly expressed principles and teachings on the one hand, and the real life conduct and practice on the other. This generalization holds, of course, whether the belief systems are religious or political. There are essentially three ways in which such contradictions can be resolved:

1   to revise conduct and practice so as to conform with the belief system
2   to revise the belief system so as to conform with the new practices or forms of conduct
3   to abandon binding principles and beliefs in order to deal with each problem individually and situationally.

Quakerism should be seen as an attempt—however modest—to use option 1 to cope with the contradictory demands of being a

Christian and a citizen in a particular place and time. Mainstream churches have often chosen option 2 when practices and beliefs clash; examples include the "just war" theory, the elevation of the sovereign as head of the church, anti-Semitism, and the role assigned to women. The political dimension of option 3 is self-evident, on both the left and the right. Quakers have always believed that it was practically—not merely theoretically—possible for people to conduct their lives and affairs, and the affairs of community and state, according to basic Christian principles. Thus, in contrast to groups such as the Mennonites and the Brethren, who have often isolated themselves from a world they regarded as intrinsically evil, Quakers have remained in the world. They did so partly as an act of conscious witness to another way of living and dealing with life. William Penn's holy experiment and the lives of Quakers such as John Bright, John Bellers, Elizabeth Fry, and Lucretia Mott come to mind as illustrations.

Remarks on Quaker History

Early Friends saw their task largely as freeing the basic Christian message from the worldly encrustations of rules, regulations, and habits that church practice rather than faith had produced over the centuries. The social climate of seventeenth-century England was one of intense questioning of established values and structures in the wake of the Reformation. In this setting Quakers rediscovered the glorious equality of all before God and the "Inner Light," the inherent ability to respond to God's prompting, to discern the truth, and to act accordingly. When Quakers speak of "that of God in everyone," they mean that every person is worthy of reverence and that each has within himself or herself a seed that will illuminate their conscience and help them to grow spiritually. Friends left behind what they regarded as lifeless forms or empty professions of faith rendered on fixed occasions and in set phrases, and refused to accept arbitrary divisions between the sacred and the secular. All life was to be lived under God's guidance and every act was equally sacred.

To Fox and the early Friends the whole of life seemed sacramental, and they refused to mark off any one particular practice or observance as more sacred than others. They took the
same stand with regard to Sunday, or First Day; it was not in
itself more holy than Saturday or Monday; every week-day
should be a Lord's Day. Their whole attitude was gloriously
positive, not negative. They were 'alive unto God' and sensed
him everywhere.[1]

Without the traditional sacraments of baptism, marriage, ordina-
tion, and holy communion, life itself became the sacrament, the
testimony of faith. In 1684 William Penn described the work of
early Friends as follows:

> The bent and stress of their ministry was conversion to God,
> regeneration and holiness, not schemes or doctrines and verbal
> creeds or new forms of worship, but a leaving off in religion the
> superfluous and reducing the ceremonious and formal part, and
> pressing earnestly the substantial, the necessary and profitable
> part, as all upon a serious reflection must and do acknowledge.[2]

Living a sacramental life, even in the most modest meaning of the
word, entails the constant presence of an internal yardstick—that
Inner Light—to which decisions, be they small or big, are constantly held up. To quote William Penn again:

> We judged not after the sight of the eye, or after the hearing of
> the ear, but according to the Light and the sense this blessed
> principle gave us; we judged and acted in reference to things
> and persons, ourselves and others, yea, towards God our maker.
> For being quickened by it in our inward man, we could easily
> discern the difference of things, and feel what was right, and
> what was wrong, and what was fit and what not, both in refer-
> ence to religion and to civil concerns.[3]

For Friends, the Inner Light, both as a concept and as a process,
represents conscience: the link between faith and practice.

The Centrality of Conscience

One cannot overemphasize the centrality of conscience in the life of individual Friends. Once the Society of Friends had rejected the detailed and prescriptive rules of conduct and structure that traditional churches provided for their members, Quakers had to develop a process of discernment in order to become sensitive to the choices each one had to make every day. Conscience therefore is the inner gyroscope pointing to the practical implications of Quaker testimonies. Throughout the centuries conscience has given direction to Quakers' lives and enabled Friends to make internally consistent choices in the small and large decisions that life brings. The process of bringing the Inner Light, the individual conscience, to bear on decisions and the growing sensitivity of the discernment can be compared with the process of tuning musical instruments. As musicians become more proficient, they tune with greater care; they also hear dissonances more keenly and find them painful. In just this manner Quakers try to tune their moral sensitivities. To them the only instruments they can use are their lives. Each life needs to be "in tune" so as to avoid the discord between faith and practice.

The Advices and Queries

The Religious Society of Friends has no fixed creeds, regulations, or prescriptive documents defining how members should conduct themselves in specific situations, but the Advices and Queries provide ongoing guidance in the perfecting and exercise of the process of discernment.[4] The following quotations from the Advices and Queries are intended to illustrate that the presence of a value system can be demonstrated by the internally consistent choices made by concerned individuals and to indicate the range of issues to which these principles apply. Decisions small and large are held up to the same light and regarded with the same seriousness.

- Bring the whole of your daily life under the ordering of the spirit of Christ.

- Live adventurously. When choices arise, take the way that offers the fullest opportunity for the use of your talents in the service of God and the community.
- In your relations with others, exercise imagination, understanding, and sympathy. Listen patiently, and seek whatever truth other people's opinions may contain for you. Think it possible that you may be mistaken. In discussion, avoid hurtful and provocative language; do not allow the strength of your convictions to betray you into making statements or allegations that are unfair or untrue.
- Endeavour to make your home a place of peace and happiness where the presence of God is known. Try to live simply. Remember the value of beauty in all its forms.
- Encourage the appreciation of music, literature, and the other arts and the development of a taste that will reject the worthless and the base. God's good gifts are for all to enjoy; learn to use them wisely.
- Choose recreations that do not conflict with your service to God and man, and in that service, be willing to lay them aside. Be discriminating in the use of radio and television and other means of information, persuasion, and entertainment. Give thought to the right use of Sunday with its special opportunities for both service and leisure.
- Remember your responsibility as citizens for the government of your own town and country, and do not shirk the effort and time this may demand. Do not be content to accept things as they are, but keep an alert and questioning mind. Seek to discover the causes of social unrest, injustice and fear; and try to discern the new growing-points in social and economic life. Work for an order of society which will allow men and women to develop their capacities and will foster their desire to serve.
- Check in yourselves and discourage in others those tendencies which lead to gambling and speculation. Do not, out of the spirit of emulation or through the offer of easy terms, buy what you do not need or cannot afford; and do nothing to encourage others in these practices. In view of the evils arising from the unwise use of alcohol, tobacco, and other habit-

forming drugs, consider how far you should limit your use of them or whether you should refrain from them altogether. Do not let the claims of good fellowship, or the fear of seeming peculiar, influence your decision. All users of the road should constantly remember that danger can arise from lack of patience and courtesy, and that any use of alcohol or drugs impairs alertness and so may imperil the lives of others.

• Be faithful in maintaining our witness against all war as inconsistent with the spirit and teaching of Christ. Seek through his power and grace to overcome in your own hearts the emotions which lie at the root of conflict. In industrial strife, racial enmity, and international tension, stand firmly by Christian principles, seeking to foster understanding between individuals, groups, and nations.

To sum up, conscience is manifest in a consistently lived life and in a large number of decisions taken in the same spirit. The exercise of conscience is central to Friends because in matters of belief they do not accept external sources of authority, such as ministers, priests, encyclicals, or sacred texts.

The Quaker Peace Testimony

Friends' Peace Testimony is a direct consequence of Quaker faith. After all, it is hardly possible to believe in "that of God in every person," and then starve, oppress, or shoot God in the guise of "others." The following quotations illustrate three facets of Friends' witness: first, that Quakers are against war because it is *wrong*, not because it is destructive, lethal, or expensive; second, that Quakers are keenly aware of the roots and causes of war that must be eliminated as preconditions for peace; and third, that Friends' stand is not, and never was, intended merely as a refusal to bear arms or to kill. The Peace Testimony is a universal testimony against conditions, such as war, violence, and preparations for war, that no one should have to face.

I told [the Commonwealth Commissioners] I lived in the virtue of that life and power that took away the occasion of all wars and I knew from whence all wars did rise, from the lust, according to James's doctrine.... I told them I was come into the covenant of peace which was before wars and strives were. (1651)[5]

We utterly deny all outward wars and strife and fightings with outward weapons, for any end or under any pretence whatsoever. And this is our testimony to the whole world. The spirit of Christ, by which we are guided, is not changeable, so as once to command us from a thing as evil, and again to move unto it; and we do certainly know, and so testify to the world, that the spirit of Christ, which leads us into all Truth, will never move us to fight and war against any man with outward weapons, neither for the kingdom of Christ, nor for the kingdoms of this world. (1661)[6]

We feel bound explicitly to avow our continued unshaken persuasion that all war is utterly incompatible with the plain precepts of our Divine Lord and Lawgiver, and with the whole spirit and tenor of His gospel; and that no plea of necessity or of policy, however urgent or peculiar, can avail to release either individuals or nations from the paramount allegiance which they owe unto Him who hath said "Love your enemies."[7]

Our peace testimony is much more than our special attitude to world affairs; it expresses our vision of the whole Christian way of life, it is our way of living in this world, of looking at this world and of changing this world. Only when the seeds of war—pride, prestige, and lust for power and possessions—have been purged from our personal and corporate ways of living; only when we can meet all men as friends in a spirit of sharing and caring can we call upon others to tread the same path.

Our Christian Pacifism, expressed in lives dedicated to the service of God and all his family, should be an experience from which we may speak to peoples and rules and which transforms a negative refusal to take part in war into a positive witness to the better way. We must by study, by group discussion, and by experience of active peace work equip ourselves with reliable knowledge to enable us not only to expound but also to apply our peace testimony.[8]

The fundamental position of Quakers against war and violence, formulated more than three hundred years ago, has been the basis of Friends' objections to military service and conscription, war taxes, war work, and military research. This testimony has also provided the motor for Quaker relief and for Friends' work at the United Nations and activities in the areas of reconciliation, peace research, and disarmament. It must also be noted that slowly, over the centuries, the position of conscientious objection to military service—to which Friends and others paid dearly in lives and suffering—has become recognized as the human right in many civilized countries where alternative service options have become available.[9]

The Nature of War in a Technological Society

The principles of the testimony against war and violence remain unchanged to this day, but the world in which conscientious objection is exercised has altered dramatically. What follows is a brief outline of these changes, particularly as they affect the nature of modern war and war preparations, and the resultant changes in the practices of conscientious objection to war and conscription in a modern technological society. As countries become increasingly dominated by technology, as they in fact become "technological societies,"[10] we see a dramatic shift in the nature of war, both as an activity and as a social institution. This shift was perceived by keen observers even before 1914 and led to the formation of the first world peace societies. By the end of the Second World War the changes were painfully apparent to all, and today it is clear that the historical notion of war as a separate and distinct activity, set apart in terms of time, territory, and participants, no longer exists.

For the modern practice of conscientious objection, two aspects of the changing nature of warfare are particularly important. The first is the disappearance of a clear boundary or demarcation between military and civil activities or aspects of national life. The second is the intrusion of war planning and preparation into "peacetime" activities of national governments, an intrusion that, in fact, blurs the temporal, emotional, and economic boundaries between war and peace. I do not wish to dwell on the fact that in modern war civilians (that is, women and children) are considered targets; the bombings of Coventry, Dresden, Rotterdam, Berlin, and Hiroshima and the attacks on refugee camps in the Middle East and Latin America are sufficient evidence. Nor do I wish to stress that nuclear fallout, be it from tests or bombs, does not respect national boundaries. For those who believe that war is wrong, these horrors do not make war any "more wrong," but they do make work and witness against war and violence more urgent. The important point is that such horrors are the consequences of the pivotal role of technology and science in modern warfare. The Second World War marked the end of a period in which science and technology provided special tools— such as gas, tanks, aircraft, and submarines—for use in more or less conventional warfare. Since then, technology has laid down the complete pattern of war and preparations for war. The arms race is driven by "technological imperative," and the intrinsic structural demands of highly advanced armament technologies have essentially eliminated "peace" as a political reality. A state of peace—in which nations do not maintain standing armies in constant readiness poised at a publicly identified enemy—has not existed for the last three decades at least, except as political fiction.

Canada—like most industrialized countries—maintains a substantial standing army in which the human component is small and the device component is large. Substituting machines and devices for human participants is a common characteristic of all modern technologies. There are highly efficient production facilities in today's industries, with a few workers operating many sophisticated devices and controls. Similarly the destruction facilities maintained by nation-states have become more and more powerful through the use of specially designed devices requiring relatively few people at the operating level. The fact that devices, rather than soldiers, constitute the core of modern standing armies is particularly evident in disarmament negotiations. The Geneva talks are centred around nuclear warheads, missiles, bombers, or delivery vehicles. The "air breathing threat" of the Canadian White Paper on Defence does not refer to hordes of foreign troops invading the nation's territory, but to air-launched cruise missiles. In military discussions "killer weapons" denote weapons designed to "kill" (that is, render non-operational) other weapons. We can reflect on the magnitude of this technological thrust by remembering the story of Stalin supposedly taunting Roosevelt at Yalta with the question: "How many divisions has the Pope?" Since standing armies, including the Canadian forces, are so heavily staffed by devices, it is not difficult to see why many countries, again including Canada, no longer extract years of compulsory military service from their citizens. Nations that still adhere to this practice most likely value the opportunity for enforced state education as highly as any benefits of military training. Current standing armies are serviced and maintained not by a stream of raw recruits but by a stream of new devices and instruments designed specifically for destruction. Note that the above reflections on hi-tech war-making are entirely based on the documentable impact of technology on all phases of society. They are valid, regardless of any moral or religious position vis-à-vis war. Whatever the sector of application, automation and advanced technological control are expensive, and the ceaseless building up of the technological powers of standing armies requires substantial funds.

Resource Conscription

Conscription is generally understood to mean the compulsory transfer to the government of goods or services for the purpose of war-making or war preparation. As shown above, the direct service of ordinary citizens has become irrelevant to the maintenance of the armies in modern technological societies, but the resources of citizens are essential. Thus governments now conscript *resources*. It is important to expose and bring into the open the current practice of resource conscription. In light of the above argument the traditional Quaker stand of conscientious objection to military service and conscription is directly transferable to resource conscription—that is, the compulsory diversion of public revenue for preparations for war. The following quotations illustrate the Quaker stand regarding conscription.

> Our conviction is that Christianity has this to say to the world: 'Your reliance upon armaments is both wrong and futile. Armaments are the weapons of organised violence and outrage. Their use is a denial of the true laws of good living. They involve the perpetuation of strife. They stand in the way of the true fellowship of men. They impoverish the peoples. They tempt men to evil, and they breed suspicion and fear and the tragic results thereof. They are therefore not legitimate weapons in the Christian armoury, nor are they sources of security.' You cannot foster harmony by the apparatus of discord, nor cherish good will by the equipment of hate. But it is by harmony and goodwill that human security can be obtained. Armaments aim at a security in isolation; but such would at best be utterly precarious and is, as a matter of fact, illusory. The only true safety is the safety of all, and unless your weapon of defence achieves this work, or works towards this, it is a source of antagonism and therefore of increased peril. (1920)[11]

> Compulsory military service is sometimes claimed as a duty attaching to citizenship. But it is not true social service. On the one hand it is part of the attempt to maintain peace by force, and on the other it is training in methods that are contrary to the highest moral standards recognised by man. The training of men to kill each other is a violation of the sacredness of personality for it is a crime against that of God in every man. It requires an inhumanity and a blind obedience that is a negation of responsible service to our fellow men. It demands much that in private life is recognised as anti-social and criminal.... Christ bids us love our enemies, government bids us kill them.... The conscript is, in effect, required to endorse war in advance. (1945)[12]

> We believe that the training of youth for war does a flagrant wrong to the young man on whom it is imposed. At a time of

life when young men should be learning the joy of freely given service on behalf of their fellows they are subjected to a compulsory negative service which will lead in many cases to a hatred or ignoring of the word 'service' and its claims in later life.... It may be suggested that our opposition is only part of our wider testimony against war. That is not altogether true. We believe that conscription for military training would still be wrong even if war were never to come. (1948)[13]

The comments expressed in the 1945 statement against the misuse of conscripted human service are strikingly applicable to the misuse of conscripted funds. Resources spent on war preparation are not available for social services at home or abroad, which is a well-known reality in Canada, where the military budgets increase while social service, foreign aid, and general research expenditures decrease. The conclusion that "the conscript is, in fact, required to endorse war in advance" applies equally to the financial conscript and the trainee. However, while trainees in Canada could claim conscientious objector status and request alternative service, the financial conscript is, at present, denied this option in spite of the provisions of the Charter of Rights regarding freedom of conscience.

The Demarcation between War and Peace

At this point we need to explore further the blurred boundaries between war and peace. In the past a war between nations began with a declaration of war and ended with some form of peace treaty. War was seen as a time-limited extraordinary state of affairs between nations and its conduct was circumscribed by a certain body of international law. In 1939 Canada began its war against Germany with a formal declaration passed by Parliament; the House was recalled from a summer recess specifically for this task. However, the state of war was never formally ended. Canada and the Western allies never signed a peace treaty with Germany. (The Soviet Union did end its state of war by signing a pact with the German Democratic Republic.) In the same vein the United States was never formally at war with Vietnam and there has not been a formal recognition of the end of hostilities between these two nations. Today the United States and Nicaragua are not formally at war, but nevertheless Nicaraguan harbours have been mined by U.S. warships. Warlike activities are initiated and carried out, and without the legal sanctions and formal signals that have, in the past, separated periods of war and peace. The practice of pursuing wartime activities in "peacetime," it must be re-emphasized, is due to the predominance of devices as combatants; devices obey orders and they don't have mothers to mount public protests.

The end of the conflict in Vietnam can, in fact, be traced to difficulties faced by the United States in trying to fight a long-distance hi-tech war against an indigenous and determined low-tech adversary. The option of dissent was much more clearly perceived and more effectively pursued when the United States needed foot soldiers and introduced the draft than it was during the preceding period of resource conscription. Since the Vietnam War immense advances in the automation and computerization of the tools of war have been accompanied by an ever-increasing conscription of resources. Canada's own role in this development is by no means negligible.

The Permanent Enemy

One final aspect of the impact of technology on the nature of war preparations must be pointed out. In *The New Industrial State*, John Kenneth Galbraith illustrated the political consequences of modern advanced production technologies. Since all such technologies are extremely capital-intensive, the government must provide the fiscal and political stability needed to bring such facilities into operation and ensure the adequate return on investments. Modern weapons technologies, including the required research and development, are particularly capital-intensive and costly. The time between initial research and the deployment of weapon systems can be as long as a decade, during which the government must provide financial security and political justification for the project. In other words the state not only provides the funding but also identifies a credible external enemy who warrants such expenditure. The practical and religious consequences of recasting the enemy as a permanent social institution have been outlined elsewhere. In the context of this paper I want to emphasize this as a further illustration of the blurred boundaries between war and peace that exist in a modern technological society. The designation by a government of nations or groups of nations as enemies in response to the needs of military procurement essentially pre-empts the option of genuine conflict resolution and reconciliation. This is unacceptable to people who, on grounds of conscience, do not give governments the power to make and unmake enemies for them.

Notes

1   Gerald K. Hibbert, *Quaker Fundamentals*, pp. 7–8, quoted in *Christian Faith and Practice in the Experience of the Religious Society of Friends* (London: Yearly Meeting of the Religious Society of Friends, 1960), no. 209.

2   William Penn, "Preface" to *George Fox's Journal*, 1694, quoted in *Christian Faith and Practice*, no. 16.

3   William Penn, "Preface," 1694, quoted in *Christian Faith and Practice*, no. 38.

4   In 1682, the London Yearly Meeting began asking representatives from Quarterly and Monthly Meetings a number of factual questions on Friends and their activities. During the eighteenth century these questions were revised so they could be used to ensure consistency of conduct among Friends and to report on the state of the Society. Further revisions and extensions took place during the nineteenth and twentieth centuries. Quotations used in this article are taken from *Advices and Queries: Addressed to the Meetings and Members of the Religious Society of Friends and to Those Who Meet with Them in Public Worship* (London: Yearly Meeting, 1964), pp. 12, 14–15.

5   *George Fox's Journal*, 1651, quoted in *Christian Faith and Practice*, no. 613.

6   Friends declaration to Charles II of England, 1661, quoted in *Christian Faith and Practice*, no. 614.

7   Epistle of Yearly Meeting, 1854, during the Crimean War, quoted in *Christian Faith and Practice*, no. 618.

8   Friends World Conference, 1952, quoted in *Christian Faith and Practice*, no. 624.

9   Seán MacBride, *The Right to Refuse to Kill: A New Guide to Conscientious Objection and Service Refusal* (Geneva : International Peace Bureau, 1971); Merja Pentikäinen, ed., *The Right to Refuse Military Orders* (Zürich: International Peace Bureau; IALANA; Peace Union of Finland; Finnish Lawyers for Peace and Survival, 1994).

10 See Ursula M. Franklin, *The Real World of Technology* (Toronto: Anansi, 1999).

11 All Friends Conference, 1920, quoted in *Christian Faith and Practice*, no. 629.

12 "The Society of Friends and Military Conscription," issued by Meeting for Sufferings, 1945, quoted in *Christian Faith and Practice*, no. 627.

13 Issued by Meeting for Sufferings for presentation to the British Council of Churches, 1948, quoted in *Christian Faith and Practice*, no. 627.

REFLECTIONS ON THEOLOGY AND PEACE

Unpublished paper adapted from an address given at the Symposium on Theology and Peace, Toronto, November 1987.

WHILE GRATEFULLY accepting the invitation to prepare a background paper for this symposium, I do not wish to hide the fact that I come to the task as an outsider. I am a Quaker, a feminist, and a physicist; my perspectives may differ significantly from those of others attending the symposium. Furthermore, I am anxious to assure you that my remarks do not imply that moral or religious insights are found solely in the Christian faith, or that persons with life-guiding religious convictions are by necessity members of organized churches. My position is that of John Woolman (1720–1772).

> There is a principle which is pure, placed in the human mind, which in different places and ages hath had different names. It is, however, pure and proceeds from God. It is deep and inward, confined to no form of religion, nor excluded from any, where the heart stands in perfect sincerity. In whomsoever this takes root and grows, of what nation soever, they become brothers and sisters in the best sense of the expression.[1]

The purpose of the symposium, as I see it, is to reflect on the daily consequences of our faith. We need to share what it is that we *do*—individually and collectively—because of our faith, as well as what we do *not* do, and do not consent to see done in our name, again because of our beliefs.

For any Quaker the direct link between faith and practice is absolutely central. To us the conduct of our lives is the only valid testimony of our faith—or lack of it. Early Friends saw their task largely as freeing the basic Christian message from the worldly encrustations of rules, regulations, and habits that church practice, rather than faith, had accumulated over the centuries. The social climate of seventeenth-century England was one of intense questioning of established values and structures in the wake of the

Reformation. In this setting Quakers rediscovered the glorious equality of all before God, and with it the "Inner Light," the inherent ability to respond to God's prompting, to discern the truth, and to act accordingly. When Quakers speak of "that of God in everyone," they mean that every person is worthy of reverence and that each has within herself or himself a seed that will illuminate their conscience and will help them to grow spiritually. Quakers left behind what they regarded as lifeless forms or empty professions of faith, rendered on fixed occasions and in set phrases, and they refused to accept any arbitrary division between the sacred and the secular: all life was to be lived under God's guidance; every act was equally sacred.

> To Fox and the early Friends the whole of life seemed sacramental, and they refused to mark off any one particular practice or observance as more sacred than others. They took the same stand with regard to Sunday, or First Day; it was not in itself more holy than Saturday or Monday; every week-day should be a Lord's Day. Their whole attitude was gloriously positive, not negative. They were 'alive unto God' and sensed him everywhere.[2]

Today none of us lives solely in our faith community. We are all part of a complex society in which we must function. From the contemporary feminists I have learned that "the personal is political,"[3] an insight that has helped me to function more effectively. We know that people interact with each other not only directly but also very strongly through social and political institutions. What happens to each of us is not simply the result of our own doing; it is vitally influenced by our social and political environment, which in turn is shaped and conditioned by our own and everyone else's responses. Consequently, a clear understanding of the realities of current social and political milieus is a prerequisite for any appropriate principled response to it. A major task of all faith communities, therefore, is the collective search for a thorough understanding of the social and political environment within which witness is to be borne.

It is the recognition of the profound structural changes taking place in our world, in addition to my Quaker beliefs and my feminist perspectives, that colours my reflections on theology and peace. I firmly believe that the structural changes occurring in the modern world are of a depth and magnitude comparable to the changes surrounding the Reformation in the seventeenth century. Technology and technique are the major motors initiating today's changes. We need a much deeper understanding of the moral dimensions of science and technology, and indeed of all knowledge, if we want to understand and modify our social and political environment.[4]

Belief Systems and Reality

All religions and belief systems reconstitute the world for their followers, giving a culturally acceptable interpretation of what life and death entail, both individually and collectively, is given, and explaining what the world *is* in contrast with what it ought to be or what it could be, and defining what stands in the way of transcending the "is" to the "ought." Troubles arise when serious contradictions occur between publicly expressed principles and teachings on the one hand, and real conduct and practice on the other. This generalization holds, of course, whether the belief systems are religious or political. There are essentially three ways in which such contradictions can be resolved:

1   to revise conduct and practice so as to conform with the belief system
2   to revise the belief system so as to conform with the new practices or forms of conduct
3   to abandon binding principles and beliefs in order to deal with each problem individually and situationally.

The brief by the Canadian Council of Churches[5] is, in my eyes, motivated by an approach similar to that denoted in option 1 above. The very title of the brief, "An Alternative View," indicates the need and the practical possibility to bring government conduct and practice closer to the beliefs that members of the churches and others hold in common. Friends have always believed that it was *practically*—not merely theoretically—possible for everyone to conduct their lives and affairs, as well as those of their community and state, according to basic Christian principles. Thus, in contrast to groups such as the Mennonites or the Brethren who often isolated themselves from a world they regarded as intrinsically evil, Quakers have remained in the world. They did so partly as an act of conscious witness to another way of living and dealing with life.

It may be useful to note some of the basic differences between a secular and a religious view of life, regardless of any specific religious affiliation. These two views differ most drastically in the understanding of "power" and "time." A religious view recognizes the continuity and timelessness of Creation in contrast to the brevity and limitations of an individual's life and power. A religious world view also recognizes the supremacy of God's power, however God might be defined in the eyes of the believer. Secular views of life tend to emphasize the short term in their time frame and the power of human institutions and human interventions in their considerations of power and power structures. Thus, whenever the churches address governments, it may be necessary to articulate the basic differences between these two world views.[6]

Citizens and Government

The task of reflecting on the Canadian Council of Churches' brief requires some comment on the role of citizens in relation to their governments. The Quaker view of this relationship is illustrated in the following three quotations.

> We are not for names, nor men, nor titles of Government, nor are we for this party nor against the other ... but we are for justice and mercy and truth and peace and true freedom, that these may be exalted in our nation, and that goodness, righteousness, meekness, temperance, peace and unity with God, and with one another, that these things may abound. (Edward Burrough, 1659)[7]

That if any be called to serve the commonwealth in any public service, which is for the public wealth and good, that with
cheerfulness it be undertaken, and in faithfulness discharged
unto God. (Meetings of Elders at Balby, 1656)[8]

We have ... in our Quaker history a lesson for our own lives of
the meaning of Christian citizenship. You can see there a twofold strand constantly interwoven: one, respect for the state as
representing authority in the community: and the other, desire
to serve the community through the state and in other ways,
but along with that, the desire above all to serve the Kingdom
of God: this means that we must be willing, when loyalty to the
Kingdom of God demands it to refuse the demands of the state
and show the highest loyalty to the state and the best citizen-
ship· by refusing demands that are wrong, because it is only in
that way that the conscience of our fellow citizens can be
reached, and in the end a better law come into being. (T.
Edmund Harvey, 1937)[9]

To me, it is important to emphasize two aspects of the relationship between citizen and government. One is the obligation that
citizens have for the appropriate conduct of the governance of
their community. The other is the overriding authority of God's
laws as they direct our conduct. It is particularly important to
stress the final sentence of the quotation from T. Edmund Harvey:
the best citizenship may be exercised "by refusing demands of the
state that are wrong, because it is only in that way that the conscience of our fellow citizens can be reached and in the end a better law come into being." In plain words this means that there is
an obligation to refuse co-operation with the state if a law involves
a violation of God's laws, and that this act of non-cooperation has
to be public so that it can appeal to the conscience of others who
may then help to change the law of the state.

   While there is a great deal of discussion about the obligations
of citizens towards the state, it should not be forgotten that the
state also has obligations towards its citizens. In our—Western
democratic—view of governments, it is the state that serves the
citizens, not vice versa. In particular, the consent of citizens to be

governed by laws drawn up with the common good in mind cannot become consent for the state to act in ways that would be illegal and immoral if carried out by individual citizens.[10] The consequences of the failure to revoke citizens' consent to immoral and illegal laws and actions of the state have been frequently pointed out with respect to Germany under Hitler, but this is far from the only illustration of the state's misuse of citizens' consent.[11] In particular, we should remember the important obligations of the state that are enshrined in Canada under the Constitutional provisions for freedom of religion and conscience. The state undertakes to provide an environment that allows any citizen to lead a moral life, constrained only by the obligation not to diminish and denigrate others or harm the integrity of Creation. We may well wish to reflect on the extent to which it is, in practice, possible to lead a moral life in any modern technological society.

In summary, then, on both religious and secular grounds, citizens have the right and the duty to speak and act on matters of governance, be it individually or collectively. The government of the day, in turn, is obligated to listen and to take seriously the requirement to establish conditions in which citizens can lead a life consistent with their moral and religious principles.

The Brief as a Mirror

We may wish to recognize at the beginning that movements of social change in Canada tend to operate in one of two modes. The first of these is the "shadow cabinet mode," in which authors of submissions to parliament or government see themselves as members of a "shadow cabinet." They address the government as members of the opposition and provide advice and suggestions, in terms of the government's activities, from the perspective of the decision-makers. The second is the "prophetic mode," in which those who address power do so on grounds of principle. They are concerned not with the practical details of government activities but rather with the principles behind these activities: the "why"— not the "how"—of an action taken or proposed is central to the discourse.

Throughout history, social movements and churches have provided both advisors and prophetic critics, but often these two groups, even when they come from the same faith community, had little communication with each other; frequently they saw each other as hindrance rather than support. In terms of the above classification, the brief of the Canadian Council of Churches to the Joint Parliamentary Committee on Canada's Foreign Relations is a "shadow cabinet" document par excellence. This brief is intended to provide the government with viable alternatives and show that there is an alternative view of Canada's foreign relations that involves feasible and doable alternative activities. As such, the brief provides an admirable blueprint in practical terms for what Canada could do and, in doing so, advance the causes of justice and peace. This document engenders great respect for the competence and integrity of the authors and it will serve for a long time as a blueprint not only for members of Parliament but even more so for members of the churches. I hope that this brief will be read and studied by all church members and that it will become the basis of discussions with friends, neighbours, and colleagues. In essentially secular terms it allows all church members to document the feasibility of another course for Canadian foreign policy.

The prophetic voice of this brief is weak, because of the audience to whom it addresses itself. While the content (written and presented in the fall of 1985) is excellent, it may need to be supplemented—and I do mean supplemented, not replaced—by an equally thorough and wide-ranging statement of the prophetic base of this submission that would do it full justice in the hands of a larger audience and over a longer period of time. It is the context, rather than the content, of the brief that may require articulation. There is, in my opinion, an urgent need to state the fundamental nature of Christian opposition to current Canadian policies, an opposition based on our faith and on the consequences we must draw from it.

The section in the brief dealing with human rights is a good illustration of what I mean. The brief urges the Government of Canada to adhere to international conventions on human rights and to work for their extension into countries and jurisdictions that, at present, do not honour them. But none of us should need international conventions to respect the humanity of others, to treat them as sisters and brothers, as members of the human family, as part of God's Creation. It may be necessary to emphasize that, for us, there is no difference between "us" and "them." The fact that on religious grounds we cannot accept the notion of "other" people may need to be prominently spelled out in a related document.

Traps of the Shadow Cabinet Approach

These reflections may serve to illustrate the traps inherent in taking a shadow cabinet approach to interactions with governments. Undoubtedly, everyone is in this bind: speaking to government may require addressing issues before the government, but acceptance of the government's agenda implies compliance with a way of looking at problems that may be non-constructive or inherently wrong. While the shadow cabinet approach allows the submission of detailed alternatives (essentially in secular terms), it does not accommodate discussion of the root causes that lie beneath the manifestations that most enquiries address. Nowhere are the generic limitations of a shadow cabinet approach more apparent than in the section of the brief dealing with security. An excellent introduction clearly defines security in terms of idolatry, but the detailed prescriptions follow an agenda not of the authors' making. The authors of this brief find themselves in the same dilemma as all those trying to lessen the dangers of war.

There is a need for coherent secular discussions and arguments to show the futility of war and the inappropriateness of the threat of war as an element of national and international policy in the nuclear age. There is a need to speak of conflict resolution, strengthening of international institutions, and the inherent dangers and fiscal disasters entailed in arming and rearming. In the course of meeting this need, many peace people have become experts in the tools, tactics, and mindset of an undertaking that they wish to eliminate. We cannot escape the sense of historical irony when we realize how much of the resources of the peace movement have gone into "studying war."

On a moral and religious level, however, technicalities begin to lose their importance. A small war is indeed just as evil as a global one; the fact that nuclear warfare is dangerous and likely lethal to much of Creation serves only as an illustration of the basic wrongness of the enterprise of war and violence, as a reason for the sense of urgency in the peace community. But if we believe that there is "that of God in every person" and that all Creation is holy, it is hardly possible to consent to seeing God— in the guise of "others"—being starved, oppressed, and shot. It does not matter where such insults occur or who in particular suffers. It is clear that participation in any such activity is indeed a fundamental violation of our faith. With this consideration the discourse shifts from an emphasis on goals—such as security—to an emphasis on means. It is well to remember the words of A.J. Muste: "There is no way to peace. Peace is the way."[12]

Removing the Causes of War

In 1953 Kathleen Lonsdale, a prominent British Quaker, gave a series of lectures entitled "Removing the Causes of War."[13] Kathleen Lonsdale was a conscientious objector, a prominent and effective worker for peace, a well-known crystallographer, and a Fellow of the Royal Society. The thrust and content of her lectures are as pertinent today as they were thirty-five years ago. She deals with the obstacles to achieving peace from a strong religious perspective, but also with a thorough knowledge of the world around us. She is basically concerned—as we are—with justice.

What do we mean when we speak of peace? Certainly there is more to peace than the absence of wars in our own country. For me, the most appropriate definition is that peace is the absence of fear, it is the daily reality of the biblical promise, "Fear not." If we look at peace as the absence of fear, we find we are linked not only to those who, like us, fear a nuclear war or a holocaust of environmental destruction, but also to those who have reasons to fear a knock on the door at night, and those who fear that there will be no food for their children or that their children may not return from school because they have been arrested and imprisoned. It links us to those in our country and abroad who have reason to fear that there may be no meaningful employment for them, that they will always be short of shelter, and that their lives will not count for much. It links us to those who fear that the delicate ecosystem of our planet will not survive the selfishness and ravages of greed. It links us to those who fear that the folly of the few will damage and destroy the lives of many.

The definition of peace as the absence of fear illustrates that the central element needed to bring peace on all levels and to reduce fear is justice. Justice means freedom from arbitrary interference but it also implies a fundamental equality of caring. In God's eyes all creatures have value and are subjects of equal care and love; similarly, in a society of justice and peace, all people matter equally. A true commitment to peace—by individuals, groups, churches, or governments—means a commitment to equal justice for all. Such a commitment entails two constituent components. One is that peace, like true justice, is indivisible. Peace, if it comes, will come to all: to those who work with us and those who work against us. Bertrand Russell defined the indivisibility of peace in his statement that "the price of peace is the happiness of our enemies," and added that he was not at all sure whether humanity was prepared to pay that price.

The second component of a commitment to peace is a rejection of the use of fear as an instrument of policy. Today the threat system is no longer a prerogative of the military.[14] Fear has become a universal management tool at all levels, from national and international governments to actions among or within corporations and procedures in local endeavours. We might wish to reflect for a moment on the scope that modern technology affords governing bodies to increase their powers in terms of instilling fear and uncertainty.

Non-cooperation with threat systems is therefore one of the central necessities of a commitment to peace. Addressing the causes rather than the tools of war means addressing uncomfortable issues of justice and threat in the light of our faith. In this light it becomes quite clear that causes of war are not found elsewhere in the world. The threat of war is *not* a problem of foreign policy. War and destruction are the inevitable outcome of the ongoing lifestyle of nations and individuals who consider the practical and moral imperatives of caring and doing justice as not applicable to themselves.

In her lectures, Kathleen Lonsdale quoted the great historian of technology, Lewis Mumford, as writing: "Between the thirteenth and the nineteenth century one may sum up the changes in the moral climate by saying that the seven deadly sins became the seven cardinal virtues . . . avarice ceased to be a sin: the minute attention to the care of worldly goods, the holding of pennies, the unwillingness to spend one's surplus on others—all these habits were useful for capital saving. Greed, gluttony, avarice, envy and luxury were constant incentives to industry."[15] No theological reflection on peace and justice—or the absence of them—can be complete without facing the challenge of this insight.

On Speaking Truth to Power

It is now about two years since the brief under discussion, and many similar interventions, were written and presented to committees and commissions of the new Parliament of Canada. The government responded in word and deed, and these responses must become part of our reflections. I do not wish us to think in terms of the "success" of this brief or any other submission. What was said had to be said and stands on its own merits. Whether or not suggestions were adopted reflects not so much on the substance of the submission as on the political reality that is the background of the churches' witness. Canada's military policy—including the recent White Paper, the Refugee Bills, government activities in the area of internal security and labour practices, and Canada's voting record at the United Nations—represents policies and policy directions opposite to the thrust of the Canadian Council of Churches brief and the many similar documents authored by peace and social change movements across the country. Instead of disarmament and demilitarization we see Canada arming and militarizing the economy. Instead of open refugee processes we see closed borders and visa requirements. The political conclusions from these events are self-evident. Here, however, we must be concerned with religious and theological reflections on this new reality. The issues then become matters of faith versus power. How should Christians—and their churches—react when the powers they address do not respond to compassion or reason? The first step, I suggest, is to "speak truth to power." Speaking truth to power requires not only spiritual clarity in terms of "truth" but also clarity in terms of the mode and locus of the secular powers to be addressed. Coming to such clarity on "power" involves a critical re-examination (underlying the activities of giving advice or submitting briefs) of the model of government.

It seems to me that in Canada today, the ruling apparatus consists largely of members of cabinet, senior civil servants, and unknown and unaccountable advisors and consultants; these constitute a genuine shift of power that drastically changes the structure of our so-called parliamentary democracy. If, upon collective reflection, this shift in power is substantiated, it seems imperative that a new modus operandi and location of power be clarified. Any dislocation of power, responsibility, and accountability needs to be shown and documented. In addition to clarifying the functional structures of power, it may be necessary, as part of the process of speaking truth, to question the motives of those in power, be they institutions or individuals.

Citizens, particularly religious groups, tend to approach the authorities under the assumption that those in power are well-intentioned but perhaps ill-informed, and that supplementary information will change views and practice. However, we must seriously consider the possibility that those in power are ill-intentioned and well-informed. This means that issues addressed by many citizens' submissions—such as justice, peace, and social problems—must be addressed in terms of the inherent attributes of the existing power arrangements.

At this point you may well ask, "How then does one, as an individual or as a church, speak truth to power, even if the structure and locus of power are less camouflaged than they now appear to be?" The answer, of course, must come out of our faith. In the end it is our lives that must speak the truth. What we do and what we refuse to do, from the smallest to the largest decisions, is the truth that we speak, the truth that nothing can hide. In terms of the individual and collective search for the truth and its effective expression in everyday life, I suggest that we focus both our practical and our prophetic witness on the means, rather than on the goals, of private and public or government activities. While the ends of our endeavours are always in God's hands, the choice of the means is frequently ours.[16]

In the light of our faith we must retrain ourselves and each other not to be overly impressed by grandiose schemes and big promises, but rather to fathom the ways and means in which such promises and projects are to be realized. Thus we will be freed from the oppression of technical details and can, with clearer sight, ask, "Who bears the burden?" and "Who benefits?" and "Who might suffer?" The answers will make the moral dimensions of our decisions much more discernable. We know that unjust means cannot produce justice, that making others fearful cannot lead to peace or security, and that the means will finally determine the ends.

I can envisage a theology of peace that focuses primarily on the discernment of means—a discernment equally valid for decisions on small and on large issues. In such a theology of peace we would find the practical manifestation of the prophetic voice; such a focus on means would expose the common roots of many issues that are now addressed separately. Speaking truth to power through a dialogue on acceptable means may allow a focused witness, according to the demands of our faith.

Any modern theology of peace must, I think, take into account the worldwide drift towards "techno-fascism," the anti-people, anti-justice form of global management and power sharing that is developing around the world. Our corporate search for a theology of peace may give us strength and help to witness against such trends. And again, it will be our conduct that will be the measure of our faith. In the words of William Penn:

> It is not opinion, or speculation, or notions of what is true, or assent to or the subscription of articles or propositions, though never so soundly worded, that ... makes a person a true believer or a true Christian. But it is a conformity of mind and practice to the will of God, in all holiness of conversation according to the dictates of this Divine principle of Light and Life in the soul which denotes a person truly a child of God.[17]

Notes

1   John Woolman, "Considerations on Keeping Negroes, Part Second," 1762, quoted in *Quaker Faith and Practice*, 2nd ed. (London: Yearly Meeting of the Religious Society of Friends in Britain, 1995), no. 26.71.

2   Gerald K. Hibbert, *Quaker Fundamentals*, pp. 7–8, quoted in *Christian Faith and Practice in the Experience of the Religious Society of Friends* (London: Yearly Meeting of the Religious Society of Friends, 1960), no. 209.

3   For an overview of feminist thought, see, for instance, Marilyn French, *Beyond Power* (New York: Ballantine, 1985); Birgit Brock-Utne, *Educating for Peace: A Feminist Perspective*, Athene Series (London: Pergamon Press, 1985).

4   See, for instance, the work of Jacques Ellul, particularly *Perspectives on Our Age: Jacques Ellul Speaks on His Life and Work*, ed. W.H. Vanderburg (Toronto: CBC Merchandising, 1981; Toronto: Anansi Press, 2003); and W.H. Vanderburg, *The Growth of Minds and Cultures* (Toronto: University of Toronto Press, 1985).

5   A brief presented by the Canadian Council of Churches in 1986–87 to the Joint Parliamentary Committee on Canada's Foreign Relations.

6   You may wish to reflect upon the use of the word "superpower" in everyday discourse and in documents issued by your church. Can you utter the words of the Lord's Prayer in worship and faith and still use the term "superpower" to denote nation-states characterized by their possession of tools for unimaginable destruction? I cannot, and prefer to use the term "empire."

7   Edward Burrough, *The Memorable Works of a Son of Thunder* (1672), p. 604; quoted in *Christian Faith and Practice in the Experience of the Religious Society of Friends* (London Yearly Meeting of the Religious Society of Friends, 1960), no. 579.

8   From Abram Rawlinson Barklay, ed., *Letters ... of Early Friends* (1841), pp. 280–81, quoted in *Christian Faith and Practice* (1960), no. 580.

9   T. Edmund Harvey, "The Individual Christian and the State," quoted in *Christian Faith and Practice* (1960), no. 583.

10 Margaret Hope Bacon, *The Quiet Rebels: The Story of the Quakers in America* (Philadelphia: New Society, 1985).

11 As an example of the wide literature on the subject, see Milton Mayer: *On Liberty, Man v. the State* (Santa Barbara, Cal.: Center for the Study of Democratic Institutions, 1969).

12 For informatin on A.J. Muste, see Net Hentoff, *Peace Agitator: The Story of A.J. Muste* (New York: Macmillan, 1963).

13 Kathleen Lonsdale, *Removing the Causes of War*, Swarthmore Lecture (London: George Allen and Unwin, 1953).

14 Ursula M. Franklin, "Women and Militarism," *Status of Women News*, (Feb. 1983). See pp. 100–03 here.

15 Lewis Mumford, *The Condition of Man* (New York: Harcourt, Brace, 1944), p. 162.

16 Susanne Gowan and George Lakey, *A New Call to Peacemaking* (Philadelphia: Friends World Committee for Consultation, 1976); Susanne Gowan, George Lakey, William Moyer, and Richard Taylor, *Moving Toward a New Society* (Philadelphia: New Society Press, 1976).

17 William Penn, *A Key to Opening a Way to Every Common Understanding* (1692), quoted in *Quaker Faith and Practice*, 2nd ed. (London: Yearly Meeting of the Religious Society of Friends in Britain, 1995), no. 26.78

THE INDIVISIBILITY OF PEACE

Adapted from an unpublished sermon given at the Pathways to Peace Conference, Timothy Eaton Memorial Church, Toronto, 2 November 1985.

... may the reflections of our minds, the feelings in our hearts, and the words in our discourse be acceptable to God.

I ALWAYS THINK it is almost a miracle that in a world that knows so little peace and justice there is a universal understanding that peace and justice do exist, ought to exist, and are attainable. In my own religious tradition, Quakers speak of "that of God in every person." We believe that there is in every person— whether well hidden or outwardly apparent—an ability to discern right from wrong that comes from God and can respond to God's will and God's word. One manifestation of this seems to me that we know about peace and justice, not necessarily because we have experienced it ourselves, but because we are struck by the difference between the realities of everyday life and what ought to be, that is, our inner and God-given knowledge of peace and justice.

We all know people who have grown into adulthood never knowing either peace or justice in their lives. Still the striving and the struggle for it is greater for them than it is for us. If we assume, which I think we have every right to, that the knowledge of peace and justice is one of the things that makes us human, that makes us members of the human family with common aims and common striving, then I think it is not difficult to define what peace is.

Peace is the absence of fear. Peace is in the message of the angel to the shepherds in Bethlehem: "Be not afraid." It is a daily reality of the biblical promise of "fear not." Consequently peace is not the absence of war—peace is the absence of fear. This again links peace tightly to justice, because it is only in the presence of peace and justice that fear can be absent. Justice, in both the temporal and the spiritual sense, is a guarantee against the arbitrariness of power that is the source of so much justifiable fear.

Once we accept that peace is the realization of the biblical promise of "fear not," we can see several things in a fresh perspective. We can see that peace has never been won, and can never be won, by instilling fear. Threatening and bullying, making some nations or peoples fearful so that others might fear less, is no way to peace. If we want to work for peace and justice we must be clear that threats and the technological instruments of threat have no place in the promotion of peace. The road to peace is not lined with weapons. The scriptures have said this; we should have known it. Furthermore, in the age of nuclear weapons, it is no longer individual nations but the survival of life on the planet that is threatened. Even for those who are unwilling to follow the guidance of their faith it is clear that "others" cannot be threatened safely. No nation can claim that it is possible to instil fear and thereby promote justice by threats. If we realize these facts, we can see why it is so difficult to promote peace in today's world, and why there is such a great hurdle between knowing and doing. The immediate answer is that it's fine to be Christian if I only had to make peace with myself.

But there is another dimension. Just as with God's love in the passage from Matthew, peace is indivisible. We have to come to terms with the fact that, like the sun, the rain, and God's grace, peace will be there for the just and the unjust. Peace will be there as we work at it with God's help both for those we love and for all those we can't stand. It will be there for our children and it will be there for all the creeps we are trying to avoid. There is no other way around, and there never has been in spiritual terms. Moreover, today there is no way around this truth in practical terms. Those of us who work for peace will have to act and speak with clarity, stressing that the work we do is not only for ourselves but for everyone. All the little games of having a small advantage here or there, arguments about whether the balance is just—and "they" get what they deserve—or whether "we" are getting the shorter end of the stick, all these considerations must be left behind. It is not for us to redistribute grace or peace. We don't run the universe; we just work here, and our work is under the guidance of fairly strict principles. One of them, as we heard in the reading from Matthew, becomes front and centre as we think and talk about peace: *Peace is indivisible.*

Bertrand Russell commented that the price of peace is the happiness of our enemies and added that he was not sure whether the world was ready to pay that price. We don't outguess God by arguing about who deserves his Love. Let us also not outguess God by arguing about who deserves peace. God's love is there for all. Who are we to work for peace just for ourselves and our friends? The willing acceptance of the indivisibility of peace removes one of the major obstacles to peace itself, because it removes the tit-for-tat judgments that stand in the way of the realization of "fear not."

We may then wonder how we can actually proceed, what can we do as we leave the house of worship and try to work for peace. First of all, we have to realize that in instilling fear, the threat system has a broader basis than just international politics. People can be threatened economically, by authority, by race, and by gender. Many of us, willingly or unwillingly, play a role in instituting such threats. Who of us has not said, "When I was your age…"? Who of us has not pulled rank or tried to intimidate someone, somewhere, through our superior economic status. This doesn't mean we cannot make choices. But I think we have to refuse participation in the threat system, be it financially, emotionally, or personally.

The other thing we must do is to realize that we are God's hands and voice. There isn't anyone else. If we don't do the work for peace, who will? And while we act in the spirit of God, it is our hands, our heads, our lives that are the testimony. God is not the equivalent of a divine maid service, mopping up the mess that we have left. God is the source of strength for those who are willing and ready to act.

Dietrich Bonhoeffer asked, "How can God speak when men and women are silent?" and it was Bonhoeffer who, explaining his faith and actions while in prison, pointed out that faith is not the waiting until you are strong. Faith is proceeding as if one has the strength of God behind every step. It is the belief that in time of need the strength to proceed will be given. Every small strong step we take is an act of faith that stimulates a new wave of strength, clarity, and a certainty of fellowship amongst those who feel concern for peace and justice. There's no other way to proceed but in faith and in the knowledge that the strength, the blessing, and the clarity will come.

There is another form of indivisibility of peace. As we proceed it will become clear to each and every one of us that working for peace is not a hobby like golf or gourmet cooking, which we do when we have the time. Peace is a way of life, day in and day out, and unfortunately there are no paid vacations. Peace becomes indivisible in our own lives, as a facet of our existence. We must remember how many people have lived that undivided life in the service of peace, how many of these were women, and how many of them have been at it for a long time. Only a few have been recognized for the momentous contributions they have made in living peace.

When the scripture speaks of loving one's enemy it doesn't mean a kiss on the cheek on Sunday morning. It means continuous respect and caring. When the scripture says, "Love your neighbour as you love yourself," it means recognizing the other person as important to you as you are to yourself. Their needs are just as important to you as your own needs, their hurts as important as your hurts. This is what guides the work for peace, and this is how we must strengthen our community and ourselves.

The great pacifist A.J. Muste once said, "There is no way to peace, peace is the way." Just as Jesus said, "I am the way," we know that indivisible peace is the way in which we have to lead ourselves, our lives, and our communities away from a system of threats. If we wish to shelter under that blessing of "fear not," we must act so that others are ensured of the same blessing.

QUAKER WITNESS IN A
TECHNOLOGICAL SOCIETY

*Originally presented as the Friend in Residence Address, Intermountain
Yearly Meeting Annual Session, Boulder, Colorado, June 1992; published
in* Friends Bulletin, *November 1992, pp. 36–39.*

THE THEME OF the 1992 Intermountain Yearly Meeting, "Be
present where you are," is a message that was frequently
offered by Fred Haslam, a much respected Friend in the Toronto
Monthly Meeting. He wanted to remind us that Friends do not
need special or heroic occasions to witness to their faith. Wherever life places us, there will be needs and openings for our witness. What is required of each of us is to be noticeably present. I
would like to explore with you what it means to be an active
Friend, living and witnessing in a technological society.

At the outset, we are faced with a curious paradox: there are
good grounds to say that Friends witness is timeless. The testimony against all war and violence, the belief in that of God in
every person, the need to practice simplicity and plain speech are
not changed by the passing of time. Yet, there are also good reasons to hold that everything has changed. Our lives are totally different from the lives of early Friends. The context within which
we need to be present poses questions that are genuinely new.
How can we respond?

Two posters that I often remember may illustrate the core of
my inquiry. One, a poster in front of a church in our neighbourhood, asks: "If you were accused of being a Christian, would there
be enough evidence to convict you?" (or, if you were accused of
being a Quaker . . .). The second poster, on the street side of the
Friends Meeting House in Cambridge, England, reads: "Do you
drive with loving care?" This, then, is our challenge: to provide
evidence of our being Friends in a world in which one drives—
and in which things are driven, usually not with loving care.

The Changing Focus of Friends Witness

Within this framework I would now like to look at some specific examples of the applications of our testimonies in today's context. I want to interlace these thoughts with some reflections on technology itself, because it is due to the changes in technologies that contexts have changed so much.

Let me begin with Friends' firm belief that there is that of God in every person and that we must answer to it. In their petitions to the high and mighty, in their work in prisons or their activities in war and conflict situations, Friends have always refused to apply permanent labels like *enemy* or *evil* to people. However difficult in practice, we are in unity when we believe that no person is intrinsically evil and beyond the grace of God. In modern societies, however, not only people but also corporations, institutions, and organizations are persons under the law. In fact, in the United States, corporations became persons under the law, with all the intended rights and privileges, before women did. Personally, I find it difficult to believe in that of God in the World Bank, the International Monetary Fund, and the CIA. I really believe that there are evil institutions in this world. The conviction might not matter a great deal, if it were not for the question of potentially good people serving evil institutions.

Friends have indeed worked with those evil institutions with a certain measure of success; some of those within became open to the Light. Some practices—notably in prisons and with respect to conscientious objection—have changed, but the evil institutions have remained. One may wish to reflect on the extent to which prison reform has helped the cause of prison abolition. The recognition of the right to conscientious objection has certainly not aided attempts to outlaw war.

At one time we could have hoped that "some day there would be a war and nobody would come." Not so today! War can, and is, fought by machines and machine-keepers. The question of whether or not "somebody" comes has become irrelevant. It is for this reason that the peace tax movement is very important for Friends, since it relocates part of Friends testimony against all wars and violence into the context of modern war preparation. This change in the focus of our witness is a direct consequence of the technology of war-making.

Technology as an Agent of Social Restructuring

Let us then reflect on the nature and meaning of technology as it affects our "being present where we are." Many of my thoughts on technology have been inspired and stimulated by the work of Kenneth Boulding, and I would like to acknowledge my indebtedness to both Kenneth and Elise Boulding. Following Kenneth Boulding's interpretation, technology is best defined as *practice*; Boulding also pointed out that there is a technology of praying, just as there is a technology of plowing. Technology as socially acceptable practice is therefore essentially "the way things are done around here." This definition eliminates the notion that technology is intrinsically linked to machines and devices. While modern ways of doing things often involve machines and devices, their presence does not create technology.

Any discourse on particular technologies, on the need for their introduction, and the values incorporated in them can benefit from defining technologies as ways of doing things and is therefore open to discussion, change, or amendment. However, contemporary technologies have now resulted in an interlocking network of machines, devices, and practices that constitute a web—or a system—in which all threads or components are affected when one is pulled or changed. An event that on the surface seems unspectacular can serve as an illustration of the interconnected effects of changing practices: the introduction of the sewing machine. When domestic sewing machines became available in the late nineteenth century, the manufacturer, like all manufacturers of new devices, wrote glowing descriptions of all the good that would come of this new invention, especially for the poor. An editorial in a trade magazine read: "In all the venerable institutions these machines are now in operation, they do or may do a hundred times more towards clothing the indigent and feeble than the united fingers of all the charitable and willing ladies collectively through the civilized world could possibly do." This technology also gave us the sweatshops that have particularly oppressed immigrant women. We must be mindful, when we hear all the glorious stuff that a new technology, a new way of doing things, will bring, because many technologies with good potential have indeed been greatly misused.

We may want to note, in passing, a few other aspects of "technology equals practice" that are sometimes not adequately recognized. For instance, social structuring through technology is one root of bias and labelling. "The way things are done around here" provides an easy and seemingly self-evident definition of the insider (who does things the way we do things) and the outsider (who does not). The social structuring by technology has also been used to justify confining women to "women's work" and to camouflage the social and moral values embedded in *our* way of doing things. It is well to remember that, from the very beginning of their public witness, Friends insisted that in the presence of the Light other ways of practical conduct will be found, not only by Quakers, but by everyone....

The intimate linking of technologies and values was beautifully described by Lewis Mumford in 1944:

> Between the 13th and the 19th centuries, one may sum up the changes in moral climate by saying that the seven deadly sins became the seven cardinal virtues. Avarice ceased to be a sin. The minute attention to the care of worldly goods, the hoarding of pennies, the unwillingness to spend one's surplus on others—all were habits useful for capital saving. Greed, gluttony, avarice, envy, and luxury were constant incentives to industry. [1]

Implications: The Need For New Modes of Response

In terms of our being present where we are in this technological world, let me address just two areas of acute interest to Friends: modern war and war preparations, and modern communications. In terms of warfare, modern technology has created a situation where there are no longer civilians, non-combatants, or innocent bystanders. In fact, in actual war situations, military personnel are often safer and better cared for than the so-called civilians. Friends witness can address these changed constellations if they wish to be present where they are.

One example comes from a Canadian event. A bunker in Debuc, Nova Scotia, is intended to house—if necessary for a pro-longed period of time—senior military and civilian officials to carry on the functions of government in case of nuclear war or intensive air attacks. A few years ago a broadly based exercise was held to test the functioning of the bunker in terms of its mission. Halifax peace people utilized the occasion to make it clear just what modern warfare involved. A few days before the exercise they distributed permission forms to those scheduled to go into the bunker. The forms, to be signed by the wives and children of the designated persons, gave the bearers permission to be safe and protected from attack while their dependants would likely perish. Not unexpectedly, the widely circulated forms created a lot of stir and also a lot of thoughtfulness. Some of the designated bunker occupants refused to go. Others squirmed. Halifax is an old navy town. When I spoke there a few days after the exercise, I tried to explain how modern war technology had turned the navy's cher-ished motto, "Women and children first," into its opposite. In modern war or war preparation, it is women and children last, if indeed their needs enter into the picture at all.

It is clear that the new technologies of war also require an economy that puts women and children last, even in no-war or pre-war times. I do not like to speak of the last four decades as times of peace, since the physical and political preparations for war have never stopped. Today Friends peace witness must include the witness against techno-structures that conscribe and allocate taxes for war and for women-and-children-last government activities. There are many opportunities for such witness.

I would be amiss if I did not acknowledge at this point the important role that the American Friends Service Committee (AFSC) has played during the past seventy-five years in terms of focusing Friends witness within a contemporary political context. Many Canadian Friends share my respect for the members of the AFSC staff and board with whom we have worked throughout the years. In my own case, as clerk of the Canadian Friends Service

Committee's peace committee during the Vietnam War, I know how much knowledgeable, practical, and moral support we received from the AFSC Peace Education secretaries. It would be hard to imagine how we could have accomplished the difficult task of sending medical aid to Hanoi without their help. I particularly count on the ongoing international work of the AFSC to expand and illuminate the new contexts in which Friends may witness to their faith.

Finally, let me give my second example of a type of activity that has been restructured technologically. Communication, as it is called in today's jargon (talking, listening, and responding to people) has always been important to Friends. Early Friends spoke and argued, listened, and proclaimed. George Fox used the phrase "This I know experimentally," as he recalled his direct experience of God's grace and presence. The power of Friends testimonies and of their rejection of formal rituals rested in large measure on the validation of the direct and personal experience of the power of the Spirit, without the mediation of saints or clergy. How often have you recently taken part in discussions that began with the equivalent of, "This I know experimentally . . ." rather than "This I saw on television"? Modern technologies, which should be called non-communication technologies rather than communication technologies, have all too often replaced the face-to-face discourse about experienced realities with discussions of one-way messages and artificially constructed images. We need to remind ourselves of the loss of reciprocity that modern technology has brought to the interchange of words and meaning between people.

When George Fox and his followers argued in the steeple houses, they argued with particular people about specific issues in the hope of changing minds and practices. The discussants argued back; there was reciprocity in the discourse. Today all radio and television-based technologies involve the sending and receiving of messages with no possibility for direct interaction between sender and receiver. We have at home a treasured cartoon that shows a little man on crutches, his foot in a heavy bandage, next to a television set with a broken screen. A second man, looking at the damaged set, says: "Next time Trudeau speaks on TV, just turn it off." Doesn't this say it all? There is no way to talk back to a television image, no way to respond directly to the message.

This absence of reciprocity that modern technologies have brought into communications between people is particularly damaging to Friends' approaches. For instance, in conflict prevention or mediation, how do we answer to that of God in every man when "he" is only an image on a screen? In view of the impact of modern technologies, Friends' tradition of making direct human contacts deserves much strengthening, as does Friends' ongoing critique of non-communications technologies themselves. Simple daily ways of witness can open. For instance, I have a special wish for the Society of Friends. Let's have a new testimony against the use of acronyms. It seems to me that acronyms are the very device that plain speech tried to avoid. Acronyms are time-saving devices that discriminate between the ins and the outs, those who know, and those who don't matter because they don't know. We should always introduce and define acronyms if we cannot avoid using them. It's a serious issue and also a good way of getting into conversation with people about Friends testimonies.

What I have tried to put before you is the thought that while Friends' beliefs and testimonies are timeless, the context in which we must witness to them is not. To be present and to witness as Quakers in a technological society involve us in two interrelated tasks. The first task is to strive for genuine understanding of the restructuring of modern societies through technology, so that we may be able to explain and to intervene. The second is to seek clarity on how to witness so that one day technology can be driven with loving care.

Note

1   Lewis Mumford, *The Condition of Man* (New York: Harcourt, Brace, 1944), p. 162.

WHAT OF THE CITIZEN?

Adapted from a talk at Beyond the Arms Race: Building Security and Peace, a conference sponsored by Dalhousie University, Mount Saint Vincent University, Saint Mary's University, Canadian Learning Materials Centre, and Halifax City Regional Library, Halifax, Nova Scotia, 22–24 March 1984.

I WOULD LIKE TO view the role of the citizen from two angles. First, I want to look at the traditional position of the citizen; then I would like to put to you what we, as citizens, might be able to do in the present context. Let me assure you that I realize that the monolithic notion of "citizens" is not always valid. Groups of citizens differ in class, age, nationality, culture, and interest. Nevertheless, there are roles that all citizens play regardless of their nationality, the political flavour of their government, their age, and their own political persuasions, particularly with respect to the arms race.

First, all citizens are, in terms of their own governments, the justification and raison d'être for the arms race. All governments justify their acquisition of weapons, their alliances, and their defence policies by the rationale of the nation-state: the state has a mandate to protect the physical safety of its citizens by all means necessary. (I will return later to the fact that today this mandate often goes well beyond physical safety to ideological safety.) This means, believe it or not, that we as citizens are the supposed reason why countries arm. (It's a bit like McDonald's, who say, "We do it all for you.") The state so justifies the arms race. Unfortunately in this case we, the citizens, cannot say, "Sorry, I am a vegetarian, I would rather do my own cooking." It is well not to forget that a central role for the citizen in the arms race is that they provide the justification for the mandate of "defence." This role, as the provider for the rationale of the need for armament to defend the physical and ideological safety of the citizen, is assigned to the population, quite globally, regardless of the particular power politics of their countries.

The second role of the citizen with respect to the arms race is that of being a basic resource. It is our money that is purchasing the arms and providing the wherewithal for this sphere. Without citizens to pay taxes and provide the wealth that can be taxed, the arms race would look quite different. While some of us have been able to refuse to have our skills co-opted, the state can always commandeer money. Thus—consent or not—the citizen provides the essential resource base for the arms race.

Thirdly, and quite importantly, the citizen is the present and the potential participant in war and in the preparation for war. Here I refer to the citizen's role as a bystander, as a civilian, as a non-combatant. One of the features that characterizes both modern war and modern preparations for war is the blurring of the distinction between what is military and what is civilian. This again is applicable to all countries. All over the world, citizens no longer have the choice of being part of the military or of the civilian population. They are drawn into bearing the consequences of war and the preparations for war, whether or not they choose to participate in it.

It is worthwhile to look for a moment at the historical development of this increasing victimization of the innocent bystander in war, because it reveals important roots of the development of the international peace movement. In the second half of the nineteenth century, the Crimean War gave Europe a first-hand look at the realities of warfare. Out of these experiences the Red Cross was formed and the first modern transnational movement of people against war as a political instrument arose. It was the beginning of appeals by citizens to their governments, arguing against war as an institution and an instrument of politics. The realization of the atrocities and suffering that war afflicted on all was particularly keenly felt by women. Bertha von Suttner's tireless activities on behalf of the first International Peace Society mobilized the conscience of citizens of her time. The realization that in war all are victims became a deep bond between citizens of different nations. We should also remember that it was Bertha von Suttner who persuaded Alfred Nobel to award prizes not only to those who had most advanced particular fields of science, but also to those who had most effectively advanced the struggle to eliminate war as an instrument of national policy. The power of the nation-state made it increasingly difficult to stress this communality of values. In the 1930s Lewis Fry Richardson, a British mathematician and a Quaker, examined the statistics of what he called "deadly quarrels" in order to demonstrate the all-encompassing nature of war in modern times, and to warn the world about the extent and potential of the next war. Richardson enumerated and counted the victims of war regardless of which side they were on or whether they were military personnel or civilians. He said simply: "Those who are dead, are dead, those who have suffered, have suffered." Suffering on the one side is in no way less horrible than suffering on the other. Richardson's approach was considered quite unscholarly at the time; in war-related studies all good academics had to separate the victims into "us" and "them." As a consequence of this attitude, much of Richardson's important scholarly work remained unpublished for more than twelve years, before two of his books were edited and eventually printed posthumously.[1]

I put these reflections on Richardson's work and on the historical roots of the international peace movement before you in order to make a plea: it is essential that we stress and gain a broad understanding of the fact that citizens play common roles with respect to the arms race, roles that are completely independent of nationality, boundaries, ideology, and individual stance. This common role and common burden that citizens globally share is the basis on which we all have to work together for peace, to lift this burden through a process of fundamental social change.

These global roles of citizens are passive roles. But questioning their underlying rationale can guide us to the active response we seek in order to move beyond the arms race to genuine security, peace, and justice. Let us first look at the self-taken mandate of the nation-state, the mandate that claims that the state is responsible for the physical and ideological safety of its citizens. This mandate may have begun as an attempt to establish a caring community, where physical safety involved looking after those who could not look after themselves because they may have been too old, too young, or too sick; it may have indicated equal access

and opportunity for all. However, the mandate has been transformed; now, more and more, it means putting people into
national or multinational fortresses under the assumption that the
threat to physical security and well-being is something "out there."

Over the past decades, states have also increasingly begun to
assume the mandate of responsibility for the citizens' ideological
security and well-being. And this mandate is in no way confined
to states behind the Iron Curtain. Recent studies by journalists
such as Barrie Zwicker have revealed how Canadian news media
deal with the Soviet Union and the Third World; it seems that the
mandate for ideological safety of the Canadian population
requires only negative reports from countries such as the Soviet
Union, Cuba, or Nicaragua. In Canada the notion of a caring
community is being supplanted by the notion of the multinational fortress. The very programs that communities have put in
place to care are being cut under a banner of fiscal restraint, and
the savings are fed into producing increasingly effective threat systems, justified by the state under the rubric of "defence," or "security," in capital gothic letters. *Defended to Death* (1983),[2] a book on
the European defence situation edited by Gwyn Prins, a young
British scholar, shows that the practice of military defence tends
to deprive a country of its finances and its values to such an extent
that eventually the external defences are perfect while the rest of
the population may be either morally or physically dying. People
all over the world are beginning to understand this and object to
it. One result is the ludicrous situation in which new missiles in
both Britain and West Germany must be defended not from
enemy action but from the anger of the population that they are
supposed to protect.

The mandate of the nation-state has gone astray and urgently
needs redefinition and focus. Part of this questioning must challenge the notion that the citizens of one country can only be
made secure through a system of threats erected towards other
countries. The idea that one achieves security by making others
insecure has led us into this ever-escalating arms race. We cannot
hope for a reversal of the arms race until the interdependence of
security in a modern world that knows nuclear weapons is fully
understood and accepted.

But beyond the issue of nuclear arms, it is the threat system itself that anyone who considers the role of the citizen must understand and reject, on a global or a local level. In this day and age it is not possible to have a world run by threats. On the local level, threats produce an attitude that sanctions and leads to the arms race, because force, shooting, overwhelming, and bullying are seen as solutions to problems. On the international level and in international conflicts, threats will always become global and can always result in the final threat of global extinction. Many people, including military planners, are today thinking about the lethal nature of global threats, but they rarely consider the wrongness of the threat system itself. Basically the threat system is morally unacceptable, even if it were to work in practical terms in the short run. In other words, even if war were safe, a safe war is just as wrong as an unsafe one.

The questioning of the nation-state's mandate to threaten brings with it the questioning of the right to commandeer citizens' resources and skills for this purpose. The refusal of consent is probably more widespread than it seems. Today we are seeing the beginning of a movement to withhold the portion of taxes that would be used for overt military application. The peace tax movement, which is basically an extension of the concept of the citizen's right to conscientious objection, is beginning to spread in many Western countries. The withdrawal of skills, on the other hand, is often done quietly on an individual basis. People change jobs, opt out, do different things in order to minimize their contribution to the threat system, be it internally or externally. It is difficult for those of us who teach to prevent the misuse of the knowledge we try to develop and pass on, but there is a good deal of scope to put knowledge at the disposal of the community in order to develop alternative skills and alternative constructive uses for our knowledge in science and technology or in the humanities.

When we speak about citizens as forced participants and unwilling victims of future wars, I think we are at the heart of the peace movement. It is out of caring not only for ourselves and our children, but also for everyone of every generation in every country, that peace people have become global allies and have rallied together to bring forward their concerns. This global refusal to participate in war brought throngs of people to the United Nations, and brought petitions from all corners of the world. The central question, "Who has given anyone the right to make us into victims?" has brought and continues to bring people into the streets.

The refusal of citizens to be cast in the role of participants is not just a projection of the acute horrors of any future war. It is also the refusal to be a participant in the preparations for war that are already so damaging to the community at large. Think of the people of Utah who felt the direct effects of nuclear testing in their own community. Think of those in Micronesia and in the Pacific Islands. Think also of those whose education, welfare, and hope have been threatened by the predominance of military priorities over social priorities. Think of the Third World countries that must accept arms in order to qualify for economic aid, that are forced to line up behind major power blocs in order to qualify as trading partners. We could describe this situation as the global bystander's dilemma. People get hurt just by being in a certain place at a certain time; they are hurt because preparations for war occur globally. This is why the move against the arms race is so universal, and why peace is such a global concern.

There is no doubt in my mind that the vast majority of people want desperately to move beyond the arms race into a time of genuine peace. To explore the road ahead I would like first to look at certain facets of the discussions of the arms race and then at the notion of peace. Discussions about the dangers of the arms race are, of course, not new. Indeed, some of us with long involvements in the peace movement experience rather sad moments of déjà vu at conferences we attend these days. But what is new is the ever-broadening constituency for whom disarmament has become an urgent personal priority. This broadened constituency may be the reason why one begins to hear the voices of mainstream politicians and members of elected governments. Some of these voices are a bit incongruous. For instance, when we hear representatives of various governments speaking about the peril of the arms race—in moving words recently uttered by our prime minister—we wonder whether the politicians have only just now woken up to this peril. It somehow seems as if one were dealing with a Victorian maiden, who, not having been informed of the facts of life, finds herself pregnant and says, "Oh dear, I wonder how this happened."

You might think that government representatives who now speak about disarmament imagine that there is a sort of "virgin birth" of nuclear weapons, that the 50,000 or so that exist around the world were catapulted onto the land by some evil force that is now threatening the universe. This is just not so. Each and every one of these weapons was designed, ordered, tested, paid for, commissioned, and deployed. It is not possible to let politicians simply say, "There is a horrible, horrible peril and we have to do something about it." We cannot absolve the political decision-makers from the responsibility of having brought about this perilous situation. There is no virgin birth of nuclear weapons; each and every piece of hardware is here by decision and design. We have before us, in the literal meaning of the word, a man-made problem.

In addition to the basic unwillingness and inability of our political leaders to comprehend that nuclear weapons create a reality that is different in kind from anything experienced before, there is the escalation of the arms race, racing from overkill to more overkill, defying reason and common sense. The madness of it all boggles the imagination. Imagine you had a couple of kids making mud pies. They put one on top of the other, and when the pile reaches eight or ten, they see the whole thing collapse. If they keep on doing this without learning from experience that you cannot pile mud pies on top of each other indefinitely without the piles collapsing, you would suspect that they might be retarded. You would be forced to have a serious talk with the teacher, the principal, or anyone else knowledgeable about such mental disabilities in order to find out what the future holds for the children and how to help them. But when this same type of thing happens with the piling up of nuclear weapons, it is called strategy. As citizens we should be reasonably clear about this, and also reasonably firm. It seems to me that we must say: "Gentlemen, you are producing a predictable collapse. Either you know how to stop it or you'd better move over, because it is too dangerous to let you continue. It is too dangerous for all of us." The freeze movement may then be seen as the sophisticated equivalent of "no more mud pies, Johnny."

It may be possible to get across to politicians what not to do, and to assert the political will to enforce it. But it is quite something else to be able to discuss what must be done instead. Now we are talking about peace. But peace, I'm afraid, is an almost unknown quantity. It may be well to reflect and realize the extent to which, for more than thirty years, the world has been preoccupied with war. At the end of the Second World War, the fear of yet another war dominated the intellectual and political scene. Everyone scurried, trying to prevent war, to prepare for war, to argue about or against war. From the point of view of those who armed and had to justify their armament, and those who argued for disarmament and had to find arguments to support their convictions, the intellectual landscape was dominated by war. But what we are talking about is peace. Peace is more than the absence of war, and it is different in kind.

The knowledge of what peace involves is far greater among citizens than it is among governments. This is because, as citizens, we can still participate in the community, in institutions and situations that operate under the basic assumption that nobody will hit anyone else over the head, either physically or emotionally. There are still situations in which you do not have to threaten or feel threatened. Thus skills of peace are still being developed in our communities. One of the most urgent present tasks of active citizens is to guard the knowledge and the skills of peace, to extend them, to be a repository for them, and to research and extend all that relates to the question of how we can live together in peace and justice as a community. Don't think that this is simple or trivial or cheap. Just giving up war does not solve everything.

I think that the development of a society that says, in principle, no to war and the threat system will be very difficult. It will only come through a profound commitment to justice and nonviolence, and through much patient trial, reassessment, and experimentation. At the moment we know nothing about the economy of peace; we do not know which of our technologies can be used to maintain a society of peace and what scales of technology can be tolerated. Our ideas on the social structures of peace are as yet undeveloped, although in this field we are far better off than in our quest for knowledge of technologies of peace.

We owe a good deal of our advances in the understanding of social structures to the women's movement. It was out of their insights and struggles that a deep understanding of hierarchical structures arose. Today many of us know that a society of peace cannot function within the hierarchical structures as we now know them. I am convinced that we will have to work within structures now being developed as alternatives, within the networks of links that have been developed, tested, discussed, and critiqued predominantly among women. As yet we know little about the extent to which these networks can be enlarged without their again becoming hierarchical.

At present it is most important to think consciously about peace as a permanent social institution. No government or nation-state will develop the skills of peace for us. As citizens it will be our role to focus on peace and justice while we vigorously oppose the arms race. There is one urgent task that we all, as citizens, must attend to. Within the framework of our search for the structures of peace, we must document those peaceful situations existing around us that do work. There is a normal tendency to document and speak only about problems, while blessed things that work without creating overt problems often remain unrecorded. Peaceful situations usually work because of a few people who flutter around and make sure that normal problems never become problems with a capital "P," but we rarely hear about such workings. The very absence of problem creation makes them invisible, so we don't notice them. We notice all that goes wrong, but I assure you that there are things that go right, often far more than we assume. There are harmonious communities, there are organizations that work, often in spite of the system in which they are situated, and there are people who are happy at what they are doing. These are the situations we should examine; we should try to learn why they work, what it is that makes them peaceful and effective, and how we can extend these processes—on what scale and under what conditions of time and place.

Peace, after all, is a process, not a product. It is not something that you can buy for a lot of money and put on the table; it is not something that you can pay somebody to design for you. Peace is a process of consent and co-operation. It is the outcome of the work of people who want peace. As A.J. Muste once said, "There is no way to peace, peace is the way." The citizen's role of searching for peaceful social structures is part of our search for peaceful social processes. We must look at ways and means that are compatible with a society of peace.

This will not be easy because I fear that we as citizens have absorbed far too much of the mentality of industrial production to recognize the primacy of means. Too often we concentrate on the end product, and we think that if we can just fiddle things the right way, everything will come out fine. The arms-control approach to peace and security weighs one weapon type against another, trying to balance weapons systems, rather than asking, "Are weapons not means of threats? Is security achieved by threats? Or what other means are at our disposal to achieve security, justice, and peace?"

If we follow the path of searching for acceptable and peaceable ways and means we will realize how much our daily lives are permeated by conflict-producing processes. Look at how situations and problems are described in our society. For instance, news-media reports seem to cast every event in a conflict model. News reports on television present the world as if everything is a conflict between people who are "for" or "against" something and the situation can be resolved only by one side winning over the other. But life is not a football match; problems are not resolved by winning. We must be very clear about the destructive influence that this sort of view and paradigm has on our daily lives. This conflict model leads to a horrible simplification of situations and it also prevents us from hearing about things that are not conflicts, or cannot be cast into a conflict model (preferably accompanied by evidence of physical violence).

Beyond media reporting of news and events, we must also look at our own language, how we phrase questions, how we talk about events, and how we describe the participants. We should consciously avoid representing all events as conflicts, and in an either-or framework. While it seems persuasive to describe things in a way that one must be either for or against, we do not live in the flat earth of an either-or world. One of the roles of the thoughtful citizen is to refuse to accept unacceptable alternatives: the alternative to nuclear energy is not simply freezing in the dark; the alternative to being a complacent and compliant citizen is not being a social outcast.

Our friends of the Green Party called themselves "green" not only because of their concern for the world's ecology, but also to indicate that they were on neither the red nor the blue side. It is clear that we must escape the either-or situation to present a totally different way of doing things. This task sits squarely on the citizen. Now it is important to introduce into the public debate the need to break away from seeing every situation or issue as a conflict and considering the victory of one side as the solution to underlying causes.

Winning is the least useful thing that can happen in any conflict. As E.F. Schumacher so eloquently told us, conflicts must be transcended in order to be resolved. Real conflicts are resolved only by transforming them into non-conflicts, but in order to transcend a conflict, to find ways of permanent resolution, one must walk around a problem, look at it from all sides, get everyone's co-operation, and begin to discover the roots of the situation. For this the either-or model won't serve, nor will the football team's goal of winning be of any help.

As we extend the either-or framework into the disarmament discussions, we find that many people are hypnotized by the mentality of zero-sum games. In this mentality, if you want to win, someone else has to lose. If you want to gain, someone else must give something up. It is not difficult to point out the many instances in which this scheme falls down. Life is full of them. Take teaching, for instance: if I teach well, my students learn, but I learn too, so all of us have gained. The most important processes in society, as far as a peaceful world is concerned, are those in which all gain. The indivisibility of peace is possibly the best example: either there will be peace for all, and all gain, or there will be no peace, and all will lose.

Let me then sum up. I have tried to show that there are passive roles for the citizen, roles that are inflicted on all, regardless of system or nationality. Citizens' security is claimed as the justification of the arms race; citizens are the resource and provide the wherewithal to feed the arms race, and they are also the victims. The inflicting of these roles and their consequences is the common cross that all carry. The resistance to assuming these roles is what binds the peace movement together, across cultures and around the globe.

This analysis has served as the base from which I have made suggestions to turn the role of the citizen from a passive to an active role that may stop the arms race and bring us peace and justice. For this to happen, it is necessary to question the assumptions under which these passive roles were assigned; it is necessary to question the mandate of the nation-state for the physical or ideological protection of its citizens; it is necessary to explore ways of removing the citizens' consent to be a resource for war preparation. It is imperative to illuminate the nature of the military threat and understand that it can only produce victims.

Together we must find means of non-participation in systems of threats, be they local or global. But more than that, we must learn to understand the structures on which threat systems are built so that we can develop structures that can become the foundations of peace and justice. In our resistance to the arms race, we should focus much of our creative energies into developing these structures along with the basics of economics, technology, laws, and the meaning of citizenship under conditions of peace.

There is a great need for us to avoid either-or presentations and images of confrontation, of teams, of winning. We must take every opportunity to point out how constraining and non-productive such images and languages are. It is clear to me that it will be citizens, rather than governments, who introduce new thoughts, fresh ideas, and human perspectives into this grim and threatened world.

What is needed is the safety net of interdependence that is built from the shared priority that *all people matter equally.* Indeed, the well-being of this planet and its inhabitants is the only guarantee for the survival of any nation, group, or family. If there is to be security and peace, it will be security and peace for all: for those we love and for those we can't stand.

Notes

1 See Lewis Fry Richardson, *Arms and Insecurity: A Mathematical Study of the Causes and Origins of War* (Pittsburgh: Boxwood, 1960); and also his important study, *Statistics of Deadly Quarrels*, ed. Quincy Wright and C.C. Lienau (Pittsburgh: Boxwood, 1960).
2 Gwyn Prins, ed., *Defended to Death: A Study of the Nuclear Arms Race*, from the Cambridge University Disarmament Seminar (Harmondsworth, England, and New York: Penguin, 1983).

WOMEN AND MILITARISM

Published in Status of Women News, *February 1983; reprinted in* Canadian Woman Studies / Les cahiers de la femme, *vol. 9, no. 1 (Spring 1988), pp. 5–6.*

SOME OF US HAVE come to the women's movement through peace concerns; others participate in the struggle for peace as feminists on the basis of their own direct experience and analysis. All of us know and understand militarism as the prototype of structures of threat and violence that are only too familiar to women.

What do we mean by militarism? *The Concise Oxford Dictionary* tells us that militarism is the "spirit or tendencies of the professional soldier; the undue prevalence of military spirit or ideals." In fact, militarism is much more than that. Beyond the traditional training for war and the preparations for "combat" (whatever that may mean), militarism today is an internally consistent system of attitudes, perceptions, and actions; it is the ultimate manifestation of the threat system that, when stripped of all its extraneous verbiage, simply says: "Do what I tell you—or else." The institutional arm of the threat system, aptly called the armed forces, provides the scope, the tools, and the logistics for the "or else." The political arm of the threat system directs and finances the development and acquisition of these tools and utilizes the knowledge of their power and availability. One arm cannot exist without the other; together they constitute modern militarism. This system operates with our money and without our consent.

Women are among those who have had much experience of being at the receiving end of threat systems designed with their resources and without their consent. It is not surprising, then, that today the most penetrating attacks on the roots of militarism and the most creative approaches to alternate structures have come out of feminist analyses.

The deepening and broadening of the structural critique of militarism seem to me a most urgent task, a task sometimes forgotten as the war-peace discussions centre on the tools of the military. After all, the fate of the Earth is at stake when nuclear war threatens. People have good reason to be frightened by the mounting stockpile of nuclear weapons, by new chemical agents, by Trident submarines and cruise missiles, by escalating responses and responses to responses. But our fundamental objection to militarism is not related to the size of its arsenal or the destructiveness of its weapons. What women must object to is the threat system *per se*. We have not consented to live in the "or else" world of threats. We want to build a "why not" world of mutual respect and diversity.

Feminist analyses of social structures, of typical situations in the workplace, schools, or the larger community, have clarified the tactics and approaches of threat-based systems. They all work under the implicit assumption that some people matter much less than others, and that all people are of interest only as long as they are needed to support the system or to justify it. Women know how hierarchical systems can threaten any opposition with social and psychological isolation, with economic penalties, and with political blackmail. Militarism should be interpreted as the ultimate development in this line of structures. The threat now is the survival of the collectivity itself. Militarism asserts a blind, diffuse, and random threat unrelated to individual people or specific issues. (If this last observation is not correct, maybe someone can tell me what a harmless female scholar like me has done that can be rectified only by the use of nuclear weapons.)

It is clear that the weapons we fear are the logical outcome of the development of the military threat system. If we want to get rid of the weapons and the danger to global survival they represent, then we must face up to the system of militarism, not just its tools. And let us not forget that facets of this system are already deeply embedded in what might be seen as the civilian sector. Just think of the incidents of blind obedience ("I'm just following orders") and automatically equating rank with competence, of disregard and lack of respect for anyone outside the system ("women, Native people, and the handicapped," as the then minister of employment and immigration put it so succinctly), not to speak of the pursuit and glorification of brutality in all its psychological, physical, and technological aspects, and you will gain an idea of the intrusion of militarism into our supposedly peaceful lives.

The twin relationship between militarism and the hierarchical structures that oppress women was clearly understood by many of the pioneers of the women's movement. In 1915 Alice Duer Miller wrote:

> Men shouldn't vote: 1. Because men are too emotional to vote. Their conduct at baseball games and political conventions show this, while their innate tendency to appeal to force renders them particularly unfit for the task of government. 2. Because no really manly man wants to settle any question otherwise than by fighting about it. 3. Because man's place is in the Army. 4. Because men will lose their charm if they step out of their natural sphere and interest themselves in other matters than feats of arms, uniforms and drums. 5. Because, if men should adopt peaceable methods, women will no longer look up to them.[1]

This is more than just a clever repartee; it illuminates the symbolic and structural roots of the male domination women are exposing. Many leading advocates of women's rights, such as Jane Addams, Sylvia Pankhurst, and Clara Meyer-Weichmann, were pacifists. Conversely, men who were opposed to war were often also supportive of women's struggles for personhood and equality. And so it should be. To me the struggle for women's rights and the opposition to militarism in all its forms are two sides of the same coin. And that coin is the promise of a livable future, a future without "aye, aye, sir, ready sir," a future without sexist or jingoist stereotypes. If this future is to be realized, it must be based on respect, not on domination, so that its principles will hold for relations between individuals, between groups, and between peoples. I am convinced that, if these goals cannot be achieved, there will be no future. Ironically this may be the ultimate "or else."

Note

1   Alice Duer Miller, "Why We Oppose Votes for Men," in *Are Women People? A Book of Rhymes for Suffrage Times* (New York: George H. Doran, 1915); reprinted in *Pulling Our Own Strings: Feminist Humor and Satire*, ed. Gloria Kaufman and Mary Kay Blakely (Bloomington: Indiana University Press, 1980).

NUCLEAR PEACE

An excerpt from "Nuclear Peace," a discussion including Ursula Franklin, broadcast on Ideas, *CBC-Radio, October 1982.*

I HAVE AN ANALOGY of the arms race and vicious dogs. You live on a street. You can't stand your neighbour, and he can't stand you. He may want to go after your carrots, and the apple tree, so you think it might be a good idea to have a dog. And since the dog is supposed to be a deterrent and you want to keep the guy from taking the carrots, you put the dog—a vicious dog—on part of your front lawn. The dog is there for all to see: "We have a vicious dog."

You can see how this works. Your neighbour says, "Now they have a vicious dog, and they may be after *my* apple tree, and anyway, they are nasty, shifty-eyed people. I'd better get myself a dog. And I'll put it on *my* front lawn." Now that man has a dog, and you have a dog. You'd better get yourself *another* dog. Soon you see that your entire front lawn is of no more use, the kids have no place to play. You have a dog, you have two dogs, you have three dogs … the place is full of dog shit. You spend your money on dog food, so you begin breeding dogs. Of course your neighbour breeds dogs, so you have to get experts on breeding dogs that are even more vicious. You sell these dogs to your friends down the street, because by now you have started processing dog food and have a small share in the dog-food plant. It gets wilder and wilder, but you say to the people to whom you sell your dogs, "It's *only* for defence."

Pretty soon, nobody can come to visit anyone. The mailman has trouble, and the kids don't play in the street anymore. You have more and more dog shit and you don't know what to do with it. In the end you spend all your money on dog food, you devote all your expertise to training dogs, you hire dog breeders, and you own your share in the dog-food plant. And that's the insanity of the arms race! In the dog scenario, very soon, someone would have said, "Listen, you're nuts. Who has given anybody the right to turn this street into a kennel?" And all the nonsense would have stopped after the third dog. The world maintains the arms race, but no street would maintain the dogs.

PEACE AS AN ONGOING ISSUE

Unpublished paper, adapted from the keynote address at the Women and Peace Conference, Toronto, 3 June 1994.

MANY OF US IN and around Voice of Women have been pre-occupied through the decades with the issue of peace. Thirty years ago, when Voice of Women entered into that arena of public discussion, the word "peace" was on everybody's mind. We had become conscious of the effects of nuclear testing and radioactive pollution, which were very much a subject of public discussion, much more than nuclear issues are today. Still, it is the issue of peace that brings us together again.

To begin, I want to reinforce the point that peace is not the absence of war. Peace is the absence of fear. Peace is the presence of justice. Because of the work that all of us have done, we are very clear that peace, in fact, is a consequence. Peace, as it was defined in 1936 by R.B. Gregg, "is a by-product of the persistent application of social truth and justice and the strong and intelligent application of love. The price of peace is the price of justice."[1]

This definition makes it very clear that not only do we not have peace in the world today, but also that the issues before us are very much issues of peace and justice: justice for people and justice with respect to the environment. Such justice allows a condition in which there is freedom from fear: fear of war and the military; fear of economic or political, cultural or sexual oppression; fear of not knowing where to find meaningful work for oneself or for one's children; fear of not knowing where there could be a public sphere in which the issues of peace and justice have priority over the issues of profit.

Thus peace *is* the overriding issue. Why then, you may ask, is it so difficult in this day and age to effectively work for peace? What has, for instance, the collapse of the Soviet empire done? Has it brought us closer to peace? I want to speak most of all about what is, in every sense, the legacy, the mortgage, of forty years of non-peace and the Cold War. We often overlook the fact that the problems we have to address today—problems that bring women together in Beijing, in Toronto, in the former Yugoslavia—are problems of trying to deal with the legacies of both the Cold War and numerous hot wars. In the following paragraphs I will enumerate five aspects of this legacy that constitutes the political, economic, and emotional landscape in which we have to work.

First of all, the legacy of the past has left the world full of weapons, and more are continually added. With a strong weapons development industry and international weapons trade, the world remains full of easily available weapons.

Secondly, the legacy of the Cold War and the preoccupation with weapons have also left the world full of unresolved problems. It is easy to forget that, for decades, the priorities of the Cold War and of a militarized world have allowed governments to postpone response to rightful demands of their citizens and not fulfil a great number of obligations of government. Governments, after all, are there for people, and not people for governments. Remember that we are their source of income and that they are our servants.

For decades we were told that a crucial service our national government must provide was to arm the country—both physically and in terms of mindset and ideology—to keep evil empires from reaching over the pole into our land and our minds to corrupt our soil and our thoughts. Although this was not quite the job description of what Canadians expected from their governments, the notion of an ever-present enemy has led, over the decades, to a large backlog of unresolved problems not only in Canada, but all over the world.

What we now face is the legacy of things undone, tasks not tackled for decades, constituting awful mortgages for the world to carry. There are mortgages of social policies, of missed opportunities particularly for women; missed openings in access to day care, to education, to training, to jobs, and to taking part in public life on terms appropriate for women. There are also unresolved problems of sustainable development, of a healthy environment, of dealing with the toxic legacies of arms production. It is also necessary to remember the pressing questions not asked and explored, the research not done, the money not made available to pursue essential explorations of alternative medicine, of alternative technologies, of different ways of arranging our lives together—

and that is a Cold War legacy I find particularly troublesome, having spent much of my life at universities.

My third point is that the legacy of the Cold War has left us with a tremendous lack of bridges. For a long time the world was divided into ideological islands and blocks, often against people's will. This state of affairs has made it impossible for two generations to speak freely to each other, to build friendships, to exchange thoughts, and to build the bridges of knowledge and trust that are essential for the development of peaceful societies.

We must never forget that the Cold War produced forty years of physical, intellectual, and emotional isolation. In some parts of the world, this isolation came on top of old colonial barriers. Some peoples never were united as communities because, in many cases particularly in the Third World, their independence came almost simultaneously with the postwar divisions. There are groups of people today who were artificially separated first by colonial powers and then by the ideologies of the Cold War. It is no surprise, then, that animosities and hostilities initially fostered by the divide-and-rule strategies of colonial powers and further perpetuated during the Cold War are now, with access to weapons and in the face of economic need, breaking out into active fighting and lack of peace.

Many efforts towards peace and conflict resolution are hampered by the lack of bridges. Among the few existing bridges are those between women in the peace movement, built painstakingly over the past decades. We need to continue to build and expand these bridges. If gatherings like those in preparation for the Beijing conference allow extensions of bridges, these gatherings will be vitally important, even if nothing else happens at the meetings.

My fourth point concerns yet another legacy: the lack of non-military perspectives in public discourse and public policy. For decades everyone focused on winning, and this perspective, transposed from territorial wars to trade activities, still prevails. Nevertheless, many of us know that winning can be one of the least constructive and most pointless activities in life. You will be especially mindful of this if your kids play competitive sports such as hockey. (My children, early on, had the good sense to be on the losing teams, which gave us the opportunity to do something else with their Saturday mornings.) The exclusive stress on winning is, in most situations, non-constructive, to put it mildly.

To focus life on winning is, if you allow this oxymoron, a losing proposition. In most situations there are far more losers than winners, and it is quite inappropriate to consider "winning" a measure of quality and worth. The perspective on winning is essentially a fighting (that is, a military) perspective. Unfortunately—again because of the Cold War mindset—this perspective has taken over public life and discourse in a very destructive manner. To me, it is unacceptable to interpret most aspects of social and political life in terms of either a war or a football match.

When I said that winning is a losing proposition, I did not intend to speak against being good at something or putting one's heart and soul into the pursuit of a worthwhile endeavour. There is a difference, and to me a very significant difference, between success and achievement. Achievement is always built on the co-operation of a group of people. One achieves with and through the assistance of others. People learn from each other. They begin to shine when there is support, when there is teaching, learning, and understanding. Achievement is always obtained with people, by people, through people. Success, on the other hand, is frequently dependent upon the absence of competitors who are more competent, more aggressive, or better known. If I succeed with my meringues, it may be only because there is nobody else who makes better ones. I hope and pray that nobody will make better meringues so my little lumps of not-quite-happy egg white will be evidence of my "success."

Unfortunately, this homely analysis applies to many other situations. I have seen with profound sadness examples among my students, some of whom begin to think negatively about classmates who are just as able or more able than they are. Students realize that their success may depend on the fact that there is nobody around who is any better than they are, regardless of absolute standards. When young people are urged to be successful, to be lean and mean, an outlook focused on success can lead them to see each other not as sources of support but as hindrances in their own path. It frightens me that success-focused people look at other people as being "in the way"—yet another military, conquering view.

Drawing attention to the lack of non-military perspectives in public life that is manifest in the emphasis on winning, we realize that the world has forgotten that, in many quarters, as people, we need each other's help desperately. This is why it is so unhelpful to look at everything on the local or the global scene in terms of a conflict model. There are other models, but after forty years of looking at society only through the glasses of conflict, alternative perspectives do not easily come to mind. It seems self-evident to cast every problem in a conflict mode, as if somebody has to win and by the same token somebody has to lose.

The absence of non-conflict models from public discourse is a bitter Cold War legacy that we need to correct. We need to re-introduce other models of social and political processes: co-operative models (which we all use day in and day out on the micro scale), eco-stress models, models that illustrate the interweaving of global issues in order to emphasize their common roots, and coping models that women have learned from history and nature. We need to ask each other: "How can we cope? Where is the best knowledge? Where is the needed support?" The world's lack of experience with co-operative models of conflict resolution is apparent in the difficulties of international negotiations. Many political leaders are like people who have not run around the block for decades and now have to do it: they cannot get up to speed, everything aches, and they limp.

The lack of articulated experience in the use of a co-operative model makes our work for peace doubly difficult. Even daily occurrences are commonly cast in a conflict model. For example, a friend of mine pointed out that even weather forecasts frequently use the language of conflict: there is a "threat" rather than a "probability" of thunderstorms. When we catalogue the problems that we need to discuss with other women, let us avoid conflict models and war language that inevitably lead to the conclusion that might is right and that winning settles the issues. Today military might may be replaced by economic might, but this substitution does not seem to be a change of approach or a move towards peace and justice.

This brings me to the fifth aspect of the Cold War legacy: the public financing of extensive high-technology projects at the expense of other items of public spending. The past decades have seen the public purse funding extensive high-technology work that was primarily of interest to the military, with additional profits ensured by spinoffs from needs created in the civilian sector.

I suggest that this trend is continuing. The much-touted information superhighway, a civilian continuation of Star Wars, is an equally unrealistic scheme put together to meet needs that were artificially created—just as needs and demands for strategic defence initiatives had to be created. Suddenly there appeared to be a need for an umbrella of missiles that nobody except the military had asked for. Now we are seeing the transposition of the same industrial support to a new scheme that will put us into a stream of mainly irrelevant information that nobody has asked for. The information highway, as an extension of Star Wars, was designed in a Cold War mindset to support a previously nurtured industry.

Having laid out five legacies of the Cold War, I will turn to the question of working for peace in this environment, because we need peace, both for healing people and for healing the earth. What must we do, and how might we do it? One step in this common task is to articulate clearly how we got where we are. The current mess in which the world finds itself did not come in a plain brown envelope by public post. It was created—and it was created primarily by men who did not listen.

One central conclusion from the experience of the peace movement must be carried into the next phase of the work, and it is this: whatever action is morally and humanly wrong is also dysfunctional. Think of all those guys who exercised power, pushing winning, leanness, meanness, and the bottom line: their schemes obviously did not work. Surely one cannot maintain that the state of the world as it is now was designed to be like this: war and strife, widespread unemployment, hunger, violence, environmental degradation . . . I do not know what those in power thought they were doing, but whatever it was, it obviously did not work out.

And it did not work out, I suggest, because the means were wrong. It is wrong to bully people; it is wrong to gain security by making others insecure. Even those who may not share our conviction that in this human family no one can live forever at the expense of everybody else need to be reminded that exploitation, brutality, and oppression do not work, even for the oppressors. These means have never worked. The Romans did not get away with it. The slaveholders did not get away with it. Unjust means may look tempting or pragmatic in the short run, but in the long run the immoral does not work. From our current vantage point, we must forcefully articulate the fact that morally unacceptable means are also impractical and dysfunctional.

Let us remember first, how we got to where we are, and second, that the means by which we got here are not acceptable, not only because we believe they are wrong but because they do not work. We do not wish to continue the present mess, and we know there are other ways of dealing with problems—co-operative, respectful, and interactive ways. Women have always known and usually used co-operative means. Approaches such as hierarchy, patriarchy, or running things from the top down have long outlived their usefulness.

What we, as women, bring to the new tasks is a horizontal solidarity. We have it here today and each of us will carry it into our own work. Horizontal solidarity is a bond that crosses boundaries and is essentially based on an understanding of means: regardless of what the situation might be, there are certain means, such as violence, that are not acceptable.

If I had more time, I would have liked to speak about the roles of the non-governmental organizations (NGOs) in the struggle for justice and peace. NGOs are important, and I find it increasingly unacceptable to characterize international organizations by what they are *not*. If we are not like governments, it may be a great compliment, but there are positive, real characterizations. Many international voluntary organizations are co-operative, many are preoccupied with facilitating social change, and many include people with whom we will want to work in order to change the world from the imperial model which still dominates the United Nations.

It is essential to transcend the present imperial approach to world problems, which will never bring justice and peace, and come to a co-operative, tolerant, confederated model. This is a task that, I am convinced, only women can do. I hope we can not only build bridges of friendship but also reaffirm the confidence that our past work so very richly justifies. We can do it and we will do it.

Note

1 Richard B. Gregg, *Pacifist Program in Time of War, Threatened War or Fascism*, Pendle Hill Pamphlet 5 (Wallingford, Pa.: Pendle Hill, 1939).

PEACE, TECHNOLOGY, AND THE ROLE OF ORDINARY PEOPLE

Adapted from an address given as the Fifth Dove Memorial Lecture, University College, University of Toronto, 18 September 1995.

I WOULD LIKE TO look at what has happened to the concerns about peace and science since 1989, when John and Lois Dove so tragically left us, by looking at three aspects of these concerns: the first one is peace; the second is technology; and the third is the role of ordinary people in the search for peace. In 1989 it seemed as if our concerns for peace were headed towards some form of resolution: that with the end of the Cold War in sight, the quest for peace would in some way be, if not completely successful, at least substantially advanced. The overall quest for peace can be seen as a set of questions to make us think, "How do we get from here to there?"—to a world in which there is "stable peace," to use Kenneth Boulding's term. We know that peace means not only absence of war, both as a threat and as a reality, but also the presence of justice and the absence of fear. Looking back, it seems that in 1989 our dream seemed closer to realization.

The peace we pray and work for is not a commodity but the consequence of a just ordering of society. There are essential political, human, and economic components that make peace possible. What would become possible through stable peace is the prevalence of justice, compassion, and fairness and with that the absence of fear.

Unfortunately the sphere of our own reality has changed drastically since 1989—mostly for the worse—although our activities in the quest for peace have not diminished. Global political realities have shifted in a strange way. Those who hoped that some of the developments we pressed for would come to pass with the end of the Cold War were deeply saddened by the turn of events. For instance, there was an expectation that money previously spent on the arms race would now become available to meet human needs, as a sort of peace dividend. We hoped for better funding for teaching and research, for arresting environmental deterioration, for building institutions of peace and international co-operation. Once the burden of the arms race was lightened or lifted, we thought, a different set of priorities for the use of public funds would emerge. Why did this not happen?

The end of the Cold War did not rechannel resources into peace, the environment, or unmet human needs. Instead of the promised peace dividend we saw a displacement, rather than an abolition, of war that occurred on two levels. On the first level, the old shooting reality of war is still painfully present in Bosnia, Chechnya, and many other places in the world; the threat of war between the big powers has been replaced by war among smaller states or regions. On the second level, we have seen the displacement of war into the economic sphere. These developments have included significant transmutations of the social institution of war. War has been updated with modern instruments to assist in the struggle for global commercial hegemony. Economic competition and conflict have taken on the characteristics of active slaughtering warfare, from propaganda and scapegoating to loss of lives, displacement of populations, and destruction of natural and built environments.

These developments put the peace movement once again in the position of struggling against the arrogance and ignorance of power, against impending destruction, occupation, and conquest. In our own country, instead of a peace dividend, we see cutbacks and layoffs along with neglect and degradation of scholarship, of the civic environment, and of nature. The so-called job crisis—the automation of work and human tasks—is, on the most profound level, a war against people. New policies of rationalization and globalization, alliances, and trade agreements are part and parcel of the type of threat system that the peace movement has been trying to expose and resist for at least the past four decades.

The mentality and the practitioners of the threat system have not disappeared with the end of the Cold War. On the contrary, the threat system is expanding nationally and internationally. What we have seen is not a decrease in the incidence of war, but rather a transposition of war into another key. Just as music can be transposed into a different key, war—in addition to its continuing presence in terms of armed struggle and the preparation for

armed conflict, complete with arms sales and the attendant profits—has undergone a social and political transposition. We, as
peace people, need to understand, explain, and confront this new
transposition or mutation of the social institution of war.

At this point you may well ask, "How come? What happened?" Surely, the justification for an arms race disappeared with
the end of the Cold War; the "evil empire" justified everything
from Star Wars to stealth bombers. Why did the major world powers not convert to peace? Why did the co-operative and constructive developments we had hoped for not come about? To come to
grips with these questions, let us reflect for a moment on the
nature of the transposition of war and the new instruments that
are playing the old tunes.

First and foremost—anyone wanting to make war needs an
enemy. Who or where is the enemy in this new war context? In
looking for an answer, we need to give special attention to the
recent manifestation of modern technologies. Let's start with the
definition of technology as *practice*—in other words, "the way
things are done around here." Current practice includes machines
and devices, computers, and every form of network and machinery, but all these instrumentalities are embedded in something
larger: the social, economic, and political workings of a society.
Clearly, the way things are done today is not necessarily the way
they have been done in the past, nor is it the way things will be
done in the future. The definition of technology as *practice* allows
us to keep both determinism and fatalism at bay.

Citizen advocacy has often involved discussions of technology
and critiques of the *way* things were done as well as *what* was
being done. Technological changes have frequently brought
groups within society face to face with the need to influence
decision-making and regulations in areas that suddenly affected
everyone's daily lives, be it nuclear weapons testing, air or water
pollution, or depiction of violence on television. The subject and
thrust of citizen interventions can be a sensitive barometer indicating incipient changes in social and political relationships.

What should be the themes of citizen interventions, particularly those involving the work for peace, in the mid-1990s? I am
convinced that it is necessary both to refocus the citizens' per-

spectives and priorities and to closely scrutinize the role played by technology in the transition from the Cold War to the present post–Cold War power relations. During the Massey Lectures on "The Real World of Technology" I tried to illustrate relationships between the development of military technologies and the economic policies of national governments by pointing out two distinct tasks for any state wanting to use military production as an infrastructure for the advancement of technology and employment. The state must ensure funding for the military-industrial complex, and at the same time ensure the ongoing presence of an enemy to justify massive outlays of public funds for research, development, and procurement of instruments and infrastructures of "defence." This designated enemy must warrant the development of the most advanced technological devices; the enemy must be cunning, threatening, and just barely beatable by novel, truly ingenious, and heroic technologies. I added then (it was 1989) that it would be interesting to see how Western "defence" infrastructures might respond to the possibility that internal changes in the Soviet Union might eliminate its role as designated enemy, and I ventured the thought that the social and political needs for an enemy might be so deeply entrenched in the real world of technology that new enemies would have to appear relatively quickly in order to maintain the existing technological power structure. Even then I was afraid that there could be a turning inwards of the war machine. After all, we must remember that the enemy does not have to be the government or citizens of a foreign state. There is a great deal of scope as well as historical precedence for pursuing an enemy within.

Unfortunately it seems that this inward turning of the war machine was exactly what happened when the "evil empire" collapsed. The technological infrastructures of the West were not dismantled; their new use, I suggest, is a new form of war (that is, the transposition I spoke of earlier) that is now called globalization and global competition. In other words, the technological tools of control and conquest function as before but in a new key, creating a new form of war. The new battlefields are "markets." These markets are not pleasant local markets like the St. Lawrence or Kensington markets in Toronto, where real people sell and buy, chat, and get to know each other. The new markets are stock and currency markets, the faceless arenas of electronic transactions. The responses of these markets have become significant indicators of the supposed well-being of people and nations, and it appears that for governments, how the stock and money markets react to elections and referenda is far more meaningful than is the so-called will of the people.

The fact that wars are being fought for access to resources, for the enhancement of commerce and trade, is not new. What is new, in terms of the transmutation of war itself, is that the battle-fields are no longer territorial; there is no physical ground that may be "ours" or "theirs." Technologies of forty years of war-making have made territory immaterial, just as intercontinental ballistic missiles have made national boundaries immaterial and neutrality irrelevant. The development we now see is an internally consistent extension of the extraterritoriality in modern weapons developments. The full arsenal of the publicly financed technologies of war, from operations research to computer systems, from satellites to space communications and integrated networks, has become the instrument of a new transposed war for global commercial power.

You may ask, "If what we experience today is indeed a war without national boundaries or defined territories, who, or where, is the enemy?" I will give my response first, and then my arguments—which you may or may not consider valid. In the war of global competition the enemy are *people*. By this I mean not *the* people (a particular class, group, or nationality) but *all* people who look at community, at work, at nature, and at other human beings as sources of meaning and interaction rather than as commodities. Whatever cannot be merely bought and sold, whatever cannot be expressed in terms of money and gain-loss transactions stands in the way of the "market" as enemy territory to be occupied, transformed, and conquered. Whatever work can be done by machines or devices will be done by machines or devices, rather than by people, who become surplus and must be "laid off," put aside like dirty dishes, or sent away to someone else ... the nightmare of ethnic cleansing in a technological transposition.

Let me now restate my interpretation of the current scene, to come to the third strand of my argument: the role of ordinary people. I hold that in the new form of transposed war there is no longer a clear distinction between "them" and "us," a distinction that passports might define. The new enemy territory being attacked is the territory of non-market forces and inhabitants. It is any and every area that is governed or informed by considerations other than the market considerations of buying, selling, and profiting. The new battlefields are found in those territories, physical as well as mental, that are the home of the common good, of art, of friendship and scholarship, of whatever is held in common and cannot be cut up into private parcels of property. This realm, and those who care for it, contains the main targets and enemies of the new war. It may be that I am wrong in my interpretation, and I would be most happy if this were so. Yet I feel compelled to make this argument, and to urge you to talk about these thoughts. It is imperative that we do not close our eyes to what is going on, both in our own country and in many other countries.

From a historical peace perspective, we are in the middle of a market-driven war on the common good. Wherever human beings see themselves as neither buyer nor sellers, neither customers nor clients, wherever they feel that their values, their vitality, and their sustenance come from a collectivity of interests, a community of shared experiences, their lives may be under attack. The attack is not always clear-cut and overt; it can be subtle or neighbourly. Yet for the peace movement, this new face of war must become as unacceptable as the old one.

When we began the work for peace as the Voice of Women we tried to speak to women across the globe about the future of all our children. We must speak about this new war in the same manner. We must ask each other, "What about the common good, the care of the environment? What kind of work will there be for our children? What is happening to the human community? How can we make common cause with other ordinary people of this world in a concerted resistance against the new war?"

You may wonder, "How can we refocus our new peace approach when so many of the 'old' problems are still with us? When there are still nuclear weapons and testing, land mines, arms sales, and weapons development?" The answer is that because the new developments are embedded in the old, both technologically and politically, both can and should be addressed together. We need to analyze the issue as clearly as possible to make it clear that market ideology and strategy are war ideology and strategy. We need to identify this phenomenon's destructiveness and its immorality, and protest its practice by our country and with our money.

Surely, the commandment "Thou shalt not kill" does not apply only to those who use guns or bombs. Peace is a most pressing issue to engage all who wish—in the words of Camus—to be "neither victims nor executioners."

GLOBAL JUSTICE CHEZ NOUS

Adapted from a talk sponsored by Ten Days for Global Justice, an inter-church coalition made up of about two hundred small groups across Canada, Bloor Street United Church, Toronto, 1 February 1997; published in Monetary Reform Magazine, *Winter 1997–98, pp. 10–14.*

PART OF LIFE is the striving for justice and peace. All of us realize that the very substance of life is made up of love and faith. I think that we have to reassure each other, now more than ever, that we aren't mad, that this is what life is all about, and it is *others* who have what I can only call "moral dyslexia." Moral dyslexia seems to prevent some people from seeing life for what it really is. Unfortunately, unlike those with learning disabilities who need and appreciate help, those with moral disabilities don't come to us for help. They don't request assistance to recover a clear moral vision. Most of them are morally disabled by their own choice.

Our struggle for justice involves the reaffirmation of not only the vision but also the reality that social life is based on mutual understanding and support, and that an integral part of life is our striving for justice in the presence of love. Just as our friends in Quebec want to be "*maître chez nous*" (masters in their own house), we want global justice here and now. George Fox, to whom Quakers trace the practice of their faith, said of the love of God, "This I know experimentally," meaning that he experienced God directly and personally. By the same token, we need to say of the practice of justice, "This I know experimentally." Most of us know what justice, or the lack of justice, is, because we have experienced it at some time in our lives. We know what it means, or could mean, to live in a family or community in which there is justice. Justice, the classic cardinal virtue, is that quality of life on which a civilized society and a loving community hinges. (*Cardo-inis* means hinge, and *justitia* = justice; thus, hinging on justice.) The four cardinal (moral) virtues upon which conduct "hinges" are justice, prudence, temperance, and fortitude.

As some of you know, I come out of the peace movement, and I have always held that peace is not so much the absence of war but the presence of justice. What we need to be concerned about today are the links between the lack of justice abroad and the lack of justice at home. Very early in my own work for peace, I discussed with a colleague the difficulty of getting my friends interested in working for peace and how much easier it was for them to support cancer research. It became clear to me during our discussion that the difference between the two modes of community work is that one is divisible: you or a member of your family can have cancer and your activities might help, but you or a member of your family cannot have peace alone. Peace is indivisible: there is either peace for all—for those you love and those you don't—or there is none.

If you work for peace or justice and new avenues of justice arise from your work, it will be justice for all, not just for those who contributed to the work. Peace and justice will come not only for your friends, but also for all those who stood in your way. This is why work for justice and peace is so unattractive in a society that glorifies individual gains and profits.

We work for global justice, not because it gives us a competitive edge, but because it's right. Justice is the hinge without which no community can live. Today most of us recognize that there are many people around us to whom justice is denied, and we realize that we had better get off our butts and do something about it. It is clear that injustice is deeply ingrained in the system within which we live, and we need a lot of spiritual and practical help to sustain our resistance to injustice. The literature provided by Ten Days for Global Justice shows clearly how the financial and monetary system opens a big umbrella of injustice over the world. Wherever people live, whether they are at the receiving end of injustice or they are perpetrators of it, the case is no longer "us" and not "them" being affected by the system ... we are all affected, because we are all under this umbrella.

Clarity and Solidarity

Since we need tools to combat the injustice that surrounds us, may I offer two? One is clarity. We must be clear about what is going on around us and put aside extraneous or irrelevant arguments, which I might classify as "censorship by stuffing." The mainstream media have, by choice, jammed the airways and newspapers with free-market propaganda. To get this message across, no matter how illogical it might be, they simply produce more and more of it, so that other voices are not heard. Rich countries specialize in this kind of censorship because they have lots of "stuff" to stuff into the airwaves and onto print media. But even they don't have a complete monopoly. Look for alternative sources of information. Clarity about what is going on around us is a necessary condition to our work for justice.

But clarity is not sufficient. We also need a second tool: solidarity. We need to recognize different manifestations of injustice and be clear that injustice—wherever it occurs and whoever is the victim—is injustice. While there is an ever-present commonality in our struggle, some injustices—such as hunger or disease—may be much more pressing than others in terms of being life-threatening for the victims. But these tragedies too are part and parcel of the same struggle for justice, and every person involved in this struggle needs to be well informed about the links between each element. And every skirmish fought with clarity and solidarity can then become a contribution to the advancement of justice. The question is, "How can we all advance the task in practical terms?"

I find the current situation both here and elsewhere only bearable and understandable with the help of two mental pictures: one is a picture I have of the reality in which we live; the other is an impression I have from looking back in history.

Occupation: The Reality in Which We Live

I picture the reality in which we live in terms of a military occupation. In an article published in *Peace Magazine* in 1996 I reflected on the question, "Why, in spite of the disappearance of the Soviet empire, in spite of the fall of the Berlin Wall, has there been neither peace nor a peace dividend?"[1] The advances that those who argued for peace had hoped for, the transfer of resources to meet human needs once the arms race had stopped, just didn't happen. In addressing this question, I suggested that the mechanism of war that brought us the planning of Star Wars and the notion of the "evil empire" was transposed—just as you would a theme in a piece of music—from what might be called the military key into the commercial key. The war that had overtly stopped with the end of the Cold War was actually transposed into an economic war in which the political hegemony became commercial hegemony. And because every war needs an enemy, and with the official enemy, "the evil empire," no longer filling the role that it played for thirty years, the new enemy is us—*people*: not a people identifiable by any one passport, but ordinary people, and their institutions, who stand in the way of a takeover by the global marketeers.

The goal of the new war is control of "the commons," and the strategy is "privatization." In the most brutal terms, it entails providing and opening up investment and profit opportunities in all the areas that people had previously set aside as commons: publishing, culture, health care, prisons, education. The purpose of dismantling the public sphere is to occupy its territory—"the commons"—and to turn it over to what I call "the empire of the marketeers." These warlords will, in the end, transform the ill health or misery of our neighbours into investment opportunities for the next round of capitalism.

In my picture of what is going on, we are being occupied by the marketeers, just as the French and Norwegians were occupied by the Germans during the Second World War. We have, as they did, puppet governments who run the country for the benefit of the occupiers. We have, as they did, collaborators. Like the French and Norwegians, we have to protect our families, and on many occasions have to work with the occupiers in order to save our lives. We, as they, need to develop strategies to build resistance under the occupation. We are, as they were, threatened by the deliberate wilfulness of the occupiers, people who have only contempt for those whose space they occupy and who see their mission as one of turning over our territory to their masters. Since our occupiers don't wear uniforms, we can't identify them as clearly as we could military occupiers of the past, but this is more of a technicality than a matter of substance.

Anyone who has lived under a military occupation will tell you that the resisters often refused to speak the language of the occupier. I think this is a good lesson to remember. We too should refuse to speak the language of the occupier, that is, the language of the market. This language reflects, as all languages do, the moral values of those who speak. For the marketeers, there are only economic values; whatever cannot be bought and sold is of no value. We can refuse to communicate in the language of the occupier, to talk about "stakeholders" and "users," "health-care providers" or "consumers of education." For us, these individuals are our teachers and students, doctors and nurses, patients and communities; they are our families and friends. This particular option of resistance is open to all of us and we should use it. We can analyze the language of public discourse and point out what those terms really mean. It is amazing how much such clarification can help to advance clarity and build a resisting community.

We can also look at how resistance worked in the past with activities designed to slow down the progress and process of occupation. One of many interesting examples is *Les Enfants du paradis* (1945),[2] a long and beautiful French film with vast, impressive mass scenes directed by Marcel Carné, who, in addition to his cinematic artistry, managed to keep people working on the production out of the clutches of the occupying army and to shield many young people from the German army or the labour camps. We must remember such tactics now, as we need to protect people, particularly those most vulnerable. We can develop, with each other, ways in which we can slow down and frustrate the occupation. In our case, such means can include court challenges, critiques and factual corrections, and creative use of electronic media to bypass the occupation forces' control of information.

At the same time we need to enlist the help of people with whom we are in solidarity in other countries and urge them not to fall for what is called "progress." Often the process of schooling or training students for production and global commerce can be the means by which marketeers get their paws on yet another conquest. Every problem encountered by people with their particular occupying army is a problem we all have. If global justice is to become a reality, we have work to do and coalitions to build and join. This image of an occupation is something that helps me to decide what I can do with my limited time and energy.

The Reformation: A Look Back into History

The second mental picture that I find helpful is a historical one. What we are going through now is a social change of immense proportions, similar to what happened during the time of the Reformation. I have always felt a closeness to those who, just before the Reformation, were living under the umbrella of a universal Church—an authority that regulated and affected every aspect of their lives. To many, the church was a worldly power that was not bringing God to the people. The question for them was how to get out from under the umbrella of power. Church reforms of the time, whether from the top or the bottom, seemed to be unable to break the stranglehold of power, but each reform movement, in its own way, was able to shake the edifice. Through the process of constant struggle and criticism, the social soil was readied for change, so that in the end it took only a trigger, a silly instant, to finally break the grip of power.

The Reformation was sparked by a clever fundraising scheme to pay for yet another megaproject: St. Peter's Cathedral, with its constant cost overruns. You can imagine that someone really smart had thought: "Why not use the dead to milk the living?" People who did not buy indulgences would feel guilty; surely everybody had an Aunt Agatha who was likely to end up in purgatory, and would want to do something about it. Indulgences had been around for a long time, but this strong promotion created such a stir that finally somebody said, "No! This is just an attempt to exploit our love for those now dead. You can't do it! Your authority does not reach into purgatory." And with this questioning of legitimacy and authority came the curtailment of power.

What I derive from this look at history is the observation that every step in that long journey had prepared the world for the Reformation. Even the most clever people of the time, working alone, could not topple the Church's power. It took the spread of words, thoughts, and deeds from one person to the next to bring about those profound changes in the structures of power. Like the people awaiting the Reformation, we know what is wrong and what must be changed. But it is hard to predict how the change will come; we don't know where or when the trigger will occur. But we do know that it will not come if we don't struggle, if we do not hold the vision of justice and peace clearly before us.

Finally, I would like you to think for a moment about the notion—recently expressed by John Kenneth Galbraith—that in this day and age the key to liberty is money. Historically, the key to liberty was the ownership of land. Those who owned land could more readily fend for themselves, and for centuries land reform was a key to social justice. In today's technological world, however, the key to liberty has become money. Only those with access to money know that they can be full participants in society and feel themselves free. "Ten Days" is correct in its focus on "people-centred" rather than "money-centred" economics. We must strive not only for social justice, here and in other parts of the world, but also for monetary justice. Without social justice and monetary justice, we can't have global justice.

Notes

1   "Peace, Technology and the Role of Ordinary People," *Peace Magazine*, January–February 1996. See also pp. 114–120 here.

2   *Les Enfants du paradis* is set in the Parisian theatrical world of the 1840s, with a screenplay written by Jacques Prévert. The film was made over a period of two years in occupied France in virtual secrecy, under the noses of the Nazis, who would have arrested several of the cast and production crew for activities in the Resistance.

HOW THE WORLD HAS CHANGED

Adapted from "How the World Has Changed," an interview with Paul Kennedy broadcast on Ideas, *CBC-Radio, 13 September 2001.*

Paul Kennedy: We've all been inundated with words and images, I think, over the past two days, and one of the most frightening words that's coming out onto the horizon now is a word that should not, I think, be used lightly. The word is "war." And many people are saying, "We're at war," that the first shot has been fired in the Third World War. Do you think this is true? Where are we?

Ursula Franklin: I'm not so sure whether we are at war, but I'm sure we are not at peace. All my life I have been profoundly committed to peace and have long learned that peace is not the absence of war but the presence of justice. The presence of justice has been missing in the world for very many people. What we may have to realize is that the other side of the coin of peace is justice, or access to justice.

Believe me, I'm a veteran of war. I lived through the bombings of Berlin. Part of my family never returned from concentration camps. I know what war, declared and undeclared, is. I can only shudder at the thought of what happened in New York. But I also shudder, and did so, when the bombs fell on Hiroshima. I'm a physicist. Between the end of the Second World War and the detonations in New York, the world has been full of absence of peace, of presence of violence, and maybe this is the time to think: "What does it take, not to avoid war, but to promote peace?"

PK: It's a difficult position to move towards, though, from the perspective that we are in right now. I don't sense that there is the kind of rational thinking from which you're speaking that can look at the world and say, "War is an absence of peace." How does one move towards peace?

UF: How does one move towards justice? Step by bloody small step. I think I would be inclined to take a position that's somewhat opposite yours. If it isn't now, in the face of horror, that one says, "Force, terrorism, more force, more violence doesn't achieve anything," when do we say it? One of the things that one tends to forget in periods of quietness is how unsuccessful violence is, even for those who have power. Nothing has been resolved by violence over the past fifty years. The rational thinking that force does not work, even for the enforcer, is staring us in the face. This crisis says, "Look at the means we use: whatever it takes!" I think this is the moment to say, "We are on a path of no return if we do not look at the roots of violence, if we do not look at the indivisibility of peace."

I learned very early in my life that peace is indivisible, as is justice. If there is peace for your friends, then there's peace and justice for all the people you can't stand. There isn't one without the other. And if this isn't the moment to see that, and to move towards it by the choice of means, there's no point in more push, more pull, more destruction. We've seen that. Sure, the United States can drop an atomic bomb on anyone and everyone if they so wish. What would then be accomplished? This is the time to think, to stand back and say: "What on earth has got us here?" If you ask me, you start your thinking after the Holocaust. You think about the atomic bomb. You think about the fact that scientists warned Truman and asked him to let the Japanese see the bomb test and its destructive power before inflicting such destruction on the people of Japan. The scientists were convinced that the sight of the test would persuade the Japanese authorities to surrender. Truman did not accept this advice, and the bombs were dropped. Truman's decision conveyed a lesson: some people matter less than others. Why are we surprised if a generation or two later, that lesson has been learned? The only question is, "Who are those who matter more than others?" This is the time to think.

PK: But it's a very difficult time to think, when the kind of peace, the kind of justice you're talking about seems infinitely far away, and the kind of violence, the kind of terrorism, are very close.

Where does one find the thoughtful solitude in which to reflect on the kinds of things you're talking about? People feel very threatened right now. One feels as though the war, the violence, the terrorism, the horror are very close to home and can be anywhere, any time.

UF: Quite. It's how the human imagination works: when I talk in times of peace about nuclear weapons, in times of tranquility about biological warfare, people go off to the movies. It's only at the time of crisis that you might get people to think.

Wouldn't it be nice if a day of mourning for what happened on September 11 was a day of quiet? It's not the thing to say to the CBC, but what about shutting up for a day? Be quiet. Let people think. Communicate the essential. The weather, okay. The traffic, okay. And then have a day of quiet. I don't think more talk gets us anywhere. Just imagine how the end of the Roman Empire looked for people during the time of the birth of what we know as Christianity. It was an awful time. People walked around and asked each other: "Who has any clue of what to do?" Not about the Romans, but about life.

So number one, shut up the trivia; number two, look at your resources. Ask, maybe, what's life all about? Is it not more important to bring up children than to see that the big machines fly faster and faster? Give it a bit of quiet. Look at history. Who has said that all people matter equally and nobody matters more than others? Most traditions. Most religions. Don't drown it out. And then begin step by small step, to increase justice, and to say: "We will not resort to violence privately, personally, collectively, provincially, nationally, globally." There's no other way. You can see how costly violence is. When people say, "Oh, it's so difficult," I reply, "Look at the cost of violence." There are also costs for peace, but the result is more than additional costs.

PK: What would you say to the people—apparently not completely rational people—but the people who perpetrated the incidents on September 11? These are not people who are interested in peace, obviously. These are people who believe in something, who were willing to put their lives on the line because of those beliefs, and who are not committed to anything like the ideals you're talking about.

UF: Quite. But they may never have had a chance to be. I think, of course, I would find it difficult to talk to them, but I may not even find it necessary to talk to them, because they are the product, they are the messengers. On the other hand, I think they may be the easiest people to talk to because one can say, "If you wish to give your life, maybe we can think of other ways of service." These are people who may have no other outlet. I think it may well be incorrect to think that the people who perpetrated this act would have no use for other ways to live if they did have the knowledge that peace and justice were open to them. I think we should not underestimate the motivations of hope. We are a country of immigrants. People go through horrors to come to Canada. Why? Because they hope for peace for their children.

PK: I'm a little bit worried though about the fact that I'm not sure how well connected the kinds of thoughts and hopes that you're expressing are with what's actually happening.

UF: Yes, you are quite right. They are totally unconnected. I have spent the best part of my life trying to put these thoughts into the stream that makes decisions, and I've been spectacularly unsuccessful. That, I think, is a reflection on my ability in the climate of the time, not on the value of the thoughts. It's unfortunate that not only I, but so many people who worked honestly for peace and justice have been so spectacularly unsuccessful. It unfortunately means that there is more suffering before we see there is no other way, there is no alternative to justice. It's like gravity. When people began to understand that they couldn't fly, it didn't mean that the dreams of flying stopped. I sometimes say, "Pigs can't fly, but pigs can be flown." It is the beginning of seeing how we get from here to there. But it cannot be done except by peace and through the means of justice. Maybe this is the time to say, "We have to learn something else."

PK: We are being bombarded with rhetoric, with images, with analyses. Many people are saying, "The world has changed. We are in a brave new world. We are in a situation that is utterly different from the situation prior to September 11." Is that so? And if the world has changed, how has it changed?

UF: Who am I to say that? I think we have to remember that the world is not North America or the people who pontificate. I think the world changes all the time, and then come these events, like earthquakes and thunderstorms, that wake people up to the changes. People begin to notice the "leaderlessness"—recognizing the intellectuals' breakdown of morale, and the absence of humane leadership—when the leadership goes underground if it gets hot and you become led electronically, when someone needs a hug, and gets a recorded message.

That's how the world has changed. We may not change back, but during catastrophes we have to recognize real changes. Unfortunately, it is suffering, like those we see now, that will be the catalyst, if there is any, for reality recognition and hopefully, for an evolution towards a less toxic and hostile reality.

ON THE FIRST ANNIVERSARY
OF SEPTEMBER 11

Published in The Toronto Star, *30 August 2002.*

A YEAR AFTER THE events of September 11, most reflections will focus not on the disastrous events themselves but on the changes that have taken place because of these events. I would suggest that these changes are not so much the consequence of what actually happened in New York and Washington a year ago, but rather of the images—the conceptual models—within which the events were reported and interpreted. Other interpretative images would have resulted in quite different consequences. ("Behavior," as Kenneth Boulding pointed out in his 1956 study, "depends on the image."[1])

Throughout the past year the image of the burning twin towers has remained synonymous with unprovoked attack, and "war" has emerged as the operative model. Thus, the "enemy" has to be identified, located, punished, and defeated: no mean task, considering that this particular enemy was not part of the U.S. consciousness on September 10. The forceful and unremitting pursuit of the enemy—however identified—has lead to more war, bombing, and suffering. It has had serious and detrimental impacts on human rights, civic tolerance, and political accountability not only in the United States but also in Canada and many other nations, without addressing possible root causes of the September 11 events.

The constraints of a war model and the notion of the enemy as the source of the problem make constructive learning from what has happened almost impossible. However, attack and war are not the only images for an interpretation of and response to the disasters in New York and Washington. What would have happened if we had perceived the events of September 11 as an unexpected and devastating earthquake, akin to the disaster that befell Mexico City on 19–20 September 1985? (Two massive earthquakes killed approximately 10,000 people, destroyed 250 buildings, and damaged more than 3,000 others.) With no human enemy or international conspiracy at hand to divert attention, response to "natural" disasters has to focus on the presence of destructive forces that need to be understood and taken into account. The Mexico City example illustrates this pattern of response. There was a remarkable increase in solidarity and tolerance, as political and social divisions were set aside to give assistance to victims. There were also political responses, such as inquiries into accountability for inadequate warning and for the disregard of building and land-use regulations. Hard questions were raised, ranging from the use of existing geological knowledge to the recognition of unexpected vulnerabilities, such as the role of the subway layout in the amplification of shock waves. Collectively and co-operatively it was possible to help victims, to understand the conditions that accounted for the magnitude of the damage, and to modify political and social conduct—including civic reforms and self-organized community projects—without inflicting further damage on anyone.

Interpreting the September 11 events as a political earthquake would have resulted in national and international actions very different from those of the past year. The disaster areas in the United States would have been sealed off, aftershocks expected and guarded against, and other earthquake-prone sites watched and protected. The nation's energy and resources would have flowed mainly into two channels: recognition and help for the victims together with restoration of normal life for ordinary people, and a thorough, dispassionate, and open inquiry into issues such as the root causes of the disaster, the breakdown of warning systems, the experience of others with social earthquakes.

Even today much could be gained from using an earthquake model rather than a war response. Once we get our mind past the preoccupation with the individuals who ignited the specific outbreak, the analogies between geological and political earthquakes are quite real, and not just the stuff of homilies. Social and political structures, like geological structures, are intrinsically unstable. They may change gradually or violently, and the overall reasons for such changes are known. What is not known in both systems is when, where, and at what level of intensity the instabilities will attempt to equilibrate. "Natural" disasters are often catalyzed and amplified by human activities; social and political eruptions build up through the interplay of internal structures and external pressures. Geological fissures and human terrorists are created in a context of forces that can be understood and—at times—mitigated. Neither can be eliminated by bombing. It is crucial to recognize that war and war measures are fundamentally dysfunctional instruments of problem-solving. Violence begets more violence, war begets further wars, more enemies, and more suffering. The practical evidence should be clear to all, including those who have no moral objections to war. War does not work, not even for the warriors. Indeed, the very presence of the option of war prevents the development and use of other images or conceptual models of response to social disasters. The notion of the enemy stands in the way of understanding the causes of social earthquakes, just as the notion of angry Gods once stood in the way of understanding the causes of natural disasters. Is it too much to hope that, in the wake of September 11, a radical change in image, away from war and enemy, becomes possible?

Note

1   Kenneth E. Boulding, *The Image: Knowledge in Life and Society* (Ann Arbor: University of Michigan Press, 1956), p.6.

PART TWO

HERE AND NOW:
THE TECHNOLOGICAL WORLD

IF, AS I BELIEVE, pacifism can provide a map of different social and political realities, then it must be a map for the "here and now"; it cannot be based solely on times past. This can put the pacifist who tries to develop such a map into a bit of a bind.

The principles of refusing to kill, to intentionally do harm, or to give consent to harm-producing actions are old and well-established in the moral teachings of many traditions. Yet if such teachings are to be usefully applied to promote justice and peace in the present tense, a careful understanding of the dynamics of the here and now is vital.

For most of the modern world, the here and now is a complex, technological society. The papers in this part illustrate my attempts to connect an understanding of this complexity with the drive for the advancement of justice and peace.

In the broadest sense of the term, the here and now is our environment, that is, all that is around us—the ever-changing overlay of nature, the built environment, the institutional and social structures within which human activities take place, as well as the activities themselves—"the ways things are done around here"—in any given place, at any given moment.

If any or all of these activities are to be guided by the tenets of pacifism, the components of the here and now deserve special study, scrutiny, and illumination.

The work in this section is part of such a process; it should be considered in conjunction with *Canada as a Conserver Society*, Report no. 27 of the Science Council of Canada (1977), as well as its background papers.

The knowledge and understanding that I gained during the years I chaired that study as a member of the Science Council of Canada have informed my approach to the mapping of the here and now just as much as have my work on ancient technologies and my interest in the practice of pacifism.

The papers are not ordered chronologically. They begin with an emphasis on the complexity and diversity inherent in nature. Clearly, we all live on the same earth, we are all impacted by nature, the seasons, the powerful outbursts of the powers of sun, rain, and wind; yet images of how heaven and earth came to be, and how human beings fit into the scheme of all things, have differed greatly and fundamentally throughout history and within different cultures. Such images are deeply imprinted in all cultures and traditions and, though their roots are distant in time from the "here and now" of my concerns, their patterns have structured the hearts and minds of those who act in the present world.

That is why I found my encounter with classical Chinese thought so rewarding. In this body of thought and instruction I could see insights and images that provide fresh sources of understanding of many environmental problems—their roots and their potential mitigation.

The paper on silence is very dear to me, not only because silence is central to Quaker worship, and is an essential part of my own life, but because of the often unintended constraints on silence that modern technologies have imposed on all people—with or without the consent of those afflicted. The assault of noise and unsolicited messages on people's souls seems to me to create an environment of violence quite akin to how aggression and war hurt innocent bystanders, those poor non-combatants caught in fights not of their own making.

That is why the struggle for a living environment that respects the place of silence is for me symbolic as well as topical. Restoring the social importance of silence represents for me part of the struggle for peace, for an environment in which care, balance, and justice are possible.

The final trio of papers in this part originally addressed audiences concerned with the role of law and regulation in shaping the social and political environment. For me it was important to draw attention to those new dimensions and constraints that modern technologies have brought to all attempts at ordering human affairs in the environment of the here and now.

ENVIRONMENTS VERSUS NATURE

Address presented as the Canada Trust/Walter Bean Visiting Professor in the Environment for 1994–95, University of Waterloo, Waterloo, Ontario, 15 November 1994.

THERE IS NOTHING greater for all of us to aspire to than to be part of the ongoing quest for learning, for human betterment, for improving the smaller and the larger community, and for being part of that great enterprise of universities—the quest for knowledge and understanding. I strongly believe that the purpose of a university is not only to be a place where knowledge and understanding find a home, but also to provide a bridge for interaction with the larger community. What is particularly important for me is that the link between knowledge and understanding is constantly kept healthy so that it does not weaken. It is quite pointless to have all the knowledge of the world and have no understanding of the problems at hand. Yet it is also frustrating and unhelpful to have a profound understanding of the problems of the world and of one's own community but not have the knowledge or access to the knowledge to do anything about these problems.

What I would like to do in the time that we have together tonight is to reflect on the knowledge and understanding gained over the past twenty-five years and what might be done with this new knowledge and understanding. I will do this primarily in terms of concepts: How do we think and talk about the environment and about nature? What questions do we ask? What actions might we take? What might be the next focus? It's a bit like a box in a box in a box. I hope to open some of these boxes; it will be for you to see if their contents are of interest and stimulation to you.

I will begin with a few reflections on the notion of "environment" as it relates to and is embedded in our older notion of "nature." I want to enlarge the notion of environment, but to do so in accordance and, in a sense, in concordance with what we have learned and can learn from and about nature. The concept of "environment" is a relatively recent one that is always defined with respect to an organism that exists within that environment. The environment for a flea is basically different from the environment of the dog that harbours the flea. Environment, in that sense, is defined by the organism to which it relates. We define "ecology" as the science of the multitudes of environments that are not only superimposed on each other but also continually interact with each other. Ecology deals with the sum of overlapping environments. "Nature," therefore, is the living dynamic of this sum total of overlapping environments.

People and their societies have also created environments for themselves. Cities, roads, bridges, and canals have changed what nature wrought and adapted nature to human needs. Such changes of the natural environment by human intervention have occurred throughout the ages. Many of these interventions involved irreversible processes that have permanently changed the real world in which we live. It is a recent idea that people need to pay concerted attention to ecology and to their environments. Today federal departments of the environment and other relatively new institutional arrangements have been called forth in response to the increased modification of nature by human intervention. The increased scale of the interventions and the realization that these activities are drastically and irreversibly changing nature's manifold and interacting environments have raised concerns.

But as the environment became a subject of study and of regulation and governance, there also appeared the idea that the environment could—and indeed should—be managed, and that it should be managed well, whatever that meant. In terms of the notion of environmental management, nature became a rather passive background to the man-made environment. (I use the term "man-made" advisedly to reflect the gender of those who, for the most part, engineered the new industrial environment.) Historically, of course, nature has not been a passive background. Nature represents an enormous power prominently in the foreground of human and social affairs. Nature has also been the inspiration for religious thought, and has posted the markers of the rhythm and seasons of life. For most of human history, nature has been regarded as independent, often dangerous, and usually unchallengeable.

Sometimes in my own darker moments, I think that if I had just one wish, I would wish that the Canadian government could look at nature in the way it looks at the United States: as a tremendous, sometimes dangerous power with which one must live. At every step it takes, our government tends to ask, "What will the Americans say? What will the Americans do? Will they retaliate?" Can you image a Canadian government, in that same spirit of caution and prudence, asking, "Will nature like that? Will nature retaliate?" Unfortunately, considerations of the power of nature have not entered Canadian political thought, even though we know full well that nature does retaliate.

The retaliation of nature tells us two things. One is that nature is a strong, independent power deserving respect, consideration, and a great deal of study. The other is that there are limitations to the tools of reductionist science—in which most of us have been trained—when applied to the study of environments. If that were not so, the responses of nature to human intervention would have been predicted much more reliably by existing scientific studies. In hindsight many of these studies appear simplistic. For instance, to study one species in the Great Lakes or one type of pollution in the hope that such information will help us to understand the workings of a complex, diverse, and dynamic system is clearly inadequate and unrealistic. In addition to the spirit of respect for the power and complexity of nature that must be brought to the study of the environment, we also need to bring a real understanding of the limitations of traditional reductionist scientific inquiry. To study the environment well we must be willing to look at other methodologies, other ways of gaining insight and knowledge that have been used to live in a harmonious relationship with nature.

Over the last decades Canadian society has developed a much greater appreciation of our First Nations' knowledge and understanding of nature. We have also begun to regard what faith communities have to say about the place of human beings within the universe with much more respect. But we also need to seek out the experiential knowledge and understanding of those who are close to the ecosystems of nature, be they farmers, fishers, or people in the Third World who live and work with nature. The fact that such knowledge rarely resides in the universities does not diminish its importance.

At the same time there have been significant changes in scientific methodologies of environmental studies. Discussions regarding the study and the politics of the environment are taking place among a much broader range of people, and the voices of those working the land and the experiences of different racial or geographic communities are becoming part of the discourse. Scientists have queried other disciplines about approaches to problem-solving and applied these approaches to environmental questions. One example concerns the application of insights from medicine to environmental sciences. When Hans Selye studied what he called "stress" and its role in illness, he realized that, regardless of the specific illness, there is a general syndrome of "being sick." He explained how the characteristic symptoms of not being well constitute multifaceted evidence of a system under stress. If some of the stress can be removed, healing can begin. This process does not necessarily require complete knowledge of the stresses, their interactions, or even their ultimate sources. Henry Regier and others have applied this approach to complexity quite successfully to ecosystems under stress, including the Great Lakes.[1]

Other perceptions are also being challenged. Today environmentalists looking at the political boundaries between countries have concluded that political boundaries are meaningless in terms of the environment, in terms of understanding and controlling pollution. It is necessary to consider the reality of bioregions, to learn from nature what belongs together, what is close, what is far, within nature's own organic reach and time scale. We are also learning that methods of traditional accounting, such as computing the GNP or tabulating monies spent or earned, are quite inadequate means of keeping track of the social and environmental effects of human intervention in nature and habitat. Traditional bookkeeping and reckoning have simply ignored factors such as resource depletion, pollution, deterioration or enhancement of the environment, and quality of life, not to mention beauty and grace. Over the last two decades at least, a movement towards total costing and social and environmental accounting has been developed. Examples include the work of Marilyn Waring[2] using time profiles rather than pay scales and monetary transfers as indicators of work contributed or values added. Such novel methodologies begin to provide a way of dealing with things that is more truthful about the environment and can better account for changes in the environment that every society "uses" as its base; and this common phrase, "use of the environment," says so much. By keeping track of just how the bounty of nature is "used," a community is reminded again and again that all people are biological creatures, deeply and closely enmeshed in and dependent on the natural environment, in both the macro- and the micro-sense of the word.

Then there is the notion of habitat. The realization that cities and towns are habitats in an ecological sense has taken hold in the field of environmental studies. The "ecology of cities," in terms of special environments that need to be life-supporting and sustainable, is as legitimate a subject of study as the ecology of wetlands or deserts. This new understanding of habitat has brought a closer co-operation and stimulation among architects, planners, and environmentalists. I was delighted to read that one of the purposes of the Canada Trust/Walter Bean Visiting Professorship is to encourage various departments within the university to work together in the study of a variety of environments. There is a great need for such cross-fertilization among the academic disciplines; the notion of habitat can act as a fine catalyst for such endeavours.

Now I would like to take you a step further in our discussion of environments versus nature. Having spoken of the achievements in our understanding and our knowledge of what nature and the environment are all about, having listened to the Aboriginal voices, to the religious community, to the extended human family, we now are at the point where we realize that environmental studies and environmental politics do not deal with questions of "inside-and-outside" or "us-and-them" situations. What is at issue is, in fact, the question of how to live in one world. All the environments of this planet—the natural, the built, and the engineered—are so intimately and irreversibly intertwined that there must be a livable world either for all or for none.

Understanding this is one thing, but the real question remains: How should we proceed? The environments of this *one* world are certainly not in good shape. In spite of new knowledge and new insights, we seem to be stuck. Why is the world not a lot better place than it is? This is a matter of action not only in terms of law and regulation. The nagging thought behind my questioning points in another direction. Possibly there is still a blank space in our thinking. Is there something we have completely overlooked? I think the answer to that question is "yes."

Let me introduce to you at this point the insights of modern ecofeminists, including Vandana Shiva in India, Maria Mies in Germany, and Judith Plant in Canada, who have linked the human/social situation and nature into a complex web of living interactions. We have already heard a fair amount about biodiversity, endangered species, and extinct plants, animals, and crops. But for ecofeminists the central focus of these reflections on diversity is not only the interplay of the great variety of species and environments, but also their existential interdependencies, their mutual protection and stabilization, their mutual enhancement and balance.

I suggest that there is a diversity in the social realm closely corresponding to the diversity in nature. I am not thinking only of the diversity among peoples and cultures. I want to emphasize that within each society there exists a particular historically and culturally rooted diversity of social forms and institutions that depend on each other's well-being and stability; just as biodiversity exists because of well-developed interdependence and mutual enhancement of its components, so, I suggest, societal diversity is part of a culture's well-being and viability. I argue further that social and political diversities are as much under threat as global and regional biodiversities. Just as we have lost biodiversity through advancing monocultures and habitat destruction, we may be faced with a corresponding threat of the loss of social diversity through the creation of a political and social monoculture. If this were so, it may well mean that a peaceful and just society—with respect to both nature and people—cannot advance without clearly understanding and safeguarding the essential functions of social and political diversity.

At this point in our deliberations, it may be helpful to consider how we talk about cultural, social, or political questions. It has been pointed out that public discourse today in most parts of the world is carried out in three "languages" (taking "language" to mean the conceptual framework of thought and argument): the language of the market, the language of behavioural science, and the language of tradition. Most of our social discourse, including the discourse on education, is now carried on in the language of the market. Whether something "pays," what will be "bought and sold," or "who gets what" are predominant parameters in debates, not only in this country, but globally. Most if not all cultural, social, and political questions seem to be discussed and decided in such terms. This predominance of market considerations is relatively recent; other languages are still available to us. The language of national self-interest has had considerable dominance in the political discourse of the recent past. Languages of history, of religion, of justice, and of compassion could also guide society's affairs, but today the language of the market holds primacy.

The language of behavioural science, which is allied to the language of the market, expresses insights into institutional structures and how they can facilitate, manipulate, and derail people and activities, including the activities of the market. The discourse of how to make things work—and indeed why things don't work—looks for answers in terms of the concepts of behavioural science.

The third language, heard often only as background noise, is the language of tradition, the language of community. It is the language of people saying: "This is us, you know. It's our life. We used to do things in this way." The language of tradition is now quite muted in comparison to the language of the market and the language of behavioural science. Social and political decisions—what to do, how to do it, what not to do—are primarily checked against the criteria of the market and the criteria of the institutional structures.

I spoke earlier about my sense that a basic piece of knowledge and understanding may be missing in our conceptual approaches to environmental questions. This missing concept, I suggest, is the concept of diversity. Diversity, as outlined above, is not just an intellectual construct. It is a dynamic reality in nature and in society, and there is far too little awareness and knowledge about the realm of societal diversity among us. One of the tasks ahead, then, is to develop and apply the language of diversity, and to compare and contrast the language of diversity with the current languages of our social and political discourse.

A language of diversity would stress very different viewpoints formed through its own concepts and its vocabulary. The question, "Is this viable?" in the language of diversity would bring to mind not market criteria but criteria derived from nature's diversity. Can "it" live? Is it situated in a supportive environment? What nourishes it? What threatens it? What makes it grow? What makes it shrivel? Nature has demonstrated to us that the mutual dependence and stability of components within an ecosystem exist because of, not in spite of, diversities and differences. Yet our current perspectives on society lack a corresponding understanding of the functioning of human and political diversities. Once you begin to think about it, you will find a number of good examples to show what happens when the role of diversity is not taken seriously, when the language of diversity is not in use.

In terms of market values, much of what happened in the course of intensifying and mechanizing agriculture looked good at first. Food production increased, and there was general rejoicing, until we discovered what was happening to the soil and to other aspects of the local ecosystem; then the hard questions about monocultures emerged. What does it mean, in terms of the larger ecosystem, when a given crop will not grow without regular applications of fertilizers? What are the costs and the consequences—such as floods, sandstorms, infestation by pests, disease—of interfering with the diversity of a particular region? Such questions cannot be addressed constructively without considering diversity as a basic structural part of nature and all environments. In agriculture the dangers of reliance on monocultures are now fully documented. In terms of environments it is understood that the susceptibility of monocultured crops to disease and their general lack of viability can be traced back to an absence of diversity, which may refer to soils, seeds, co-plants, or animals, in their environment.

None of this is really new. You only need to study forests as ecological systems, as Vandana Shiva has done, to realize that the viability of a system depends on its healthy diversity, that is, on the well-being of all its dissimilar parts. Little of the meagre knowledge about nature's diversity has yet been taken seriously and transposed into the social and political environments. Thinking in terms of a language of diversity would demand respect for individual and collective differences. It could also express the understanding that any political or social monoculture will be as susceptible to damaging infestations of ideologies as large wheat plantings are to attacks of rust. No society can ever be immune to all ideological infections, but surely it is not necessary for us all to get mad at the same time, to go bananas over the same thing, or to hate in the same manner. In farming, the best defence against birds or bugs may lie not in more chemicals but in a diverse natural environment that includes elements that are not to the liking of birds or bugs. It seems strange that civil society is so blind to the benefits of genuine political diversities and differences.

I suggest in all seriousness that we need to look at social systems from the viewpoint of environmental studies—that is, from the viewpoint of seeing viability as a consequence of diversity and, as the other side of the coin, seeing monocultures as threats to survival. Our modern social and political systems encompass a wide variety of institutions that have evolved in order to meet particular societal needs. But institutions, like some crops, can become inbred and lose some of their vital characteristics. Gertrude Stein made it clear that a rose is a rose is a rose, but it is not always self-evident that a university is a university is a university. Yet, just as in nature a rose differs from a lilac or a violet, within the social fabric a university differs from a business or a church; a church, in turn, serves functions in the social ecology that a university or a business cannot fulfil, and the functions of a government cannot be provided by a business or a school. It may be that because all social and political institutions are judged in market terms, there seems to be a noticeable loss of social diversity. There seems to be an increasing crossbreeding and drift towards monoculture in our institutions: universities try to act like business enterprises, banks speak out on education and the future of research.

This is dangerous from an ecological point of view. I fear that we will not make major progress in using our hard-won knowledge and understanding of nature, the physical environment, and the human impact on the environment if we do not address the problems of the social sphere as environmental questions. There is a pressing need to reach an ecological understanding of the societies in which we live, particularly the technological societies. We should study them as local micro-environments and in a global context, realizing that air currents and stock markets may not be so different that we cannot use similar mathematical tools to study pollution in one and perturbation in the other. But, most of all, we should study human societies as part of nature, subject to the same laws and considerations, governed by the same ultimate dependence of one on all.

What has been relearned and rediscovered through the years of environmental studies is the respect for nature, for diversity and complexity. These lessons need to be translated into the human sphere, into the sphere of social structures and the sphere of individual relations. Such an incorporation of knowledge, based on a language of diversity, seems a necessary condition—though not likely a sufficient one—to move towards a stage in world history where people can live and work together in peace with nature and with one another. If the knowledge of how to get from here to there is in any way advanced both by my being here and by the gracious gift of this lectureship, I couldn't be happier.

Notes

1   Hans Selye, *The Stress of Life* (New York: McGraw-Hill, 1956); Clayton J. Edwards and Henry A. Regier, eds., *An Ecosystem Approach to the Integrity of the Great Lakes in Turbulent Times*, Proceedings of a workshop supported by the Great Lakes Fishery Commission and the Science Advisory Board of the International Joint Commission, Ann Arbor, Mich., 1990.

2   Marilyn Waring, *If Women Counted: A New Feminist Economics* (San Francisco: Harper & Row, 1988).

EARTH WITHOUT A CREATION MYTH:
THE VIEW FROM CHINA

A lecture delivered at Earth and the Mind's Eye, *the first interdisciplinary conference presented by the Institute for Advanced Study, University of King's College, Halifax, Nova Scotia, 19 March 1988; published in* Earth and the Mind's Eye, *ed. Kathleen Jaeger (Halifax, 1988).*

THE JUSTIFICATION for my taking part in this conference comes primarily from my wish to bring into our discussion evidence of a different cosmology: that of the Chinese. As we exercise our privilege of studying the material, organizational, and philosophical views of Chinese civilization, we have the opportunity to examine an ongoing civilization with a continuity of at least five thousand years during which the common tasks of community—city planning, health, justice, religion, art, philosophy—were achieved with remarkable levels of success. This civilization, moreover, is built on a cosmology that is essentially different from that of Western tradition: a different view of the universe, how it works, and how people fit into that universe. In our modern era it is to me a source of optimism to recognize that the tasks of community can be accomplished from different bases, particularly as we face tasks new to us—tasks not yet managed as well as we have hoped—with the realization that we are moving into a society that cannot sustain itself unless it learns to look at the earth very differently. In this situation, Chinese civilization offers a body of experience we can turn to, not to copy but to find fresh inspiration.

Chinese cosmology, like all cosmologies, is very old; the human need to see how the world works was established early on and very profoundly. In my opinion, once a particular view is taken, it sets down roots that do not change. What grows from those roots may be elaborated, or have other elements grafted onto it, but the roots remain ever-present. Accordingly, I want to begin my discussion around 1200 BCE, when the Shang Empire began to leave oracle bones for us to interpret. Oracle bones are pieces of cattle scapulae or tortoise shell. A groove was carved in the bone and a question inscribed in the groove; the diviner then applied a hot twig or a bronze rod to the bone until it cracked. The diviner then interpreted this crack as the ancestors' oracular answer to the specific question asked. The script in which these questions were written can now be deciphered and directly linked to both later and modern Chinese scripts, and scholars have determined the questions posed, the answers, and the ways in which diviners interpreted the cracks. The diviners also noted whether or not the prediction came to pass; this candid record gives us an idea of how the Chinese at that early date thought the world worked. We see the Chinese concept of cosmology, first through their technology, and much later, from an increasing body of texts, the authenticity of which has been confirmed by archeological evidence.

Let me now outline briefly how the earth appeared in the mind's eye of the Chinese, and define their essential parameter. In the classical and medieval Western traditions, this essential parameter was the concept of order. That desired order, undisrupted and understood, is paradise, "perpetual spring." The Chinese, however, regarded this perpetual spring either as a huge joke—since there is no such thing in the universe—or as an absolute horror—since the concept defies their belief in a right cycle of things. Where other cosmologies think of eternal order, the Chinese think of time and change. They are preoccupied with time and with an understanding that everything is cyclical. For them, what must be understood is how the various cycles fit together; hence the Chinese are deeply concerned with the mechanics of change, and desire to learn how changes actually happen. They see the universe, heaven, and earth, as a unit, and believe that its dynamic is one of phases of change.

All human affairs—those of individuals, of the state, of the entire civilization—have the same cyclical nature, reflecting these phases. Later the Chinese called these changes the "yin" and the "yang," coming and going, light and dark, waxing and waning. But in this cosmology we find no idea of something coming out of nothing, of something being created, or of something being static. Nor is there a conception of a pilgrimage towards something that will never change. Eventually one learns to understand change and to conduct oneself so as not to get in the way of change.

The whole later Confucian emphasis on *li*—the right way of doing something—is consistent with this early cosmology. From this concept flows a view of nature in which there is no separation between humanity and the earth, but rather a belief that we are here and must understand the dynamics of change in order to achieve the right way of conducting our affairs. Because of this felt need and the Chinese belief in continuity between the living and the dead, the diviners addressed their questions to the ancestors; the more remote those ancestors were in time, the more universally applicable their answers were thought to be.

The great ancestor Ti, who was everyone's ancestor, was the appropriate oracle to pronounce on questions of universal import. But individually pertinent questions were also put to close personal forebears. "Do I have this toothache because I have inadvertently offended Grandfather Wu?" Grandfather Wu after death was regarded as being very like Grandfather Wu before death. Yet in the Chinese concept of the continuity of living and dead, a near ancestor was also not essentially different from one who was very remote.

The Chinese ancestors were there to see that things were done right, so that no action would disturb the changes generated by the overall principle of balance. When things got out of whack, one said, "Oh! We have done something wrong." But that "something wrong" was seen not as "sin" but rather as "wrong process." From this concept comes the idea that the legitimacy of rulership—for the Chinese, the so-called "mandate of heaven"—is in fact a job description. The ruler's task is to do certain things more correctly than anyone else. The mandate of heaven is a temporary justification of rulership to be judged ultimately by behaviour. Thus, under the general principles of Chinese cosmology, there is nothing divine in kingship. Indeed, if the mandate of heaven, the task of just and right processes in government, is not carried out, the good citizen is obligated to draw attention to the situation; eventually the dynasty must be overthrown and rulership entrusted to a better house.

Somewhere around 600–700 BCE a disgruntled courtier decided that the king's mother-in-law had too much power, and that in consequence the universe would send signs that things were going wrong. So he went about the countryside tut-tutting about the situation at court and recording the incidence of floods, earthquakes, and other disasters in an attempt to show that the number had so increased that surely a fresh ruler should take things in hand. In making his case, he gave us our first description of an industrial accident: a magnificent account of how a previously kind and tame furnace suddenly fumed like a volcano, throwing out molten metal and killing workers over a wide range. His description is so accurate that we can reconstruct what must have happened and even produce a fair estimate of the size of the furnace. Clearly, the bottom of the furnace must have got wet; the steam was trapped and the metal melted through the heat from charcoal on top. The action of the compressed steam on the molten metal blew the whole thing up.

This episode reflects a relationship in which people, even monarchs, are seen as a part of nature; when their behaviour—which can extend to detailed practical things such as taxation or mining—offends the harmony of the universe, the earth will give signs that the mandate of heaven has not been properly discharged. Thus dynasties change at fairly large historical intervals, and their decline is always retroactively attributed to one of two forms of inappropriate behaviour: drunkenness or mismanagement. In these explanations we find no concept of personal sin, but rather of a failure to work in harmony with earth and heaven. Excess mining, for instance, was severely frowned on, not as an instance of greed, but because it was seen as destroying the harmony of the earth. Whatever the political reasons, the underlying reason for the change of dynasties was the concept of unity between human beings and all things of the earth and the belief that the task of the learned was to understand the dynamic of the cosmos and instruct others how to live in accordance with it.

This cosmology, in which the concept of order holds no privileged place, but is simply one phase like all other phases, has an obvious practical consequence, clearly illustrated in Chinese medicine. In dealing with a state of imbalance, one has a situational choice. If somewhere the dark, the yang, dominates, the physician can advise on either increasing the light or decreasing the darkness as he seeks to restore balance. There is no doctrinal preference for one path to harmony over another. Such a system rules out a dogmatic approach that says "You must do this." Instead, the prime consideration is the end that is sought, a view that is totally related to process, the right way of doing things according to Chinese cosmology. This emphasis on right process holds for the greatest tasks to the smallest. Chinese medicine offers a prime example, but we also see these cosmological principles at work in the question of the appropriate siting of dwellings or tombs. The experts called in not only give advice and map the terrain but also consider the occupant, his family background, his birthday, his general state, and his occupation in choosing the proper site. Their manuals have titles such as *Of Wind and Water* and *Of Mountain Slopes, Wind and Streams*, and reflect a conviction that human housing, in life or in death, must take account of the surrounding natural elements if happiness is to be a possibility. There is no question of controlling the environment through an act of will. The aim is to understand what is around you and to orient yourself in harmony with it.

Like all experts, these specialists in siting came to believe that they knew everything, and discredited themselves because they did, in fact, aspire to know more than is humanly possible. It has been characteristic of the genius of the Chinese to prune back such excesses and respond with remarkable openness to other influences, taking from them what would fit into their deeply rooted concept of earth and heaven and rejecting what would not. Thus Taoism grew quite naturally out of the simple ancestor worship of the Shang, but whereas in the Shang the priestly caste was also the ruling caste, Taoism separated the two, making the priests the teachers of the rulers. Yet what these priestly interpreters were to teach the monarchs remained much the same. Indeed, much of both Taoist and Confucian literature deals with right process, and thus strongly reflects the early cosmology. Part, but not all, of the new thought from Buddhism was also grafted onto the rooted cosmology. Some ideas of reincarnation were accepted, but the Chinese continued to reject a creation myth and to retain their belief in the basic unity between heaven and earth, life and death.

Into this already highly bureaucratized, scholarly culture came the Jesuits, who arrived in 1582. In their subsequent relations with the Chinese the Jesuits recognized with real understanding that they were dealing with a sophisticated and learned society. Along with Christian teaching, they also brought seventeenth-century European mathematics and astronomy, with its advanced techniques of measurement. In China they found a willing, eager, and respectful audience that became deeply impressed by their learning and skill. When the Jesuits turned from astronomy to the Gospel, the Chinese found much of the teaching of justice and compassion to be congenial, but they had difficulty with the Judeo-Christian creation myth. They could not believe it possible that these Jesuits were, on the one hand, studying the heavens with more insight and precision than the Chinese had achieved, but, on the other, subscribing to such folly as the idea that something is created at a certain point and ends at a certain point. The Chinese were more puzzled than anything else at what they saw as the incomprehensible gulf between the Jesuits' sophisticated study of the heavens and their apparent conclusions concerning the nature of the universe.

I am indebted to the work of the great sinologist Jacques Gernet for this account of the Jesuit experience in China. The following passage from Gernet's article "Christian and Chinese Visions of the World of the Seventeenth Century" provides a clearer picture of how the Chinese reacted to the Jesuits. About 1610 one of the Chinese literati spoke of the missionaries in these terms:

> They are extraordinarily intelligent, those people. Their studies concern astronomy, the calendar, medicine and mathematics. Their customs of loyalty, good faith, constancy and rectitude, and their marvelous skills are certainly ahead of many of our doctorates. It is simply a shame that they speak of the lord of heaven, a crude and obnoxious conception that leads them into absurdities and which our literati have great difficulty in dealing with.... If they could only put aside this conception, they would very well fit into one of our Confucian traditions.[1]

Such was the general Chinese view of Christianity: there was nothing so very wrong that they could not graft it onto their rooted convictions, except the doctrine of creation, which seemed to run so counter to their own sense of the universe.

They did not, of course, see the root of the Christian tradition in earlier traditions. Naturally, too, they could not see what that tradition meant in terms of subsequent development, when the West turned to modern science and China retained the concept of wishing to understand the dynamic of what is there. The Chinese had been early masters of technology but they did not follow the route of the West, which led from the wish to understand and admire God's work, to using God's work for the benefit of man, to seeing scientists as God's little helpers, and finally to permitting scientists to play God.

It is in this context, I think, that it is salutary to consider how the earth appeared in the mind's eye of the Chinese, and to recognize how that earth's place in human life profoundly differs from our vision. To those of us who are concerned about the earth and feel that our approach to it cries out for some fundamental change, I suggest that we can benefit from looking at the deep-rooted conviction of the ecology of all things that we find in Chinese cosmological tradition.

Notes

The original lecture was informal and delivered without script. An edited version of this talk appeared, with permission, in *Earth and Mind's Eye*, ed. Kathleen Jaeger (Halifax: University of King's College, 1988).

1   Jacques Gernet, "Christian and Chinese Visions of the World of the Seventeenth Century," *Diogenes*, vol. 105 (1979), p. 115. This article is reprinted in *Chinese Science*, vol. 4 (1980), pp. 1–17. For a fuller discussion, see Gernet's *A History of Chinese Civilization*, trans. J.R. Foster (Cambridge: Cambridge University Press, 1982), pp. 438–59.

SILENCE AND THE NOTION OF
THE COMMONS

A lecture presented at The Tuning of the World: The First International Conference on Acoustic Ecology, *Banff Centre for the Arts, Banff, Alberta, 11 August 1993; published in* Proceedings: The Tuning of the World *(Banff, 1993); reprinted in* Soundscape: The Journal of Acoustic Ecology, *vol. 1, no. 2 (Winter 2000), pp. 14–17.*

IN A TECHNOLOGICAL world where the acoustic environment is largely artificial, silence takes on new dimensions, be it in terms of the human need for silence (perhaps a person's right to be free of acoustic assaults), in terms of communication, or as the intentional modification of the environment. This discussion consists of two separate but interrelated parts: Silence as Spiritual Experience, which draws largely but not exclusively on the Quaker tradition of religious worship; and Silence as a Common Good. The notion of silence will be examined in terms of the general patterns of the social impact of modern technology. Silence possesses striking similarities with aspects of life and community, such as unpolluted water, air, or soil, that were once taken as normal and given, but have become special and precious in technologically mediated environments.

I am very obviously an outsider, and wish to come to this group to talk about something that is central to all the work that you people are doing. I come in a way as a friend and colleague, in a field where I am fully aware that silence has been the subject of many publications. I know the chapters on silence in Murray Schafer's *The Tuning of the World* and I know that John Cage and others have written books on silence. If I had my senses about me I would have taken as a title for this talk something much more like "The Anatomy of a Soundscape: Dissecting Silence," because what I really want to do is to see how both our concept and our practice of silence have been influenced by all the other things that have changed as our world has become what Jacques Ellul calls a "technological milieu," a world that is increasingly mediated in all its facets by technology.

Let me, then, give you an idea of what I hope to do during this hour with you. I will first of all very briefly say something about sound and the technological system, but I want to spend the bulk of my time talking about silence, to define and analyze it. I hope to be able to show you that we are faced with two domains in which silence is important, and I want, as I describe how those two domains impinge upon each other, to talk about the notion of the commons, common needs, and our common heritage. I want very quickly to talk about technology as practice because this has something to do with the last point —"What Now?"— if I am able to convince you that there is an issue, what might we do? I don't ask you to agree, though I ask you to follow me for this hour, to accept my definitions and assumptions. I am happy if you question them, but just for this hour we will take them in and see what evolves from them.

Let me begin with sound and the technological system. Before we had a technologically mediated society, before we had electronics and electromagnetic devices, sound was rightly seen as ephemeral; sound was coupled to its source, and lasted only a very short time. This is very different from what we see in a landscape: however much we feel that the landscape might be modified, however much we feel that there is a horrible building some- where in front of a beautiful mountain, on the scale of the sound- scape, the landscape is permanent. What is put up is there. That's very different from the traditional soundscape. Modern technol- ogy has brought to sound the possibility of doing two things: to separate the sound from the source, and to make the sound per- manent. In addition, modern devices make it possible to decom- pose, recompose, analyze, and mix sounds, to change the initial magnitude and sustainability of sound, and to change all the char- acteristics that link the sound with its source. Murray Schafer called this separation of the sound from the source "schizopho- nia." We now have easy access to the multitude of opportunities that result from overcoming that coupling.

These techniques are pretty important when you think about the social impact of technology, because prior to these develop- ments there was a limitation to sound and sound penetration. If you heard a bagpipe band there was a limit to the amount of time the band would play; you could wait patiently until eventually the players got exhausted. On the other hand if you heard a recording of a bagpipe band, you were out of luck; it's never going to be exhausted. So in terms of the social and civic impact of technology, electronics make an awful lot of difference; they change the modern soundscape. Modern technology is a source of joy for modern composing and the opening of many doors for expression. Modern technologies are also the source of a good number of problems related to the soundscapes, and to the way society as a whole adjusts, copes with, and possibly ameliorates sounds. And in there sits the tale of what occupies us.

But there is not only sound; there is also silence. Silence is affected by the same technological developments, the same factors that make it possible to separate the sound and the source, and to overcome the ephemeral nature of any soundscape. I said that I would try to define silence and to analyze the attributes that we would keep in mind, related to the value of silence. I struggled with the definition; defining silence as the absence of external or artificially generated sound is fine but a little bit shallow. You can say, "So what, silence is the absence of sound," but silence in many ways is much more than the absence of sound. I feel that we come to the root of the meaning and practice of silence only when we ask, "Why is it that we address, that we value, that we try to establish silence?" The absence of sound is a necessary but not a sufficient condition to define what we mean by silence. The second attribute, the second parameter, comes out of the question, "Why is it that we worry about silence?" The reason is that silence is an enabling environment. When we think about the concept of silence, we note the fact that there has to be somebody who listens before we can say there is silence. Silence or the absence of sound is defined by a listener, by hearing.

In a way, the modern soundscape, along with the modern understanding of silence, divides itself into two domains. There is, of course, the silence imposed by fear or apprehension, its domain ranging from the "shut-up-or-else" to the polite preference not to speak out. However, my preoccupation is with the other domain, with silence as the *enabling condition* in which *unprogrammed and unprogrammable events* can take place. That is the silence of contemplation; it is the silence in which people get in touch with themselves; it is the silence of meditation and worship. What makes this domain distinct is that silence is an enabling condition that opens up the possibility of unprogrammed, unplanned, and unprogrammable happenings.

In this light we understand why, as Christians, traditional Quakers found it necessary in the seventeenth century, when they were surrounded by all the pomp and circumstance of the Church of England, to reject it. We understand why they felt any ritual, in the sense of its programmed nature and predictability, to be a straightjacket rather than a comfort, and why they said, to the amazement of their contemporaries, "We worship God in silence." They justified the practice of silence because they required silence in order to hear God's voice. Beyond the individual centring, beyond the individual effort of meditation, there was the need for *collective* silence. Collective silence is an enormously powerful event; there are contemporary accounts of Quaker meetings under heavy persecution in England when thousands of people met silently on a hillside. Then, out of the silence, one person, unappointed, unordained, unexpected, and unprogrammed, might *speak*, to say, "Out of the silence there can come a ministry." The message is not essentially within that person, constructed in their intellect, but it comes to them out of the silence. This isn't just history and theory. I think that if any one of you attended a Quaker meeting, particularly on a regular basis, you would find that suddenly, out of the silence, someone will speak about something that had just entered *your* mind. It's an uncanny thing, but the strength of collective silence is probably one of the most powerful spiritual forces.

In order for something like this to happen, a lot of things are required. There is what Quakers call "to be with heart and mind prepared." But there is also the collective decision to be silent— to be silent in order to let the unforeseen, unforeseeable, and unprogrammed happen. Such silence, I repeat, is the environment that *enables* the unprogrammed. I feel this environment is very much at risk. I will elaborate on this point, but first I want to say that there is another silence at the boundary of the two domains mentioned above. It is the silence that enables a programmed, a

planned, event to take place. It is the silence in which you cour-
teously engage so that I might be heard; in order for one to be
heard all the others have to be silent. In many cases the silence is
not taken on voluntarily; this is the false silence that I am afraid
of. It is not only the silence of the padded cell, the silence of the
solitary confinement, but also the silencing that comes with the
megaphone, the boom box, the PA system, or any variation that
silences other sounds and voices so that a planned event can take
place.

There is a critical juncture that I hope you will keep in mind
between the planned and the unplanned, the programmed and
the "unplannable." I feel strongly that our present technological
trends drive us towards a decrease in the space—be it in the soundscape, in the landscape, or in the mindscape—for the unplanned
and unplannable to happen. Yet silence must remain available in
the soundscape, in the landscape, and in the mindscape. Allowing
openness to the unplannable, to the unprogrammed, is the core of
the strength of silence. It is also the core of our sanity, not only
individually, but collectively. I extend this to the collectivity because as a community, as a people, we are just as much if not more
threatened by the impingement of the programmed over the
silent, the enabling of the unprogrammed. Much of the impingement is unnoticed, uncommented upon; and in some ways it happens much less obviously than an intrusion of a structure into the
landscape. While we may not win all the battles at City Hall to
preserve our trees, at least now there is a semi-consciousness that
this type of struggle is important. Where could one go to get away
from the dangers of even the gentle presence of programmed
music, or Muzak, in our public buildings? Where do I protest that
entering any place—from the shoe store to the restaurant—
deprives me of the opportunity to be quiet? Who has asked my
permission to play that slop in an elevator that I may have to use
umpteen times every day? Many such *background* activities are
intentionally manipulative. They are not just noise that can be
dealt with in terms of noise abatement. I want to stress two aspects
in this context. One is that the elimination of silence is done
without anyone's consent. The second is that we really have to

stop, think, and analyze in order to understand just how manipulative these interventions can be.

For instance, in a sports arena, friends tell me, the sound environment is coupled and geared to the game: if the goalie misses there are mournful and distressing sounds; when the home team scores there is a sort of athletic equivalent to the "Hallelujah Chorus." Again, the visitor has no choice: the programmed soundscape is part of the event. You cannot be present at the game without being subjected to that mood manipulation. I wonder whether music will soon be piped into the voter's booth: perhaps an upbeat, slightly military tune to say, "Get on with it, get the votes in." Joking aside, soundscape manipulation is a pretty serious issue; in any case, who on earth has given anyone the right to manipulate the sound environment?

Now I want to return to the definition of silence and introduce the notion of the commons, because the soundscape essentially doesn't belong to anyone in particular. What we are hearing, I feel, is the privatization of the soundscape, in the same manner in which, in Britain, the enclosure laws destroyed the commons of old. There was a time when every community had what was called "the commons," an area where sheep could graze, a place important to all, belonging to all. The notion of the commons is deeply embedded in our social mind as something that all share. There are many "commons" that we take for granted. Millennia have taken clean air and clean water as a norm. Because of the ephemeral nature of sound, silence was not considered part of the commons in the past. Today the technology to preserve and multiply sound and separate it from its source has resulted in our sudden awareness that silence, too, is a common good. The silence that we need so that unprogrammed and unplannable things can take place is taken from common availability without much fuss and civic bother. It is being "privatized," if you allow that expression.

This apparent acquiescence is another illustration of an often-observed occurrence related to the impact of technology. Because of the impact of modern technology, things considered normal or ordinary in the past become rare or extraordinary, while things once considered rare and unusual become normal and routine. Flying is no longer a big deal, but a handmade dress or a home-cooked meal may well be special. We now consider polluted water essentially as normal, and people who can afford to will drink bottled water. It is hard to have bottled silence. But money still can buy distance from sound. Today, where there is civic anger with respect to silence, it involves "noise" (such as airport noise), not with respect to the manipulative elimination of silence from the soundscape.

And this is, I think, where we come in: we have seen and acknowledged the deterioration of the commons as far as silence is concerned; we have seen that the soundscape is not only polluted by noise—so that we have to look for laws related to noise abatement—but also increasingly polluted by the private use of sound in the manipulative dimension of setting and programming moods and conditions. There is a desperate need to be aware of this, and to be aware of it in terms of the collectivity rather than in terms of individual needs. I feel that this is a time for civic anger. This is a time when we have to say, "Town planning is constrained by bylaws on height, density, and this and that. What does town planning have to say about silence?" What, you may ask, would I suggest? First of all, the insistence that as human beings in a society we have a right to silence. Just as we feel we have the right to walk down the street without being physically assaulted by people, and preferably without being visually assaulted by ugly outdoor advertising, we also have the right not to be assaulted by sound, and in particular, not to be assaulted by sound that is there solely for the purpose of profit. Now is the time for civic rage, as well as civic education; now is also the time for action. Think of the amount of care that goes into the regulation of parking, so that our good, precious, and necessary cars have a place to be well and safe. That's very important to society. But I have yet (beyond hospitals) to see a public building that has a quiet room. Is not our sanity at least as important as the safety of our cars? I think we should begin to think. Are there places, even in conferences like this, that are designed as hassle-free, quiet spaces where people can go? There were times when one could say to a kid: "Where did you go?"—"Out"—"What did you do?"—"Nothing." That sort of blessed time is past. The kid is programmed. We are programmed. And we don't even ask for a quiet space anymore.

One possibility relatively close at hand is to set aside a quiet room in those buildings over which we have some influence, as a normal matter of human rights. Further, I would highly recommend that we start the inevitable committee meetings with just two minutes' silence and end them with a few minutes of silence as well. I sit on committees that have this practice; it can not only expedite the business before the committee, but also contribute to a certain amount of peacefulness and sanity. One can start a lecture with a few minutes of silence, and can close a lecture in silence. There can be a few minutes of silence before a shared meal. Such things help, even if only in a small way. I do think that even small initiatives make silence "visible" as an ever-present part of life. I now invite you to share two minutes of silence before we go on to the question period. Let us be quiet together.

Question: School libraries have become very noisy. Aside from a general disrespect for knowledge, why do you think this has come about?

Ursula Franklin: I have always thought that libraries are and must be places in which there is quietness. The automation of the libraries is largely responsible for the current increasing noise level. As long as you had a sizable number of librarians around, when you asked them a question, their voices would moderate your voice. But when you are sitting in front of a computerized catalogue and the screen reads "error message 23," you will likely ask one of your chums, "What's error message 23?" and she might call across the room, "Jeanne, do you know what error message 23 is?" And there goes the silence of the library. I think the absence of knowledgeable and caring people is frequently at the root of this sort of problem. The moment there is a substantial reduction in staff there is noise.

Q: In other cultures there are openings for silence. Can you suggest openings for silence in Western culture?

UF: I'll begin by correcting the word "culture" in terms of "Western culture," because the lack of opportunity for silence comes from our "non-culture," our *not* caring for human beings. We have to create that space beginning with small things, like a bit of silence before a meeting. I think I am developing a considerable suspicion of grand designs and plans. We are at a stage where, in a sense, we are taken over by the occupation force of the program. So it is the small things that we can do, the small things at a reasonably local level. But we must also be aware that we have rights; we are not just bags of potatoes. The change has to come first from seeing injustice as injustice. I think it is an unwarranted intrusion in my life to be programmed by people who have not asked my consent. Why should I be subject to that? Part of the obligation of government, as the guardian of the commons, is to not allow citizens to be assaulted. We have no problem defending that on the street. Why do we have a problem defending not only the assault on our ears but also the assault on our minds?

Q: What I appreciate most about the Quaker silence is that it is not just the silence, but the witness that comes out of the silence. But there is that point when the silent person is called upon to witness but refuses to witness. Then it seems to me that the silence no longer has this good aura, but becomes a recalcitrant silence.

UF: A point well taken. Silence then becomes quietism, and the importance of the unruffled self takes precedence over the need to witness, that is, to care about the state and well-being of silence, and of the values that we hold. There is a distinct danger in forgetting to remind each other that silence is an enabling environment; it is not a purpose in itself. It is what happens in the silence that makes the difference.

Q: I'm a sound-maker and it's my business to make noise. How do you feel about the role that sound artists play in finding a balance between silence and sound in public places?

UF: As long as you make or perform your sound on request, it is, I think, the contribution of any artist, any writer, any performer. It is the performance of sound without request that I find problematic. If my consent is that I come to your concert and other people's consent is that they are quiet because they want to hear your art, then your sound is a contribution to the life of the community, and there can be nothing better. But it requires the invitation and the consent.

Q: How do we apply this call for civic anger against the creeping privatization of the soundscape that has no legal basis when we have no legal footing?

UF: That's where a good deal of thought has to go. I am not sure that we do not have a legal basis. For instance, in his book on democratic theory C.B. Macpherson has what I consider a helpful definition of what public property and private property are; he says private property is the right to exclude others from the use and benefit of something, whereas public property concerns the right not to be excluded from the use and benefit of something. That, I think, you can find in law. Now we would like the sound environment in an elevator to be seen as public rather than private property.

Q: How can silence and sound co-exist?

UF: They don't have to be in the same place. In the case of beaches I can well see a quiet part of the beach, just as there is a shallow end of a swimming pool. It is certainly possible to respond to the different needs that people have, even the different needs a single person has at different times, by setting aside a part of a park or a beach as a quiet section. I don't think that we need to put ourselves in an either/or situation, but on the other hand we cannot be in a situation where certain needs are excluded because other needs are incompatible with them. We are fortunate enough that among ourselves we have enough imagination to think and negotiate ways of co-existence of different needs.

The world lived without elevators, as well as elevator music, for quite some time. Where there is a bank of elevators, can you have one quiet elevator? In a well-known and good Jewish hospital in Toronto the elevator systems take into account the fact that Orthodox Jews do not work on the Sabbath, and that pushing an elevator button is considered to be work: on the Sabbath, one elevator stops at every floor going up and down. This is a respectful solution for the presence of people who may be a minority, but who must not be disenfranchised. Similarly, we could negotiate one quiet elevator.

Q: I know many people who are anxious about being quiet, who need sound and music. What would you say might be the essentials of teaching people an appreciation of silence?

UF: I don't think you can do that. I think you can invite them to share silence with you. Quaker children are an example. We take our youngsters to meetings, and they sit there for half or three-quarters of an hour. They are fidgety but they manage, they are quiet, and they get quite addicted to it. But the fear of silence, I think, has to be overcome by people themselves. I'm not a great believer in teaching except by the example of friendship, and I suggest that you simply sit quietly with somebody. Sit with that person who you care about, quietly, just with a cup in front of you, for five minutes, and again in a week's time for ten minutes. There's nothing to fear from quiet, and there is no need to fear silence. I have always found that people begin to be grateful for silence and become quite dependent on it. The only way I can see teaching is to be with somebody you care about and say, "Why don't we try it?" I have no other answer.

Q: I was interested in your understanding of silence as leaving room for the unprogrammed and the unexpected, and was thinking about the role of technology in programming. Is it necessary that technology have that role?

UF: I think that apart from some isolated, cocooned, individual situations, technology requires conformity. You can be creative only within a set of quite closely defined parameters that includes the computer itself. I think we have to realize that as the world gets more and more structured by technology, the possibility of the unexpected is reduced. The nooks and niches in which things can happen become more and more constrained. I don't deny that there may be individual detours around this constraint, but we have to talk more about it, to see whether it is not just a manipulation of an environment, like an umbrella you put up so that, while it still rains, it doesn't rain on you.

Note

This lecture was transcribed and edited by Gayle Young, with the assistance of Ursula Franklin, for the publication of *Proceedings: The Tuning of the World* (Banff, 1993).

LIBERTY, TECHNOLOGY, AND HOPE

Keynote address presented as the 22nd Viscount Bennett Lecture, Fredericton, New Brunswick, 17 February 2000; published in UNB *Law Journal, vol. 51 (2002), pp. 35–47.*[1]

IN REFLECTING ON ideas of liberty, technology, and hope, I want to offer some thoughts to help us engage in an interesting civic conversation about our community. I am not certain that the title "Liberty, Technology, and Hope" was a wise choice on my part, as it is much too broad. What I want to look at, in even the most elementary way, is the notion of liberty and of the law as social instructions. I understand the term "social instructions" to mean a set of concepts and practices that express people's wishes as to how they want and need to live together. The social instructions expressed in notions of liberty and in legal provisions intersect with other kinds of social instruction, such as technology—the way we do things in the course of living together. I thought that it would be interesting to engage in this civic discussion as we attempt to look after the common good of our community.[2]

It is well to remember that none of us are free to do whatever we wish. This is not only because of our lack of liberty, but also because the very activity of doing things links us together in work and delineates what we can and cannot do in a certain place and at a given time. In adopting this viewpoint, I thought it would be useful to look at the two sets of social instructions and at the notion of hope. I use the word "hope" not in the sense in which a strict Methodist such as R.B. Bennett would have said "Salvation is our hope," but rather in the sense in which Karl Polanyi states in *The Great Transformation*: "Hope is defined as the vision of perfectibility."[3] Hope is the dream that one can work towards betterment, that things can get better and that they will get better for everyone. Such hopes and dreams of perfectibility are a pretty tall order and difficult to visualize or actualize, but it is nonetheless important for us to try to envision ways of advancing our dreams of perfectibility together. Before considering how these sets of instructions overlap, let me begin with some definitions. For instance, what do we mean by liberty, and how do we picture the social impact of technologies?

If someone had asked Bennett what is meant by liberty or hope, he could have spoken in a Methodist, British lawyerly way about what liberty and hope meant to him or what he meant by these terms. But I think he would have been puzzled if someone had asked him about technology. In spite of being a man who, in the words of F.R. Scott, "hitched his wagon to the CPR"[4] and derived wealth and power from the opening of the West that the railways brought about,[5] he would probably have replied, "Technology, you know, that's the sort of thing workers do for a living; they get dirty doing it and they get rather nasty when they are unemployed." In spite of his imaginably cavalier attitude towards technology, new technologies were the source of his personal wealth and power. Technological change was the reason for his New Brunswick upbringing; the formative imprint on Bennett's childhood was a change in transportation technology. His father, a sea captain and a wealthy builder of sailing ships, was pushed out of business by the steam engine. When the large seagoing steamers became common, boat builders and captains like Henry Bennett lost their livelihoods and their status. Bennett Sr. started a fairly modest and unrewarding farming business in New Brunswick.[6] R.B. Bennett probably did not envision the family's fate as a human consequence of technological change, but such reflections could have altered the path of his political career, including his defeat in the Depression. Bennett's fall from power was rooted in his inability to grasp the structuring effect of technology on economic life in the world.

This reflection is not intended to diminish Bennett's record as an important Canadian statesman. However, Bennett was quite helpless in the face of the Depression. His problem is not unlike the helplessness vis-à-vis globalization that we find amongst today's political leaders, who may also not consider the social impacts of technological change as thoroughly as they should.

Turning to definitions of liberty, Ann Denin reminds us, using John Stuart Mill's own words, that the modern spirit of liberty is a love of individual independence.[7] A century later, in *Four Essays on Liberty*, Isaiah Berlin introduced negative and positive liberty.[8]

A negative liberty indicates that one needs freedom "from" something. In fact, Berlin said that freedom was the absence of oppression. When he turned the coin to speak about positive liberty—the freedom "to"[9]—he insisted that the freedom of an individual was located in his ability to be his own master. In 1952 Berlin wrote, "I wish my life and my decisions to depend on myself and not on external forces of whatever kind. . . . I wish to be a subject, not an object."[10] Of course, for a worker in one of the call centres in this province or for a woman who is unwillingly pregnant with her fifth child, Berlin's views will appear hopelessly idealistic.

C.B. Macpherson, Canada's pre-eminent political theorist, picks up where Berlin left off, recasting that freedom "from" oppression. Macpherson, being much more attuned to the power of economic structures, viewed freedom in terms of immunity from the extractive powers of others, including those of the state. He rephrased Berlin's freedom "from" as a counter-extractive liberty, and took Berlin's positive liberty, the freedom "to," as a developmental liberty—the freedom of people to develop and use their full human capacities.[11] Yet Macpherson was equally aware of and eloquent about the impediments that stood in the way of realizing liberty for all, and the impediments that inhibited the use of a person's full human capacity. He classified the impediments into three groups.[12] The first group is rooted in the lack of adequate means of life. Life needs energy, both physical and psychological. Lack of food, shelter, and community can be a primary and very serious impediment to the development and use of human potential. The second group pertains to the lack of access to the means of labour. A situation in which there is such a lack of access, with no way for an individual to obtain the means of life even if they are generally available, constitutes, in terms of society, a genuine impediment to liberty. The third group consists of items that relate to an individual's lack of protection against invasion by others. Such invasions need not be territorial; they can be ideological or economic, social or police-directed. Whatever their form, the lack of protection from invasion is an impediment to the pursuit of liberty.

Macpherson's view of freedom essentially maps out the territory of liberty and constitutes what people consider when they worry about its pursuit. Interestingly, when one thinks about liberty it is assumed that there is a constituency or society. In the most simple terms, there have to be others. The concept of liberty only makes sense vis-à-vis others. It is pointless to sit on a desert island and pontificate about freedom of speech when there is no one to hear you. The whole notion of liberty, of being free from oppression or being free to think and act according to one's own convictions, assumes the existence of society as a reference system. While laws and law enforcement may address the protection or promotion of liberty, their means are most likely based on regulating the conduct of citizens and institutions, in other words regulating society. There is little point in talking about liberty when there is no viable society.

If we look at law as a body of social instruction, we can make the case that the goal of law is the advancement of liberty. But again, the existence of a society is assumed. The composition or the politics of that society may change but, in terms of a fixed reference point with respect to liberty, there must be a society. Yet, in the modern technological world, the existence of society as a reference system should not be taken for granted. ·

It is well to remember that the law is not our only codex of social instruction. The other great source of social instruction is work: not so much the outcome of work or the products of labour, but the process, the way we do things together. It is the complex set of activities and arrangements that we often consider under the rubric of "technology." It is helpful to define technology simply as "practice," as the way of organizing work and people. There has always been technology. The problems of civilizations throughout the ages are often very similar, but how those problems were dealt with has differed significantly through time and culture. Whether you write on clay tablets or send somebody an e-mail, what is said is probably quite similar. It is how you say it, the way both the work and the task are structured, that has changed. Perhaps it wouldn't be a bad idea to go back to clay tablets for a while. People might be a lot more succinct if they had to write, bake, and carry their communications. It would be amazing to find out how many things could be left unwritten.

It is important to reinforce that technology is practice. It is the way we do things. Certain technologies may involve devices, machinery, or computers; nevertheless the focus should be practice. What matters is how we do and share the work, who instructs and who obeys. Such arrangements and the practices they imply are profound social instructions.[13]

In *The Real World of Technology*, I distinguish between two different forms of technological development: holistic technologies and prescriptive technologies.[14] These two categories involve distinctly different specializations and divisions of labour, and consequently they have very different social and political implications. Holistic technologies are normally associated with crafts. Artisans, be they potters, weavers, metal-makers, or cooks, control the process of their work and make the decisions from beginning to end. They draw on their own experience, each time applying it to a unique situation. Holistic technology involves specialization by product.

Prescriptive technologies, on the other hand, involve specialization by process. Here, the making or doing of something is broken down into clearly identifiable steps. Each step is carried out by a separate worker or group of workers who need to be familiar only with the skills of performing that one step. In Europe, this type of division of labour took hold during the Industrial Revolution and it underlies most modern technologies. Take as an illustration the modern manufacture of a car. The seats can be made in one plant, the body may be made somewhere else, as would be the brakes, and all parts may be assembled elsewhere again. What happens in this example is significant on two levels. One is the tight prescriptiveness of the process: all the separately manufactured parts have to fit together to make a functioning car. Training in such work nurtures what I call the "culture of compliance," an acceptance of the obligation to conform to detailed instructions because "things have to fit."[15]

At the second level, there is the fact that none of the workers see the total project; thus there is a need for co-ordination and management. Managers emerge who can instruct the workers, whether or not the managers themselves have the technical skills to carry out the tasks. The Industrial Revolution gave rise to a massive body of new social instructions that were quickly transferred from the factory to other workplaces. Prescriptive technologies transformed not only manufacturing but also administration and governance, instruction, and inquiry. Many of these technologies utilized the new scientific insights of the time. It is well to remember that the first applications of new knowledge to the workplace were more often than not in what I have called "work-related technology"—technical changes, such as the digging shovel or the tractor, that actually made it easier for workers to accomplish the task.[16] On the other hand, many of the later technologies are "control-related."[17] Their aim is not so much to make the work easier for the worker but rather to facilitate the control of the labour process itself. Most people know from their own experience the extent to which modern electronic technologies are control-related. Monitors and smart cards are not the only examples. The very replacement of workers by devices can be an essentially control-motivated development. The bank machine cannot hand you money more efficiently than a bank teller; however, the bank machine does not unionize, it does not need to go to the washroom, and it does not need to sleep. While the machine is likely more expensive than employing a teller at a reasonably decent wage, the determining factor is control. Control through technology is not a new consideration. Looking back at writers of the Industrial Revolution, such as Charles Babbage,[18] it is clear that a number of them dreamt of a workerless factory where nobody had to deal with unruly workers who might drink or want a raise or better housing.[19]

Another important facet of the real world of technology is the role of planning. Planning, as an activity involving "planners" and "plannees," originated within prescriptive technologies. As prescriptive technologies have taken over most of the activities in the real world of technology, planning has become society's major tool for structuring and restructuring, for stating what is doable and what is not. A common denominator of technological planning has been the wish to adjust parameters so as to maximize efficiency and effectiveness. Underlying such plans is a production model, with production typically planned to maximize gain. Holistic planning strategies, on the other hand, are usually designed to minimize disaster rather than to maximize gain.

Let me now move to a discussion of global structures. It is not just individual manifestations of the culture of compliance, which everyone who lives in a technological society recognizes, that is at issue here. As the question of liberty is before us, I would like to inquire into what happens when new technologies move into broader spheres. To facilitate the discussion, consider a simple model. Imagine the whole world as a plain round cake, cut in wedge-shaped slices that represent states, countries, or regional entities. One slice is called "Canada." Many of our institutions and social images can be visualized within such a model. You may think of yourself as a raisin in the cake, as one of the crumbs at the bottom, or maybe as part of the icing on top.

Much of what we perceive as identity, including our language, has been anchored in our slice, in a definable locality. The notion of "foreign" languages is an interesting variation on the theme of identity as locality. Consider the phrase often used in Atlantic Canada, that somebody is "from away." In the cake model, the slice locates "us." It defines our representation: the Members from Kicking Horse Path or Bonavista-Twillingate are identified in terms of their location within the slice, as are our law courts and school boards. Notions of social mobility, the image of a trickle-down effect, fit well into the cake model. It seems obvious that "our" slice is closer to its adjacent slices than it is to slices on the opposite side of the cake. Such proximity matters when it comes to questions of contact and exchange. While many of our social activities, social instructions, customs, and laws relate to actions and movements of people within the slice, there is, and has always been, a certain amount of overlap of activities and ideas with adjacent slices.

Moving beyond local interaction, individuals have always traversed great distances, from the Apostles to Marco Polo. Some have returned to their own communities bearing new ideas and stories. In terms of the cake model, such travel and exchange amounts to a horizontal slicing within the cake. Throughout history small horizontal cuts have been made by individuals or small groups of people, and have often been followed by more organized trade. Think of the Silk Road, which dates back to Roman times, as an important trade route along one of those limited horizontal cuts. Modern science, from navigation aids and communication to land and air transport, has improved the ease of horizontal movement within the global cake, New technologies have pushed the boundaries of space and—using the cake model again—horizontal cutting becomes easier as time passes. An increasingly rapid exchange of people, ideas, goods, and habits has taken place along such horizontal cuts. For a long time the national entities, states, and empires—the vertical slices—were defined and governed by boundaries, passports, and tariffs. This was the model within which R.B. Bennett functioned. His solution to Canada's problems during the worldwide Depression was to increase Canada's ties to Britain; he wanted to strengthen the Imperial Slice and protect it by instituting high tariff walls.[20] For him, it was the vertical slice that had to be protected by regulating and restricting the horizontal movement of people, ideas, goods, and money.

It is well to remember that in the past it was easier for people to move, notwithstanding the practical problems of getting from here to there. However, the movement of goods was strictly limited by physical constraints, and money was almost impossible to transfer because of the reluctance to accept foreign coinage. Today the situation is basically reversed. It has become almost impossible for individuals to move from slice to slice, except when their speedy return is assured, while it is easy and almost trivial to move goods and money across the horizontal cuts.[21] The protection of the vertical slice, pre-eminent for Bennett and his successors, began to crumble as horizontal movement became easier, mainly through the increase in air traffic. Yet it was the electronic technologies, beginning with the telegraph, radio, and telephone, that produced a quantum leap in the importance of horizontal versus vertical activities. Electronic technologies have made it possible to send instructions without sending people. You can trade on the stock exchange in Tokyo by telephone or computer link without being there. The ease of conveying instructions has made previously unthinkable transactions across horizontal slices possible.

However, the same technological changes have substantially increased the problems of maintaining the integrity and cohesion of the vertical slices. National entities have become unable or unwilling to regulate the intrusion of horizontal activities into patterns of life within the vertical slice. Yet it is in the vertical slice that law and governance, the bearers of social instruction, are embedded.[22] The increased ease of horizontal slicing occurs in parallel with a vastly increased fragmentation of work and production and is directly related to, if not caused by, this fragmentation. Technological innovations that make it easier to achieve horizontal movements combined with modern production technologies and their prescriptive fragmentation lend themselves well to global capital mobility and the subcontracting of work.

Here is a brief and graphic example. Recently a friend of mine in Toronto went to buy a pair of winter boots. Checking where they were made, she found that the left boot came from Indonesia and the right one from South Korea. Though the shoes fitted well, she went to the sales person, only to find out that there was no mix-up of orders. It was an intentional design. This incident illustrates the ultimate in prescriptive technology and its impact. My friend commented later that it was probably quite a clever way of subcontracting, since it undercut the black market. You cannot swamp a country with left boots. The problem is that while the horizontal pull weakens the vertical slices—as there is no shoe industry in Canada—it is in the vertical slice that authority and all legitimate tools of intervention are located. Law and liberty are embedded in the vertical, but the most crucial social and political activities are taking place along horizontal segments.

Where does this leave the members from Kicking Horse Path or Bonavista-Twillingate? What should they do if they value the cohesion of their communities and feel that there is a precious identity in the vertical slice? The representatives of the vertical cannot give up on the constitutional obligation to authorize or legitimize activities that impact on their locale, on their constituency. Yet, the power to forge new social instructions and new demands of compliance has gone increasingly to horizontal activities. It is this change in authority and constituency that is at the core of present world problems. In every country the ruling apparatus has divided itself into "horizontalists," who are often from the upper part of the slice, and "verticalists," who may identify more with the crumbs at the bottom and resent the "horizontalists" who divide their country in the name of commerce.

The ease of horizontal activities has developed in part because those who have the power to maintain the cohesion of the vertical slice have divested themselves of the very powers that could regulate the new activities. Here is the central problem of developing a contemporary approach to liberty, technology, and hope. On the one hand, there is a new body of social instruction—new technologies—that could address the pursuit of liberty in light of the impediments that Macpherson points out. Clearly, liberty makes no sense for those who do not have enough to eat and thus lack the means of life. While there is now a large body of new knowledge and with it fresh hope for human betterment, global developments have not removed the basic impediments to liberty for many people. Furthermore, progress towards the pursuit of liberty depends on the presence of a viable society. Yet the same technologies that could give the tools to assure a sustainable means of life may also disempower society, at times quite intentionally. None of these observations should be interpreted as technological determinism or a belief in the autonomy of technology *per se*. I am not implying Margaret Thatcher's "TINA" (there is no alternative).[23] There are alternatives, but such options must be discussed thoughtfully and knowledgeably.

Thus, the situation in which we find ourselves presents on one hand a clear desire among people to pursue liberty for themselves and others. Many make the case that a horizontal cutting of the global cake can improve the chances of an adequate means of life, bringing food and shelter to all. Yet it is becoming quite clear that the very reference system for liberty, or a viable society vigorously guarding against the erosion of liberties, has itself become endangered. With fewer and fewer activities embedded in vertical slices, those who work horizontally must question the location of their society or community, as well as to whom they are ultimately responsible.

In a discussion of a more expanded version of the cake model during a talk in which I was quite critical of the use of electronic systems in the classroom,[24] someone asked, "Don't you think there could be a community of like-minded people on the Net?" Because I was just moving house, I responded by saying, "I can certainly see that one can make friends on the Internet and collaborate with them, but they won't help me pack my books next week." It is easy to forget that there is a physical reality in community and society, but it is dangerous to do so. We all depend on the physical reality of our community for our well-being much more than we often realize or admit.

The social instructions of technology intersect with law and tradition in the reality of our communities. The hard task before us is to find a way in which these often contradictory instructions can be sorted out and cobbled together so that liberty can advance. Those who wrestle with issues of intellectual property or with the effect of research transmitted across institutional boundaries will understand the enormity of this challenge. Hope, as the expectation of perfectibility of people and institutions, will help with this task, and so will clarity. It is important that we become clear as to what is going on around us, at least in a structural sense.

There are ways of resolving the current contradictions between the demands of liberty and the demands of modern technology. In fact, we should be discussing them with a great sense of urgency. Personally, I do not want to believe that vertical slices are acquirable, particularly not in Canada. All people have the right to be governed, and governed well, rather than to be administered for the benefit of somebody else. It would appear that at the moment Canadians are not governed but administered.[25] In terms of liberty, I firmly believe that there is no substitute for "good government" in the sense of peace, order, and good government. There can be new options to make good government work well in a technological society. For instance, in response to C.B. Macpherson's first and second impediments, there may now be a place for a basic incomes policy[26] as a way out of the dilemma of vanishing employment in an efficiency-driven system.

There is significant practical and intellectual scope in striving for clarity in the face of assessing which endeavours should be entrusted to horizontal arrangements, as well as how to activate and strengthen the vertical sinews. If there is any real hope that modern standards of liberty, such as human rights for all, can co-exist with modern technology, then there must be the option to assert the authority of community. In other words, it must be possible to reject social instructions that come at us horizontally by saying, "No thank you, we don't want it." Now is a time to look at technology, not as an instrument to maximize gain, but as an opportunity to minimize disaster. The disasters that I fear most are the threats to the sustainability of society. Minimizing such threats is, I hope, one of the true aims of liberty.[27]

Notes

1   Beth Beattie, an L.L.M. student at Osgoode Hall Law School, kindly provided editing and footnoting assistance for the version published in the *UNB Law Journal*.
2   I define "common good" as indivisible benefits—justice and peace, clean air, sanitation, drinkable water, safe roads, and equal access to education—as opposed to divisible benefits for private and corporate profit; see Ursula M. Franklin, *The Real World of Technology*, (Toronto: Anansi, 1999), pp. 66, 117.
3   K. Polyani, *The Great Transformation* (Boston: Beacon, 1957), p. 84.
4   F.R. Scott, "Ode to a Politician," in *The Selected Poems of F.R. Scott* (Toronto: McClelland & Stewart, 1981), p. 68.
5   Bennett was a lawyer for the Canadian Pacific Railway; he made millions of dollars defending the CPR and other big corporations and investing his fees: G. Donaldson, *The Prime Ministers of Canada* (Doubleday: Toronto, 1997), pp. 132, 135.
6   Donaldson, *Prime Ministers*, p. 134.
7   John Stuart Mill, *On Liberty*, ed. E. Alexander (Peterborough, Ont.: Broadview Press, 1999), p. 117. It is interesting to note Mill's comment on human nature and machinery: "Human nature is not a machine to be built after a model, and set to do exactly the work prescribed for it, but a tree, which requires to grow and develop itself on all sides, according to the tendency of the inward forces which make it a living thing" (p. 114).
8   I. Berlin, *Four Essays on Liberty* (Oxford: London, 1969).
9   Ibid., pp. 122–23.
10 Ibid., p. 131.
11 C.B. Macpherson, *Democratic Theory: Essays in Retrieval* (Oxford: Clarendon Press, 1973), p. 53.
12 Ibid., pp. 59–60.
13 Technology can be a catalyst for the spread of control and management. The fact that citizens are more and more stringently controlled and managed is often considered normal and fundamentally beyond question, as a necessary feature of technological societies.

Technology has been the catalyst for dramatic changes in the locus of power. See Franklin, *Real World*, p. 49.

14 Franklin, *Real World*, pp. 10–12.

15 For a fuller discussion of the culture of compliance, see Franklin, *Real World*, pp. 16, 17, 19.

16 When work is organized as a sequence of separately executable steps, the control over the work moves to the organizer, the boss, or the manager. The process must be prescribed with sufficient precision to make each step fit into the preceding and following steps. Only in that manner can the final product be satisfactory. See Franklin, *Real World*, p. 16.

17 Control-related technologies are developments that do not primarily address the process of work with the aim of making it easier, but rather to increase control over the operation: workers can be timed, assignments broken up, and the interaction between operators can be monitored. Since most modern technological changes involve control, new control-related applications have increased at a much faster pace than work-related ones. See Franklin, *Real World*, pp. 9–10.

18 C. Babbage, *On the Economy of Machinery and Manufactures* (London: C. Knight, 1832).

19 For a more detailed discussion of the emergence of new social patterns in the seventeenth and eighteenth centuries, the massive changes of the Industrial Revolution, and commonalities between that era and the present time, see Franklin, *Real World*, pp. 55–58. Respective proponents in both ages have voiced irrationally high expectations of the beneficial effects of science and technology.

20 Donaldson, *Prime Ministers*, pp. 136, 138.

21 For a discussion of the speed of monetary transactions and the resulting increase in global financial trading and profit-making, see Franklin, *Real World*, p. 162.

22 For a further discussion of the relationship between technological innovations and horizontal movements, see Franklin, *Real World*, p. 159.

23 "TINA" refers to the famous retort of British prime minister (1979–90) Margaret Thatcher to critics of her free-market economic strategy. When pressed about economic injustice, she was dismissive, arguing, "There is no alternative." This defence of the status quo was soon nicknamed "TINA," meaning that there is no alternative to capitalism and that a globalized economy is inevitable; The Media Channel <http://www.mediachannel.org> (accessed 20 May 2002).

24 If there ever was a growth process, if there ever was a holistic process, a process that cannot be divided into rigid predetermined steps, it is education. See Franklin, *Real World*, pp. 23, 169–70.

25 The major decisions that affect our lives are not made by the House of Commons or as a result of public deliberations by elected officials. We have lost the institution of government in terms of responsibility and accountability to the people. We now have a bunch of

managers who run the country to make it safe for technology. See Franklin, *Real World*, p. 121.

26 See S. Lerner, *Basic Income: A Primer* (Toronto: Between the Lines, 1999); Franklin, *Real World*, p. 177.

27 There are few practical difficulties in planning to minimize disaster, and such approaches are possible in today's real world of technology. Examples include the inquiry led by Thomas Berger into the building of the Mackenzie Valley pipeline, and the 1977 study of the Science Council of Canada, *Canada as a Conserver Society*.

NEW ISSUES OF ACCESS TO JUSTICE
RAISED BY MODERN TECHNOLOGY

A talk presented as the Annual Distinguished Access to Justice Lecture, Faculty of Law, University of Windsor, Windsor, Ontario, 25 October 1994; published in Windsor Yearbook of Access to Justice, *vol. 14 (1994), pp. 243–54.*

THE WIDESPREAD USE of modern technologies has given rise to a set of new and inherently different problems of access to law and justice. These problems will require not only changes in and adaptations to existing law but also a rethinking of the very concept of justice as well as the notion of individual access to it. The task of addressing these problems will demand new forms of awareness and new forms of coping with the social and political impacts of technologies. I will not attempt to deal with all such issues in this paper, but will try to illustrate the *problématique* of access to law and justice in a technological society through several examples, chosen from some of the less obvious and somewhat routine facets of everyday life.

Definitions and Context

To begin with some considerations of terminology, the term "justice" is used in the following paragraphs in its original classic meaning of *justitia*: one of the four cardinal virtues on which the well-being of a civilized society hinges.[1] Recent extension of the original term to concepts such as social justice, environmental justice, and economic justice seems to indicate the timeless importance of justice and the quest for it.

Since I grew up in the shadow of Hitler's Nürnberg Laws, the difference between law and justice has always been very clear to me. In this paper, law and regulation are considered one possible instrument of justice—not as *the* instrument of justice. It is also recognized that other instruments of justice, such as compassion, tradition, common morality, and the notion of a common good are presently somewhat in eclipse, while economic instruments such as markets and tax systems are gaining ascendance as perceived tools for social justice. It will be argued that the very nature of modern technology limits and circumscribes the scope of law and regulation in terms of their enabling access to justice.

"Technology," as used here, is best defined as practice: that is, "the way things are done around here."[2] To focus on technology as practice, rather than falling back on other definitions of technology,[3] makes two attributes of technology explicit. One is that technology is a form of societal structuring that is historically much older than mechanical or electronic devices and is not intrinsically dependent on them. The other attribute concerns the definition of legitimate practitioners and of the content of social practices through the technologies employed. To illustrate this point, take education as an example: the technology of schooling is well established. While it is generally understood that learning can take place in a multitude of ways and locales, "teachers" as practitioners have to be accredited; they then operate entirely as part of the technology of schooling. The certification of any acquired knowledge becomes the prerogative of those institutions, set up as components of the educational technology.[4]

The gendering of workplace and profession is rooted in the possibility of restricting access to particular technologies and the potential of being able to claim that those working outside a particular technology are "unqualified" practitioners: the fields of medicine and nursing respectively are indicative examples.

It is at times useful to divide technologies into work-related and control-related categories.[5] The aim of work-related technologies is, in the main, to make the process of work easier for the worker. Control-related technologies are developed and implemented largely in order to facilitate external control and monitor the work and the worker. As the complexity and sophistication of technologies increases, control functions frequently outstrip work-related functions. This is particularly evident when considering administrative and organizational technologies. It is the aspect of actual or potential control, embedded in new technologies, that raises many of the novel issues of access to justice. In other words, the application of findings of modern science has yielded significant instruments of power and control not previously available.

General Attributes of Technologies

Common to many technologies is their ability to manipulate time and space. Whether it is fast flight, replaying events in slow motion, hearing voices of those no longer living, viewing images gathered from outer space, or examining details of structures discovered by means of electron microscopy, traditional human boundaries of duration and distance have been altered beyond recognition. Furthermore, from the sending and receiving of messages across the globe to playing back past events, technologies have imposed hitherto unknown complexities on everyday life, complexities that have profoundly influenced the citizen's sense of reality.

Different modern technologies are linked to each other in a complex technological system—what Jacques Ellul has called a technological milieu[6]—so that changes in one technology affect all other operative technologies. In an intricately woven fabric the tension on one thread affects all other threads and the patterns they form; similarly, a complex technological society responds to changes in one technology with structural changes that go well beyond the intent and scope of the altered technology. Consider, for example, the changes initiated by the general availability of cheap and easy photocopying or the impact of the transistor radio.

In human terms, one dramatic attribute of technology is the interposing of devices and processes between humans. Technical devices and systems, such as telephones or telegraphs, can act as conduits between people, but they can also be substitutes for people, as in the case of answering machines or automatic bank tellers. These developments are, in some ways, the price of overcoming the constraints of distance and time, but such technologically altered social relations can have serious consequences in the quest for justice.

A further important attribute of many modern technologies in consideration of access to justice is their tendency to fragment technical, social, and economic processes. Much of the social and political impact of the Industrial Revolution can be traced back directly to changes in the division of labour instituted at that time. The rise of prescriptive production processes that divided industrial production into a series of well-defined steps, each carried out by a different worker, profoundly changed the culture and politics of work.[7]

To this day the fragmentation of tasks and decision-making that technology demands is a major source of our problems in access to justice. Maxine Berg gives a compelling account of attempts by the British parliament to grapple with public policy issues raised by the introduction of machinery into British factories.[8] These debates, which are well worth rereading, were clearly perceived as arguments between profitability and justice. Profitability carried the day.

Finally, many technological processes frequently have irreversible effects on nature and society. If such effects are known to be detrimental to those subjected to them, justice may demand a pre-emptive rather than a penalizing approach to such processes. In summary, living and working in a technological milieu means that all human, social, and political activities are mediated by a system of highly interconnected and interdependent technologies. These technologies, defined as socially sanctioned practices, structure and restructure social and economic relations to construct a new reality that is often difficult to mitigate by means of law or regulation.

Considerations of Access to Justice

The impact of technologies on justice concerns in everyday life often leaves seemingly trivial footprints. Take, for instance, bar codes, those ubiquitous strips of lines and bands that, when affixed to objects, allow their computerized classification and registration. We see them used at checkout counters in stores and in libraries, on credit cards and access cards, apparently only to speed up and automate routine transactions. There seems to be no restrictions on their use or area of application, but the information that can be collected from the routine use of bar codes can have serious consequences. Two examples may suffice to illustrate the point. The first one dates back to the 1970s in the German Federal

Republic. In several jurisdictions, during an investigation of the loyalty of teachers and their political acceptability (with the potential of denying employment as teachers or civil servants, a provision called *Berufsverbot*), it turned out that dossiers of those under scrutiny contained lists of books borrowed from public libraries as evidence of questionable political leanings. Such lists were compiled without the library users' knowledge or consent, using the bar code identification of the borrowers' library cards. Thus a seemingly innocent cataloguing technique became a potent instrument of control and surveillance.

A number of authors have discussed such technological threats to individual privacy,[9] but the question of responsibility and accountability of those who may choose, for routine applications, technologies with strong surveillance capabilities also needs to be raised. Are there, one might ask, techniques that could satisfy the cataloguing and bookkeeping needs, while minimizing the surveillance potential? Are there public responsibilities of those who use particular technologies to guard against their potential misuse? Should those who benefit from the use of new technology be obligated to include safeguards at the design stage of the system? We need a much clearer understanding as to who should take responsibility and be accountable for the installation of a technology that has the potential for serious misuse, in terms of justice and infringements of human rights. There are, after all, not only regulatory but also technical methods to address the problem of potential misuse. Bank notes and passports, for instance, are issued on paper that makes forgeries difficult. Design constraints and their enforcement could similarly limit the control potentials of specific bar-code-based technologies.

The second bar-code example concerns so-called smart buildings. We all know them; occupants have cards with a special bar code that allows access to the building, the elevators, and those parts of the building that the cardholder is entitled to enter. Often such buildings house commercial or government offices. Those without an appropriate card cannot get through the building's entrance; those with a card may still be confined to certain parts or floors of the building. They may, or may not, have been informed of this.

The point I want to make here is that the use of a very simple and seemingly trivial piece of magnetic tape to regulate access to and movement in otherwise public and unrestricted buildings can be obtrusive. Imagine now that at every point in a building where an access card is needed to proceed further, the slot for the card is replaced by a guard, a soldier, or a concierge asking for identification and authorization. It would not be long before someone would refuse compliance; many would heatedly inquire who was in charge and on what authority such restrictive practices operate. Restriction of movement or access enforced by a guard or a soldier affects our sense of justice dramatically, while the same restrictions enforced by a piece of plastic seem normal and non-controversial: but technologically packaged restrictions are just as restrictive as those enforced by human beings.

There is an added dimension of the technologically packaged constraints: they are often much less transparent in terms of their origin, their purpose, or the responsibility for their initiation and enforcement than are those enforced by identifiable human beings. It is this lack of transparency that contributes so much to the public perception of technology as a headless tyranny that renders the citizen powerless and without access to justice.

The Fulcrum of Planning

One crucial aspect of modern technological systems is their link to and dependence on planning. Technologies that make for the functioning of modern life are rooted in planning. They are put in place according to detailed plans that are rarely examined for their relationship to issues of justice. In his reflections on planning Kenneth Boulding[10] reminds his readers that in the technological world there are not only planners but also plannees: those who— whether they like it or not—must live with and conform to plans that others make for them. More often than not it is the planners' lack of concern for the welfare of the plannees that raises issues of access to justice.

One example of the technological packaging of bias and prejudice is the construction of the New York parkway, a system of roads in New York State designed and built in the late 1920s and

1930s under the leadership of Robert Moses, the state's legendary commissioner of public works. The bridges and underpasses of the parkway system were too low to allow buses to pass under. The political statement of the design was clearly evident: those who had access to private cars could enjoy the "public" amenities of the parkway; those who had to travel by bus could not. R.A. Caro, the biographer of Robert Moses, makes it clear that the racial and class bias of the bridge design was fully understood by the public at the time of the opening of the parkways.[11] Yet, the bridges had to be constructed before they could be recognized publicly as a technological manifestation of bias or lack of social justice. By then, of course, little could be done. The decisions regarding bridge design had been made long before the opening date, during the planning phase of the project by a technical staff far away from public scrutiny. Those affected by justice issues arising from the design were totally outside the planning circle. In this case, as so often, access to justice depended on access to planning.

Since the days of Robert Moses much planning and land-use regulation has been put in place, providing for some public participation and the occasional technical discussion. Certain design biases—for instance, preventing access by persons who are disabled—have been identified and at times corrected. At the same time the scope and scale of technological developments have accelerated and irreversibly altered both the public sphere and the workplace. In terms of planning, if issues of access to justice are dealt with at all, they are still handled situationally—by means of a site-specific inquiry—rather than systemically—by critically examining the features of the technologies to be employed. This need not be so.

A possible model for a public and principled planning process can be found in the 1977 Royal Commission Inquiry into the Proposed Mackenzie Valley Pipeline.[12] Here, issues of justice and access to justice were addressed as an integral part of a planning process that involved planners as well as plannees. Unfortunately, the undertaking was never repeated with a similar thoroughness, nor were the systemic insights of the Berger Commission and its approach incorporated into legislation. There remains a need to address access to planning as a major facet of access to justice in terms of public policies in a technological society.

Inclusion Caused by Technology

Problems of access to justice are also encountered by citizens who are involuntarily included in, or conversely excluded from, particular social activities. Many inclusions or exclusions occur as an inevitable consequence of the scope of modern technologies and the intrinsic systems character of technological structures. Well-established citizens' rights and freedoms may be significantly altered by technological developments. I will outline one or two examples to illustrate the characteristic features of the genre of these problems, features that make access to justice difficult or impossible for the individual citizen.

Modern warfare and its technology provide probably the most dramatic case of the inclusion category. No longer can one draw a line to separate civilians from soldiers. The distinction between soldiers and civilians began to disappear during the bombings of the Second World War, as population centres were destroyed in order to demoralize the civilian population. With the use of atomic weapons, the customary distinction between combatants and non-combatants became totally meaningless, not only within and between countries at war, but also globally. As clouds of radioactive debris crossed national boundaries and jurisdictions, neutrality or distance no longer provided protection from the consequences of other people's wars or from events over which the potential victims had neither control nor sway.

The rules of war and international conventions of past times, which were once drawn up in an attempt to protect civilians by restraining military activities in terms of space or type of weapons, can no longer address the technological dimensions of war. The development of weapons systems since the Second World War has increased the inclusion power of war even further, so that the largest fraction of casualties and victims of recent wars have been civilian "bystanders." It is clear, in the systems of modern warfare, that neither national nor international law can, at present, provide access to justice for those who are included against their will.

In terms of their impact on the individual's access to justice, modern warfare and its technology should be seen merely as a dramatic prototype of many pollution-related justice issues. Indeed, technical and industrial activities frequently involve wars against nature on both local and global scales. The analysis of involuntary inclusion, as sketched above, is thus equally applicable to many problems triggered by uncontrolled or uncontrollable technological interventions in the citizens' environment.

In most parts of the world, the law protects citizens against unauthorized entry into their homes, against stealing or defacing their property. Yet the law has no answer when a citizen asks, "Who has given anyone the permission to foul the air I have to breathe, or to put acid in the rain that waters my lawn?" The fact that water and air are common rather than private properties should not place their misuse outside the realm in which individuals or communities can seek access to justice. In technology's war against nature the innocent bystanders are as much in need of care and protection as are the non-combatants in the wars between nations. Modern technical developments have made justice-based responses to these problems exceedingly difficult to design, let alone to enforce.

There are essentially three reasons that make it so hard to apply the current instruments of regulation and law to the control of technologies involved in the unwanted inclusion of citizens. The reasons are related to the range and scale of the phenomena, the irreversibility of the processes, and the cumulative nature of the causes and contributions. Global warming may serve as an example of the class of non-military activities that bring about the involuntary inclusion of citizens, an inclusion that is often perceived as unfair, unjust, and undeserved. Global warming is a generic term that summarizes the observed and the anticipated changes in the world's climate due to changes in the composition of the Earth's atmosphere.[13] A significant portion of these changes are due to the increasing presence in the atmosphere of carbon dioxide and other compounds released, for instance, during the burning of fossil fuel. It is the increased industrialization—directly attributable to the spread of modern technologies—that accounts for the accelerated discharge of carbon dioxide and other gases into the atmosphere. Once released, the pollutants have irreversible effects on climates and soils as well as on the distribution and filtering of radiation through the atmosphere. While the rate and intensity of industrialization have varied greatly in different parts of the world, the effects of the altered composition of the Earth's atmosphere are roughly the same for the contributing and non-contributing regions and their citizens. Furthermore, the individual or local contributions to the changes in atmospheric composition become a cumulative burden for the entire planet, each contribution adding to all others regardless of place or nature of its origin. Thus a large number of essentially unrelated causes are—by virtue of the technologies used and because of the nature of the physical world that all of humanity shares—integrated over space and time to produce commonly felt effects that now require prevention or mitigation.

The traditional notions that underlie justice concerns, such as notions of individual intent or provable and transparent links between cause and consequence, are not applicable to the inclusion situations described here. Yet harm is being inflicted on people who have no power to affect the situations that cause this harm, nor a means to escape the detrimental consequences that are seen as fundamentally unjust and unacceptable. The present state of environmental law and its enforcement, as well as the non-compliance of nations with the few existing international conventions related to global warming and the limitation of atmospheric discharges, illustrates just how difficult it is to address—even conceptually—the access to justice issues that technologically caused inclusions entail.

Exclusions Caused by Technology

The most prominent example of a technologically triggered exclusion of citizens from certain essential activities has a longer history than that of global environmental problems. The replacement of workers by machines was recognized as a justice issue at the beginning of the Industrial Revolution and directly linked to the introduction of new technologies.[14] The response of some of the "technologically excluded" workers, who attempted to

destroy the machines that threatened them, was equally direct. In
1812 Lord Byron cast one of three votes in the British House of
Lords against a bill proposing the death penalty for destruction of
industrial machinery. In a letter to Lord Holland, Byron stated his
intention to speak out and vote against the bill, noting that one
machine frame could perform the work of seven weavers, thus
employing one and throwing the other six out of work: "My own
motive for opposing the bill is found in its palpable injustice and
its certain inefficacy. I have seen the state of these miserable men
and it is a disgrace to a civilized country."[15]

The early nineteenth century saw a number of efforts to
address justice issues implicit in the technological exclusion of
workers from labour. Robert Owen and his followers attempted
to use machines in a manner that would confer the benefits of
mechanization primarily on the workers, enhancing their work
and the quality of life of their families and communities.[16] Other
reformers proposed a tax on machinery levied in proportion to
the displacement of workers, with the proceeds used to mitigate
the effects of the new technologies.[17] While Owen emphasized
that productive work was an essential part of a fully human existence, other reformers tended to separate the income and work
components of employment. The state eventually addressed in
part the income component of exclusion from work through the
provision of welfare or unemployment payments, but failed to
face the justice issues inherent in the technological displacement
of workers by devices. Discussions of a guaranteed annual income
can be regarded as searches for mechanisms to cope with existing
and anticipated exclusions of citizens from waged or salaried
employment. Such mechanisms operate without intervening on
the level of the individual technology or the market system itself.[18]

The Future of Work

Consequences of automation, because of the increased use of
computers, the interlinking of electronic technologies, and the
phenomenon of exclusion from work, have spread from the
physical to the mental and intellectual workforce. This spread has
resulted in the contemporary feeling of acute crisis, well illustrated

by the title of Jeremy Rifkin's book *The End of Work*.[19] Rifkin offers suggestions on how to deal with the crisis, such as taxation and the redirection of public funds towards voluntary or non-profit activities. These remedies, which are not dissimilar to some of those suggested 150 years ago, are proposed in terms of economic justice within the framework of the existing global and competitive market economy. But Rifkin does not address the more fundamental justice issue: the need for meaningful work as part of human existence. Apparently it is not seen as part of the crisis or as an essential component of any approach to a solution.

E.F. Schumacher, on the other hand, sees the lack of meaningful work opportunities as a major feature of the current crisis, not only as it relates to unemployment and poverty, but also in relation to environmental deterioration and the disintegration of communities. In *Good Work* Schumacher defines the three purposes of human work: "First, to provide necessary and useful goods and services; second, to enable everyone to use and thereby to perfect their gifts as good stewards; and third, to do so in service to and in co-operation with others, so as to liberate ourselves from our inborn egocentricity."[20] For Schumacher, the central question to be addressed is not how to mitigate the effects of modern technologies on the nature and availability of work through income supplements or appropriate taxes. He sees the task of restoring the place of "good work" in society as one of modifying technology so as to make *good work* possible. Thus human considerations—issues of justice, equity, and the requirements for a full human life—take precedence over considerations of efficiency or economics of scale. Projects employing intermediate and appropriate technology were initiated by Schumacher and continued after his death by a number of other groups.[21] All these projects considered the human and social parameters as primary design criteria and sought to adapt the technology to them, rather than expecting social and human relations to adjust to whatever changes the adoption of new technologies might entail.

Schumacher's interpretation of the essential role of meaningful work resonates through a series of events that took place in Sicily in 1956. These events provide a dramatic illustration of a collective response to issues of access to justice arising from exclusion from productive work. Under the guidance of Italian architect and social reformer Danilo Dolci, citizens in one of the poorest and most neglected parts of Sicily had long agitated for government help and reform. With no help forthcoming, the situation in the community worsened and incidents of violence increased. A group of unemployed men decided to stage a "strike-in-reverse." Instead of withdrawing their labour in protest against unacceptable conditions, they insisted on using their labour—unpaid and out of their own free will—in the service of their community. They set out to restore a long-neglected road not only to protest government promises not honoured but also to establish their moral right to work for the common good. The work was stopped by the police. Dolci and other organizers were arrested, tried, convicted, and imprisoned for allegedly resisting police. Dolci's statement at his trial gives a powerful account of the moral injustice inflicted on those excluded from meaningful work.[22]

When we consider access to justice in the case of technologically forced inclusion of citizens in the impacts of war and pollution, the traditional distinctions between combatants and non-combatants, actors, and bystanders are no longer tenable. Equally, the distinction in law and regulation between the human and the non-human workforce becomes questionable. Why, we might ask, are there regulations governing the use of "replacement workers" during workplace disputes, when "replacement devices" can be employed freely and without constraints? Within the broader context of global sustainability, does it make sense to promote birth control among people without considering, at the same time, birth control of machines and devices?

Concluding Reflections

I have attempted in this paper to construct a map of the impact of technology on issues of access to justice. I hope it has become apparent that while some of these issues, such as the concept of public health, could be addressed by appropriate extensions of current regulation, many other issues may not be susceptible to such approaches. The greater and more profound question that must be tackled soon is this: Can justice be a hinge for ecological and human well-being in a technological society that does not examine and regulate technologies as components of social and political structures?[23]

Notes

1   "Cardinal" from the latin *cardo*, meaning "hinge." The other three cardinal virtues of antiquity are prudence, temperance, and fortitude, to which the theological virtues of faith, hope, and love/charity were later added.

2   Ursula M. Franklin, *The Real World of Technology* (Toronto: Anansi, 1999), p. 12.

3   See, for instance, C. Mitcham, "Philosophy of Technology," in *A Guide to the Culture of Science, Technology and Medicine*, ed. P. Durbin (New York: Free Press, 1980); G. Grant, "Knowing and Making," in *Royal Society of Canada, Proceedings and Transactions*, 4th series, 12 (1974), pp. 59–67.

4   Franklin, *Real World*, p. 9.

5   D.F. Noble, *Progress Without People* (Toronto: Between the Lines, 1995).

6   J. Ellul, *The Technological Society* (New York: Vintage, 1964); see also Ellul, *The Technological System* (New York: Continuum, 1980).

7   Franklin, *Real World*, pp. 10–19.

8   M. Berg, *The Machinery Question and the Making of Political Economy, 1815–1848* (Cambridge: Cambridge University Press, 1980).

9   D. Lyon, *The Electronic Eye: The Rise of the Surveillance Society* (Minnesota: University of Minnesota Press, 1993).

10 K.E. Boulding, *Beyond Economics* (Ann Arbor: University of Michigan Press, 1968).

11 R.A. Caro, *The Power Broker: Robert Moses and the Fall of New York* (New York: Knopf, 1974).

12 T. Berger, *Northern Frontier, Northern Homeland: Report of the Mackenzie Valley Pipeline Inquiry*, 2 vols. (Ottawa: Supply and Services Canada, 1977).

13 C. Mungall and D.J. McLaren, eds., *Planet under Stress* (Toronto: Oxford University Press, 1990).

14 E.J. Hobsbawm, *Industry and Empire* (London: Penguin, 1968). See also M. Berg, *The Machinery Question*, particularly chap. 8 and the discussion on Charles Babbage.

15 For the full text of Lord Byron's letter and his speech, see Noble, *Progress Without People*, appendix 5.

16 R. Owen, *A New View of Society*, ed. V.A.C. Gattrell (Harmondsworth: Penguin, 1969); see also J.F.C. Harrison, *Robert Owen and the Owenites in Britain and America* (London: Routledge and Kegan Paul, 1988).

17 For the debates around the taxation issue, see Berg, *The Machinery Question*, pp. 232–36.
18 R. Theobald, *The Guaranteed Income* (New York: Anchor, 1967).
19 J. Rifkin, *The End of Work* (New York: J.P. Putman, 1995).
20 E.F. Schumacher, *Good Work* (New York: Harper and Row, 1979), pp. 3–4.
21 G. McRobie, *Small Is Possible* (London: Jonathan Cope, 1981); see also P.N. Gillingham, "The Making of Good Work," epilogue in Schumacher, *Good Work*, pp. 147–217.
22 D. Dolci, *Report from Palermo* (New York: Orion, 1959); D. Dolci, *Outlaws* (New York: Orion, 1961). Dolci's trial statement is also reprinted in P. Mayer, ed., *The Pacifist Conscience* (Chicago: Holt, Rinehart and Winston, 1966), pp. 391–401.
23 Ursula M. Franklin, "New Threats to Human Rights through Science and Technology: The Need for Standards," in *Human Rights in the Twenty-First Century: A Global Challenge*, ed. K.E. Mahoney and P.J. Mahoney (Dodrecht, Netherlands: Martinus Nijhoff, 1993), pp. 733–37. See also pp. 198–203 here.

NEW THREATS TO HUMAN RIGHTS
THROUGH SCIENCE AND TECHNOLOGY:
THE NEED FOR STANDARDS

Address presented at Human Rights in the Twenty-First Century, a conference sponsored by the Faculty of Law, University of Calgary, Banff, Alberta, 9–12 November 1990; published in Human Rights in the Twenty-First Century: A Global Challenge, *ed. K.E. Mahoney and P.J. Mahoney (Dodrecht, Netherlands: Martinus Nijhoff, 1993), pp. 733–37.*

DISADVANTAGED GROUPS who have spoken earlier articulated their disadvantage very well. We have heard about *how* they are disadvantaged. But we have heard less about *why* they are disadvantaged. The work for human rights needs to know those reasons. We have to concern ourselves with why it is that dominance and oppression seem to be growing. One of the reasons is doubtless that the maintenance of privilege requires continued dominance and oppression. Another reason—and that is the thesis of this short paper—is that recent advances in science and technology have increased the machinery of dominance and oppression. The tools of that machinery that are now available, and the ways in which human rights can be infringed in manners not foreseen or foreseeable in the liberal, democratic pseudo-tradition that we assume must be understood. In particular, the advancements of science and technology have changed the context in which human rights are placed and must be defended. The ensuing discussion attempts to show, on the basis of some examples, what this change in context is and what new tasks and new standards are needed in the work of protecting human rights.

The Significance of Science and Technology
for Human Rights

Science is an endeavour that separates knowledge from experience. That is both the glory of science and its greatest drawback, because in many ways science finds it impossible to bring experience back into the newly acquired knowledge. As a consequence we must now struggle with the application of non-contextual, scientific knowledge to the very context-bound problems of human rights.

It is the application of scientific knowledge, not the knowledge itself, that impacts on human rights. What this overview is primarily concerned with, therefore, is applied science and technology. In my book *The Real World of Technology*,[1] "technology" is defined not just as devices, machinery, or electronics, but as socially sanctioned practice. Technology, for present purposes, is to be understood as the way we do things, because we have translated the advances of science into a host of infrastructures and mechanisms that can incorporate new threats to human rights. Technology, then, is, as Jacques Ellul[2] called it, a milieu. And the technological order is distinctly different from the liberal, democratic order that we consider to be the basis of human rights.

Implications of Technology for Human Rights

One of the important aspects of modern technological practice is that it allows the control of people in ways that make the control invisible. Big Brother no longer blares out of loudspeakers. Today Big Brother barely beeps. The invisibility of control ought to concern us very profoundly. Even the most undramatic, trivial examples show how this control, this headless tyranny, has permeated "normal" life and become invisible. One of my pleas for new standards is to make these occurrences visible, to name them and to make the process open and transparent.

For instance, the bar codes in the magnetic strips of the plastic cards are very much a part of life. The single bar code on a card that lets car owners into the parking lot is an electronic key; it is not really different from the old lock and key, it is just easier. Now think of the combination of two bar codes: the one on your library card and the one on the book you borrow. Suddenly you see the possibility that someone can track what you read. Even a decade ago, when the question of the *Berufsverbot* (a check of the political loyalty of teachers) formed part of the attack on human rights of our colleagues in Germany, dossiers of the books they had taken out of the library were used as evidence showing their divergent political views and their potential disloyalty to the constitution. Consequently, even a simple library card can become a pervasive control mechanism activated by purely technological means without the consent and knowledge of the user.

Another familiar example concerns security of "smart" buildings. Here cards allows those who occupy the building access to certain floors; if they want to go elsewhere, they may find that their card does not provide access. This exclusion of people from particular parts of the building is automatic and mechanical; it is not possible to knock on some responsible person's door to ask, "Why can I not enter there?" A couple of months ago, I was in the building that houses the Canadian International Development Agency in Ottawa, with an employee of that organization. We wanted to see someone in a different part of the building, but we found that my colleague's card would not let us in. "Trivial," it might be replied. If, instead of the card, access was controlled by an armed guard who demanded identification and refused entry, blood pressures would rise. People would say to the guard, "Who has given you the right to exclude me?" But in the "technological" example there is only a bar code, a bit of magnetic tape. Replacing the armed guard, or even the traditional concierge, by a bar code means that the control potential is much greater. People can be tracked all around the building. Real surveillance can be carried out with no human face, instituting a headless tyranny.

Replacing the armed guard by a mere bar code also has another consequence: it trivializes arguments of principle. What was previously a human rights argument, namely as to who has the right to exclude categories of citizens, suddenly becomes the sum of small and trivial steps. It is characteristic of the impact of technology that principled decisions and the locus for principled decisions become hidden in a multitude of small trivial steps.

An old and quite blatant example of technological exclusion is found in the New York State parkways designed by Robert Moses.[3] The bridges were deliberately designed to be too low for buses to pass. The effect is racial bias technically packaged: those who own a car are able to enjoy the amenities of the park; those who are black, poor, and take the bus cannot. Nobody has to say,

"I don't want them Niggers around here." The bridges are simply made low enough not to allow it.

This example is also cited to make the point that those who defend human rights in a technological order must shift their intervention from the point of infringement to the point of planning. Once the bridges are built, it is too late for protests to the New York authorities. It is too late to say, "You should have put in higher bridges. This is an affront to civil rights." These arguments must be made before the contract for bridge construction is given. This shift of locus from the infringement to the planning and the intent, from the action to the potential, is one of the important impacts of technology.

Even more serious than technological exclusion of groups is the compulsory inclusion of groups in situations that may infringe their human rights and from which they cannot escape. The technology of war first showed us the extent to which the range of violence can be extended. The radius increases—through planes, through bombs, through nuclear weapons—in both space and time. The notion of the innocent bystander, the distinction between combatant and non-combatant, totally disappears. Today the world is faced with many variations of compulsory inclusion in life-threatening attacks. There is no way to be a refugee from pollution, from global warming, from the threat of nuclear war. The very basis of the right to have control of the destiny of one's life, and to have control over the time and the mode of one's death, is taken out of the hands of all people. The rights to live in peace and health, to associate with those with whom one wishes to associate and not with those with whom one does not, have all been limited by technology.

We must realize that technology and the technological order have separated human rights issues into macro- and micro-situations. Human rights organizations may prevent the torture of individuals in specific micro-situations. But the human rights movement has no handle on the macro-torture of those subjected to gas warfare or the effects of nuclear radiation. The linkages have not been made.

It is my view, however, that it is possible to begin to link the micro- and the macro-levels. An understanding of technology would underscore the need to move from the incident of infringement to the intent of a particular technological situation. This would allow intervention on behalf of human rights at the point of planning instead of the point of execution.

An illustration of this point is the position of the conscientious objector in a technological world. To a certain extent, conscientious objectors have successfully convinced civilized nations that those who, on grounds of conscience, object to war should be allowed alternative service. In the past that possibility included alternative service not only in war but also where military conscription existed in peacetime. The situation today is different. No longer can conscientious objections begin if and when war is declared. War is fought primarily by machines and devices, by bombers and missiles, not in hand-to-hand combat. The bombers and the missiles are built in peacetime. They are prerequisites for war. What does a pacifist do when her taxes are used to pay for the instruments necessary for war? "When war breaks out," she is told, "we will take account of your pacifism; we have some laws." The point is, however, that people are no longer needed for war; devices are needed. So instead of the conscription of bodies in wartime, there is conscription of money in peacetime. This is the basis on which we must now test the right to conscientious objection. The right to conscientious objection has been tested in Canada by those who chose to put part of their income tax into a peace trust fund so as not to deprive the public revenue of that portion that they, like all citizens, owe the state. The object is to keep that money out of preparations for war. That is a matter of conscience. As yet, Canadians do not have the option to exercise conscientious objections to the new technologically determined focus.

We need discussion and debate on these dilemmas. If we cannot devise instruments to accommodate the new reality of the technological milieu, our ensuring of human rights to our own citizens is compromised and the larger question of the compulsory inclusion in a threatening non-human-rights environment will not be addressed.

Conclusion

The new standards we need must first of all derive from the recognition of how technology changes the context and the environment of human rights. Attention must shift from the occurrence to the potential of an occurrence. Then, as Professor Cotler points out in his paper,[4] we need fact-finding mechanisms. We need to make clear, at a sufficiently early stage, the relationships between specific technologies and their potential for the abuse of human rights. We cannot allow states to hide evidence of technological infringements as some have hidden evidence of murders or disappearances. We must begin to develop the apparatus that will enable us to realize if and when we are faced with the risk of technologies becoming intrinsically unmanageable in terms of their impacts on human rights. These are technological threats to which the international community must respond, because humanity cannot afford to allow them to materialize.

Notes

1   Ursula M. Franklin, *The Real World of Technology* (Toronto: Anansi, 1999).
2   Jacques Ellul, *The Technological System* (New York: Continuum, 1980).
3   Robert A. Caro, *The Power Broker* (New York: Knopf, 1974).
4   Irwin Cotler, "Human Rights as the Modern Tool of Revolution," in *Human Rights in the Twenty-First Century: A Global Challenge*, ed. K.E. Mahoney and P.J. Mahoney (Dodrecht, Netherlands: Martinus Nijhoff, 1993), pp. 7–20.

PART THREE

COPING WITH AND CHANGING THE TECHNOLOGICAL WORLD

WHENEVER I HAVE spoken or written about technology I have tried to clearly define my use of the term. *Technology*, for me, is *practice*: "the way things are done around here." This definition, which I learned from Kenneth Boulding, makes it easy to recognize that there have always been technologies, specific ways in which things were done by people who made choices that made sense to them. Their choices become comprehensible to us when interpreted within their context of place and time, priorities, culture, and resources. All social activities, viewed as the collective practices of people living and working together, have altered and do alter the world. Throughout time, every new technology was shaped by the interplay of social activities and available resources—using the concept of resources in the broadest sense of the word.

A historically new dimension of this process is the all-embracing systems nature of modern technologies, which turns them into a milieu from which it can be impossible for people to escape.

Practices and processes, *how* things are done, are socially and morally as important—and occasionally more important—than *what* is being done, that is, proclaimed purposes and political rationales.

We should not forget the remarkable similarity of most of the tasks—such as providing food and shelter, exercising power and control, promoting cohesion and stability, and expressing and celebrating common beliefs and visions—faced throughout history by societies. The very richness of human history arises from the broad tapestry of *how* such tasks were structured and carried out.

My overriding preoccupation with understanding the meaning of the *how* is in many ways a convergence of my religious quests, my feminist perspectives, and my scientific interests in the relationship of the structures and properties of materials. My belief in the potential of modifying collective practices is also at the root of my obstinate optimism.

It is a given that all life involves change. Starting with this reality, it is within our common human potential to use a combination of solidarity, compassion, and a realistic understanding of the impact of contemporary practices to direct social and political changes towards justice and peace, and away from war and violence.

The first four papers in this part attempt to highlight different facets of coping with and changing the here and now. They seek to consciously understand and compassionately alter social and political practices, beginning with an elaboration of the concept of technology as practice. "New Approaches to Understanding Technology," a talk I gave in 1984, furthers the distinction to be made between *work*-related and *control*-related technologies. "All Is Not Well in the House of Technology," presented at a 1997 symposium of the Royal Society of Canada, pleads with academics to give some of their serious scholarly attention to the phenomenon of technology per se. I tried to interest them in studying technology as text, with its own syntax and vocabulary. Such studies could open fresh ways of discussing and foreseeing morphologically similar impacts of different technologies.

Those papers are followed by two talks that address the same need to step back from the details of particular innovations, and to focus on their overall systemic impact. When I spoke to community workers and members of Parliament respectively, my emphasis was on the inevitable social and political consequences of seemingly purely technical changes—this time, however, on the human condition. I tried to direct the listeners' awareness not only to those activities that a novel technology would permit, but also to specific practices and options that would be foreclosed by the new system.

In the following three papers the accent shifts from general considerations of technology as practice to the role of those involved in the practice, that is, to the importance of considering those who will be required to comply with practices, imposed with or without their consent, as well as those who choose to work in new ways. None of these actors are pawns on a strange chessboard. The actions and images of all participants shape social and political practices for better or for worse.

Women and their special contributions to new ways of social ordering are the primary focus. Historically women, on account of their different human and social experiences, have developed different modes of work, different ways of knowing and coping. As a feminist, I am convinced of the value of women's insights and patterns of relating. As a pacifist, I look at them with hopeful expectations, viewing them as a pool of potentially helpful new approaches. As an engineer I know how much the applications of new scientific findings need novel, collaborative practices in order to be truly helpful. The question is then: Can feminist practices shape and change technological practices, and, at the same time, can practising feminists function and survive as feminists in the contemporary here and now? "Will Women Change Technology or Will Technology Change Women?" tries to map the essential dimensions of the question for an audience of feminists, many of them academics.

"Stormy Weather," on the other hand, speaks to teachers and school administrators who were pioneering the implementation of equity and non-hierarchal practices into a traditionally patriarchal institution. Part of their daily work and struggle was to try to understand the dynamics and the turbulence of the social changes that their work entailed. My image of the transition to a new social order was offered in support of and in solidarity with my colleagues.

One of the most tragic results of the violence of these structural changes was the murder of fourteen women, all engineering students, at L'École polytechnique in Montreal on December 6,

1989. My commemoration address was given a few weeks after the tragedy at a service by and for members of the Faculty of Applied Science and Engineering of the University of Toronto.

I got into a lot of trouble with my fellow engineers for pointing out that the murdered women had been abandoned by their male classmates, a fact well documented by the inquiries, but not well publicized. Yet clarity and truthfulness seem to me essential prerequisites of any resolution of gender issues. Many of the measures subsequently instituted to address problems for women in the professions have their roots in the shock of the Montreal massacre.

The final papers in this part are specifically concerned with the role of citizens in coping with and changing their technologically mediated environments. The basic conviction informing my contributions is that good government is possible; furthermore, one facet of good government is that citizens can have the legitimate expectation that their views will be taken into account before decisions affecting their communities and environments are made. The discussion of a green energy policy served to illustrate the different criteria that civic concerns and expectations could bring to issues of energy demand and supply.

The processes of citizen politics and their evolution in Toronto are the subject of the next two talks. Regarding citizens' expectations to have a say in municipal decision-making, it was important for me to emphasize the overriding importance of planning activities. It is at the planning table that not only citizens' practical preferences but also their social and moral convictions are tested.

"Planning and the Religious Mind" and "On Speaking Truth to Planning" look at present-day planning and what it involves. The process, so essential for any modern technological society, carries heavy conceptual mortgages: among them the fragmentation of tasks that the Industrial Revolution brought, and the technologically focused allocation, control, and foreclosure of options, perfected in, and for, war. And then there are the asynchronicity and the limitation of individual and collective moral autonomy that globalization entails.

If facets of all these attributes are of necessity embedded in present-day planning, is this really the process that we, the citizens, want or need? Is this the only process that is possible in the technological here and now? "Planning and the Religious Mind" suggests other planning criteria that could be more compatible with a map of pacifism.

NEW APPROACHES TO UNDERSTANDING TECHNOLOGY

Keynote address delivered at Technology, Innovation and Social Change, an international seminar sponsored by the Institute of Canadian Studies, Carleton University, Ottawa, and the Centre of Canadian Studies, University of Edinburgh, 26–27 October 1984; published in Technology, Innovation and Social Change: Proceedings *(Ottawa: Carleton University, 1985), pp. 6–11; reprinted in* Man-Environment Systems, *vol. 16, nos. 2–3 (March–May 1986), pp. 65–67.*

ON THE CONFERENCE program, my talk has the title "New Approaches to Understanding Technology." Actually, it is not that these approaches are new, but that they may be different from what is normally heard. It is for this reason that I want to put them before you. The perspective that I want to take is a historical one, using the word "historical" in a very general sense. Though I am not one to think of history as a series of continuing "onward and upward" movements, it is still possible to define such a thing as a historical trend. One of these trends is the increasing emphasis that societies have placed on the importance of the individual human being. This trend is observable and discernable as we move into the phases of modern history.

It is in part due to the development of technology—particularly in terms of communication and travel—that we now speak about the global village in the sense of Marshall McLuhan. This global village in which all of us are neighbours and citizens has made "other people" into more real and definable human beings. Modern society has seen significant movements that initiated social change on behalf of "others," such as the abolition of slavery and the restriction of child labour. Many social reforms were initiated by people appalled by the conditions in which others had to live, and who found that it was inconsistent with their own view of human dignity and human potential to look aside when such inequalities occurred within this global village. I hope the recent recognition of the equal rights and equal potentials of women is part of the general historical trend towards considering and respecting the importance of all human beings.

It is in this perspective that I would like to discuss technology, and therefore I would like to subtitle my talk "Technology as if People Mattered." This subtitle, of course, is based on the subtitle of Ernst Friedrich Schumacher's book *Small Is Beautiful: Economics as if People Mattered*. Before outlining how our understanding of technology might change by taking this differing perception, let me say that technology is not always a helpful concept for discussion. Those who have heard me speak about the systems aspect of technology may find it peculiar that I now say that technology per se is not always a helpful concept. In spite of the need to keep in mind the systems aspect of technological developments, the very notion of technology can be too broad and diverse to serve as an appropriate parameter in discussions on social impact. I am reminded of the generality of the concept of humanity, and of Charlie Brown's comment "I love humanity. It's people I can't stand!"

Instead of speaking about technology, I will, as far as possible, speak about particular technological developments—about machines, devices, and computers—because I want to focus on the impact on *people*, rather than the impact on humanity. What would change if we were to look at machines, devices, installations, and processes from the point of view that people matter? First, the questions we ask might be phrased differently; second, there might be new questions from this perspective, questions that were not asked before. In terms of phrasing questions differently, consider a discussion about costs and benefits. Instead of discussing the overall costs and benefits of a particular development, we could look much more closely at the groups to whom benefits accrue, and could ask much more precisely, "Who is paying the costs?" We would be concerned not only about what risks are politically acceptable or socially condonable, but also about whose risks we are discussing. If this were done consistently and applied to specific instances related to devices and machines, computers and word processors, it would become obvious that technological developments fall into two broad groups.

The first group contains work-related innovations: the machines and devices that make an individual's work easier, more effective, or more enjoyable. The transition from the mechanical to the electrical typewriter, for instance, falls into this category. The second group of technological developments contains control-related technologies: developments and devices that affect the control of the workplace and the work environment rather than the work of an individual. One example might be the electronic checkouts at the supermarket; these devices assist inventory and labour control, but they do not really change much for the person standing at the cash register.

A significant proportion of the control-related technologies are designed to control major aspects of our social and political environment. At present control-related applications of modern devices are increasing much more rapidly than are work-related innovations. I need not remind you of the amassing of personal files and of the data-collecting activities of various agencies, official and otherwise. There are great difficulties in developing constraints that would keep the application of such control-related technologies within the framework of a democratic society. Working under the assumption that people matter, in such cases of control-related technologies it would be imperative to ask not *how* the new technology will be introduced, but *why* it should be introduced at all.

There is more to the perspective I have taken, however, than the rephrasing of existing questions and the hope for different and more meaningful answers. There are a number of new questions to be asked, questions that did not come to mind in the old frame of reference. I would like to put just one of these questions to you. It relates to an area of inquiry that I have always found surprisingly absent in discussions on technology, innovation, and social change.

Although there is a keen public awareness of the range of new technologies, there is amazingly little real information in terms of the numbers and categories of the devices, machines, and systems that constitute these technologies. It is self-evident that machines and devices are an integral and real part of our environment, both physical and political. Nevertheless, as a society we seem to see through them as if they were socially and politically transparent. In simplistic terms, we might define a machine as a device that uses energy and performs work. But in spite of the fact that machines increasingly take the place of people in the workforce, we do not count them in the way that we count people. The science of population demography has flourished for centuries: people are counted periodically; birth rates are projected; we know the average lifespan, the average income, the average food rations in different countries; we can rely globally on a large amount of well-collected, well-analyzed, accessible data on population changes. But we do not have a science of machine demography. There is no national or international machine census. We know nothing about the lifetime or life cycle of any particular device. We know nothing about birth rates in various technological areas. Thus while the danger of a human population explosion can be discussed in terms of factual evidence and projections, the possibility of a machine population explosion is not discussable in a similar framework.

Much of the required information, I suggest, could be generated from existing data. The fact that at present there are no machine demographic statistics[1] is an indication of a certain lack of reality in assessments of the social consequences of technologies. But machines and devices are real, as McLuhan often reminded us. They are there, they use our energy, they do our work, they listen to our telephone conversations. I think it is time to concern ourselves with the mechanical citizens and, as a society, to devise some rules of conduct for them, some social norms and constraints for the part they take in our lives. We should be mindful that at a time when human citizens are subjected to increasing pressure towards conformity, law, and order, the corollary to this development should not be an increasing lawlessness of mechanical citizens.

So much for the questions that might emerge from a different perspective. Let me now touch on one other facet of the problems we are discussing. If we assume that people matter, then *people* should be a central reference point in the development of technologies. It is then imperative to design technological innovations in such a manner as to enhance the truly human attributes and qualities. Decades ago Norbert Wiener spoke about "the human use of human beings." In his spirit, I would like to compare the values and attributes of the technological order with those of the world of women. I draw on the experience of women particularly since they are in many ways still much closer to the human realities of everyday life. The purpose of this comparison is to illustrate the contradictions that can arise in the perceptions of tasks and values depending on whether we take, as the base, the technological order or the human order, as symbolized in the world of women.

Examining tasks and values, it is evident that in the technological order tasks are fragmented. Whether executed by humans or by devices, tasks are specified and prescribed. These tasks are predictable, non-random, fully scheduled, and carried out without reference to context. The narrow specialization of technological tasks usually offers little scope for initiative or improvisation. The strict categorization of tasks and procedures and the interchangeability of people and devices leave no room for spontaneity. The functioning of the technological order depends on the integration of hierarchal structures of increasing complexity. Planning and scheduling are absolutely essential. Authority is derived from access to and control of various levels and interfaces of the structure.

In the women's world, tasks are defined by the context and specific needs from which they arise. These tasks, more often than not, are flexible, unpredictable, non-specific, and integrated. They cannot be scheduled and there is a high degree of randomness, both in reality and in expectations, since the women's world is to a large extent unplannable. This world is horizontally structured and full of the unexpected. Diversity in skills is valued, as is personal loyalty and a sense of continuity. The world of women puts great stock in experience, and experience is seen to be transferable to new, unforeseen, or unforeseeable tasks. Inventiveness, spontaneity, and improvisation are equally highly valued.

It is also important to realize the existence of basic differences in strategy. While the technological order and its subsystems are normally geared to maximizing gain, the strategies within the women's world are more often than not aimed at minimizing disaster. In summary, then, the work by and with mechanical citizens requires conformity, predictability, and specificity, as tasks are prescribed without reference to context. The work with and by human citizens, on the other hand, requires integration, judgment in terms of context, and interactive inventiveness. Without wishing to go further into these problems, I hope that I have indicated some of the genuine and basic incompatibilities between the technological order and the tasks and values that have evolved within a human context. It seems to me that, at the moment, we live in a situation in which the technological system, with its own structures and values, and the human systems exist precariously side by side.

In the powerful trends of the new industrial revolution, people have to adapt to the work, habits, and values of the machines. People are generally regarded as sources of problems, while devices are considered as means to solutions. Thus the intellectual, political, and financial investment is in devices rather than in people. In this process, workers lose skills or jobs as the machines take over many of their tasks, and certain social settings are also eliminated in the process of redesigning the activities of production. The elimination of some of these social settings also eliminates the opportunities of developing those human skills that are fundamentally different from the skills of machines: abilities such as listening, interpreting, instructing, and working out mutually acceptable accommodations. But it is these skills, more than anything else, that the global village needs.

If we do not wish to let the technological system totally erode and destroy the realm of people, some clear and conscious political decisions must be made. If the word "paradigm" were not such an overworked term, I would say that what we need at this point is a drastic paradigm shift. There is an urgent need for technological societies to examine their historical roots and their cultural and political assumptions. There is also a great need for clarity as to the role of the mechanical citizens in the political and social systems. If we believe that people matter—and that all people matter equally—then priorities must be discussed, agreed upon, and implemented so that the structure and daily workings of communities reflect the way in which the human and mechanical citizens are treated. This will not be an easy task, but not facing it will mean turning away from the trends of history that I spoke of at the beginning of this talk.

Note

1   When I was working with the Science Council of Canada in 1976 on *Canada as a Conserver Society*, a report that dealt with resource allocation, I wrote letters to the editors of *Nature*, *Science*, and *The Canadian Science Forum*, explaining my interest and requesting contacts with machine demographers. I received no reply, other than several letters saying, "That sounds interesting. Would you mind sharing with me whatever information you might obtain."

ALL IS NOT WELL IN THE HOUSE
OF TECHNOLOGY

Address to The Well-Being of Canada: A Symposium of the Royal Society of Canada, Ottawa, 22 November 1997; published in Transactions of the Royal Society of Canada, *6th series, vol. 8 (1997), pp. 23–31.*

THERE IS A CERTAIN amount of open-endedness in the title of this symposium, surely intended to allow the perspectives of different discussants to illuminate the theme. My notion of the well-being of Canada is not expressed by the GNP or international credit ratings, much as these measures may have their place in the scheme of things; even employment data, infant mortality statistics, income distributions, or levels of pollution can convey to me only part of the picture of the well-being of a country. It is the degree of real hope and scope of the least powerful members of our society that is my indicator of the well-being of my country.

Having been asked to examine how well Canada is doing in "the area of technology," I realized that, had the president of the Academy of Science asked another of our members, this lecture might have begun with statistics on the number of computers, telephones, or television sets in Canadian homes, or with the number and areas of high-tech patents filed by Canadian inventors, and maybe the fate of such intellectual resources. However, I do not intend to hand out merit or demerit points. Rather, I would like to look at "the area of technology" as both a field of specific knowledge and a field of general interest, because I want to emphasize those facets of the question to which we, as members of the Royal Society of Canada, might be able to make a contribution. We are, after all, intellectuals and academics for whom the temptation of analyzing problems and coming to the conclusion that someone—not us—*must* do A, B, and C is always present. But we do not need to yield to this temptation since there is something specific for us to do. I am convinced that the problems in what I call the House of Technology are not all "other people's problems." This morning I wish to argue that much of what is unwell in the House of Technology may be traced back to a lack of academic and scholarly attention to technology per se. I would also like to make the case that Canadian scholars may be in a very good position to give such fresh and focused attention.

At this point, I need to define "technology" and my use of that term: I have always defined technology as *practice*, that is, "the way things are done around here."[1] This definition, while including all the elements of design, of devices and systems, of purpose and control, emphasizes that technology is a social phenomenon not confined to the application of modern scientific knowledge. Technology, defined as culturally and socially rooted practice, is thus an integral part of every society. As a societal activity, technology—that is, practice—is interactive; it involves and structures the collectivity. You cannot have technology alone, just as you cannot have literature alone. (The very act of writing assumes a reader separated from the writer in space and/or time.)

Technologies have always been important to the well-being of societies, and yet there is a stunning discrepancy between the amount of intellectual attention, the level of methodological scrutiny, the extent of care and scholarship that is devoted to what people have *done* and how they have *done* "it," compared to what people have *said* and *written*. There may be a great deal of talk about technology and technological change, but how much do we actually know about technology per se, or about the interactive structuring of society and technology? Let me illustrate my argument with the help of two drawings created almost a century apart.

The first comes from a series of cards commissioned in 1898 by a French publishing house[2] illustrating aspects of life in the year 2000; the illustrator, Jean Mark Côté, was asked to depict the changes in society under the impact of new anticipated technologies. On one particular card we see the futurist concept of "airmail," the new way of moving a letter from place to place in the year 2000. Evidently the artist expected that this new way of doing something, this new technology, would not change anything else within the social fabric; it would be home delivery as usual, probably twice a day. The second drawing is a cartoon on a flyer announcing a public meeting on technological unemployment in Toronto in November 1997.[3] A librarian presiding over a room full of readers, each sitting in front of an individual video display terminal, answers an inquiry with, "Sir, this is a library. If you want a book, go to a bookstore." Here again a new technology is applied to an established activity ... but can we assume that there will be public libraries "as usual," just as a hundred years ago a French artist assumed there would be home delivery of letters in the year 2000? If we no longer believe that one social practice, one technology, can be changed without affecting other social practices, how do we study, describe, or assess the interplay of technologies in general and systemic terms?

If we imagine the interdependent technologies as rooms in a house, connected by doorways and corridors, then I hold that this House of Technology is not well lit; it seems to be full of trap doors, and it lacks exits, windows, and, most of all, signs or direction indicators. Although we live in a country—and in a world— that is increasingly and rapidly restructured by new practices, by new technologies, we have few if any intellectual tools to address technology as a social force, not in terms of good, bad, or indifferent, but in terms of its attributes, statements, and internal consistencies or inconsistencies. Without analytical tools and methodologies it is almost impossible to contemplate an answer to the question, "How well is Canada doing with respect to technology?"

In other words, I argue that nothing has had a greater impact on the events of the past hundred years than changes in technology. Dramatically different and novel practices have been used to accomplish what one might call the basic tasks of civilization. These tasks have really not changed profoundly over the millennia: human communities have always tried to provide food and shelter for their members, direction and instruction for their young, myths and signposts that validate their traditions, and safety, care, and scope for the collectivity. What has changed so profoundly over time is *how* these tasks have been and are being carried out. Advances in knowledge or access to new resources have been translated into new practices, new ways of doing the task at hand. Yet where do we turn for an analysis of these technologies? It seems to me that we cannot inform ourselves on technology as technology in the same way that we can, for instance, on literature as literature, or on language as language.

The domain of "doing"—its context and its actors—has not had the degree of intellectual illumination that the domain of "declaring"—the world of the spoken and written word, with its context, rules, and meanings—has had. There may be historical reasons for this lack of systematic scholarship of technology as a field of inquiry: the Euro-centred emphasis on literacy in education, compared to conduct and action, may have something to do with it. But whatever its roots, this imbalance in transparency needs to be addressed.

There is, I suggest, a new and major field of scholarship in the making, a field that is transdisciplinary more than interdisciplinary, because it will cut across the traditional boundaries of disciplines and academic faculties. Its new knowledge, while building on scholarship and insights of existing fields, will transform and extend the scope and method of the inquiry into the nature of technology. I am conscious of the contributions already made. No one will labour in this area of study without being influenced and stimulated by Lewis Mumford, Michel Foucault, Ludwig von Bertalanffy, Jacques Ellul, and many others.[4] The notions of technology as a system, or Ellul's concepts of technology as milieu, have particularly influenced thinkers and practitioners alike. But we are still, I feel, without adequate methodologies to analyze technology in general terms. I would like to indicate how the mapping strategies of other disciplines might provide fruitful morphological parallels for the work of those concerned about the structure of technology.

Why not look at technology as *text*? We all are aware of the simultaneous presence of declaring and doing, of word and deed in our lives. We have the artifacts of the word as well as the scholarship to evaluate and critique the written record. We also have the artifacts of the deed, the physical, social, and institutional evidence of technologies past and present, although only a much less developed scholarship of analysis and critique. Think for a moment of the introduction of a new technology as *doing* a text. Looked upon as a *text*, does a given technology, a particular practice, not have substantive and/or relational components in its *language?* Surely there are also subtexts and assumptions here, just as there is context, meaning, consistency, or inconsistency to be discerned in any technological process or activity.

In my own work, I have put forward a general distinction between holistic and prescriptive technologies, but there is so much more to be done to discern the recurring elements, the words, and the vocabulary of technology. We need grammar, syntax, and structure as well as the signs and the symbolic components of technology as text and/or language. In the past, technology has been "read" by those, including myself, who commented on it mainly as social instruction, the how-to manual that outlines a task and its context. Now it is time to read and interpret technology as literature, as text per se. It is no longer solely a matter of content, but also one of an analysis of the constituent elements, both visible and implied.

In the examples that follow I have tried to indicate how one might approach a textual analysis of technology. Carrying out such a new methodological work is obviously beyond the reach of my own scholarship. The examples and their discussion are intended mainly to stimulate my colleagues who master different intellectual instruments to re-examine the discourse about technology. Let me assure you that I am not trying to revisit the debates about structures in literature and science[5] or the discussions on ways of knowing.[6] What I am wrestling with is the need for an anatomy of technology that could stand in a point-counterpoint relationship to the anatomy of literature, in the broadest sense of the term. As I try to understand the world of technology I am grappling with the lack of intellectual tools and look to the humanities for help. The domain of *doing* requires mapping and orienteering instruments that the world of *declaring* begins to take for granted. It may, in the end, turn out to be a quest for an appropriate taxonomy.

My first example relates to the ski lift. When I came to Canada I was astonished to see the effects of rather severe skiing accidents among my fellow post-docs. Though I had skied in Germany, I had never known ski lifts and it took me a while to see the link between the availability of a lift and the severity of the accidents encountered on the downward path. Quite simply, the process of getting up a slope without mechanical help seems to convey skills that are adequate to get down reasonably safely. Mechanizing the "up" part of the practice changed the risks of the "down" part.

How might one analyze this simple change in technology as a *doing text*? There is a *task* (the plot, the story): to get up to a certain point on a mountain and down again. There is an *activity* associated with the task: to do the climb and descend on skis. The prerequisites for the activity (in addition to trivialities such as having skis, a mountain, and snow) are skiing skills and skills of informed observation, assessment, and collaboration. The text may be divided into two parts—chapter 1, the ascent; chapter 2, the descent—and we have two versions before us: the Pedestrian version, in which the task is carried out without mechanical assistance; and the Ski Lift version, in which the ascent is mechanized. The task is the same in both versions, but in the Ski Lift version the ascent is accomplished externally: the Ski Lift version contains something different, another actor, another voice, tense, or language. This change does not affect the task level of the text; the ascent is readily accomplished. The change in technology, though, does affect the activity and skill level of the text. It becomes clear that although the task of chapter 1 can be more readily completed in the Ski Lift version, with the help of the new technology, the very use of an external mechanism diminishes the activity and skill content. Chapter 2, the descent, is the same in both versions as far as task and activity are concerned.

Yet in terms of context and form, there is a significant discontinuity (might it be in vocabulary, language, grammar, or syntax?) between chapter 1 and chapter 2 in the Ski Lift version. This discontinuity is not apparent in the Pedestrian version, where chapter 1 and chapter 2 seem to flow without a break (pardon the pun) in either the skill or the activity levels (subtexts?). Actually *doing* chapter 1 in the Pedestrian Version confers the skills required to do chapter 2. The Ski Lift Version, though lacking the activity that allows the acquisition of the necessary skills, implicitly assumes their presence. A textual analysis would note the changes in voice (style, grammar) as well as the new unstated and possibly unwarranted assumptions. One could request clarification through footnotes or other editorial devices in order to draw attention to the significant changes between apparently identical texts (plots). This discussion is intended not as an argument against ski lifts but as a plea for clarity, using as case in point a simple and transparent illustration. Any good analysis of a simple situation ought to identify structural elements, signifiers of discontinuities, or conceptual gaps that could be transferred to more general and complex considerations.

In my second example, I want to extend the ski lift analysis to the much more complex situation of external aids for teaching and learning, to the realm of the development and transfer of knowledge and understanding. There have, of course, always been external aids for teaching and learning: books and dictionaries, mathematical tables, charts, and slide rules. But the scope and capacity of modern computers and their linking must be seen as much more than a vast increase in the number of standard aids and their uses. The structure of teaching and learning has so changed that we may want to examine the new text of education and compare it to the previous version. For the sake of transparency, I would like to confine myself to certain aspects of education in a school setting: specifically to the introduction of electronic spellers and calculators, or their equivalents, into the classroom.

Looking at the situation as a *text*, we can again discern a specific task: the mastery of spelling or the competence to carry out a mathematical operation. As before, the tasks involve an activity level (learning) and a skill component (applying what has been learned). The specific tasks arise within a larger context: writing and composition; setting and solving numerical or mathematical problems. As in the ski lift case, part of the larger task can be accomplished today by external devices. Therefore the consequences of the task-related skills—spelling or calculating correctly—come into use in spite of bypassing the task-related activities—learning how to spell or calculate correctly.

One of the questions arising from the new technological possibilities is this: "How is the overall text, its content, its internal logic and consistency, its credibility and conclusions affected by the external task substitutions and transpositions? To answer this question, we have to go back to the main *text* of education in which the specific tasks are embedded. In the context of this analysis I will define the purpose of classroom education as the growth of the students' knowledge and understanding. Thus the tasks of spelling and calculating correctly are only part of the overall plot or story of the text.

In the ski lift case, mechanizing the ascent may leave the skier with inadequate skills for a safe descent; the classroom case is similar, though less transparent. The activities related to learning how to spell and calculate teach more than simply mastering the tasks at hand. These activities include implicit lessons for the student on how to work in a group and how to learn, as well lessons in tolerance and anger management, inventiveness and response. Such implicit social learning must be accomplished even if the explicit tasks of spelling and calculating are forever relegated to external devices. Physical injuries resulting from the imprudent use of ski lifts can be identified relatively easily and remedial measures undertaken. But in the case of the teaching aids, must we await the appearance of potential social injuries and their tracing back to changes in explicit and implicit learning before we discuss the new teaching technologies and perhaps supplement them with new sources of skills? Can we not analyze the changes in "syntax" of the new text of education—as text—to illuminate its structure, gaps, or discontinuities, and compare this text to other texts with similar plots or stories?

Other examples that I could give, such as the use of electronic communications and transactions,[7] are of greater complexity, but I could see them being analyzed and discussed in terms of the elements and motives identifiable in the simpler cases. Here again comes my plea to colleagues in the humanities for their help. Serious methodological research into technology as text would be brain-intensive, but not capital-intensive. It would promote a new kind of interdisciplinarity and transdisciplinarity and encourage a fundamental approach to our most relevant problems.

Canada, as a country, could provide many examples for such a textual analysis of technology: examples of new practices and novel ways of doing things, as well as of their structuring impacts on society and governance. Such examples might range from

roads vs. railways to radio, telephone, fax, and Internet penetration
of the North and of the southern regions of our country. Both
French- and English-language analysis of the realm of "declaring"
is well represented among our colleagues, and I am confident that
they will be able to adapt their scholarship to the realm of
"doing." I am also sure that this Society will welcome the practitioners of the new discipline and will even come to a decision
about which of our academies they should belong to.

Notes

1   Ursula M. Franklin, *The Real World of Technology* (Toronto: Anansi,
    1999).
2   This illustration is found in Isaac Asimov, *Futuredays: A Nineteenth-
    Century Vision of the Year 2000*, illustrations by Jean Mark Côté (Lon-
    don: Virgin Books, 1986).
3   Flyer created by the Coalition Against Technological Unemploy-
    ment, announcing a public meeting in November 1997 in Toronto.
4   Lewis Mumford, *The Myth of the Machine: Technics and Human Devel-
    opment* (New York: Harcourt Brace Jovanovich, 1967); Michel
    Foucault, *The Order of Things* (New York: Random, 1970); Ludwig
    von Bertalanffy, *General System Theory: Foundations, Development,
    Applications* (New York: Braziller, rev. 1968); Jacques Ellul, *The Tech-
    nological Society* (New York: Knopf, 1964); Ellul, *The Technological Sys-
    tem* (New York: Continuum, 1980).
5   See, for instance N. Katherine Hayles, ed., *Chaos and Order: Complex
    Dynamics in Literature and Science* (Chicago: University of Chicago
    Press, 1991), particularly the editor's introduction; and Bruno
    Latour, *Science in Action: How to Follow Scientists and Engineers through
    Society* (Milton Keynes, U.K.: Open University Press, 1987).
6   Gregory Bateson, *Steps to an Ecology of Mind* (New York: Ballantine,
    1972); William R. Poulson, *The Noise of Culture* (Ithaca, N.Y.:
    Cornell University Press, 1988).
7   See Ursula M. Franklin, *Every Tool Shapes the Task: Communities and
    the Information Highway* (Vancouver: Lazara Press, 1996); and "Beyond
    the Hype," *Leadership in Health Services,* vol. 5, no. 4 (July–August
    1996), pp. 14–18. Both are reprinted here, pp. 225–34 and 235–42.

EVERY TOOL SHAPES THE TASK: COMMUNITIES AND THE INFORMATION HIGHWAY

Keynote address presented to Community Access to the Information Highway, a conference in Ottawa, 7–9 May 1995; published as Every Tool Shapes the Task: Communities and the Information Highway *(Vancouver: Lazara Press, 1996).*

COMPUTERS AND the application of computer technology are, of course, something we all have seen coming and that we have lived with. In many ways it is a technology of the young, and I consider myself, to phrase it politely, chronologically challenged, so that I really don't know whether much of what I can say will be of help to you.

Who Are Community Groups?

I think the subject of this conference is very important. It is very serious. It is also very broad. I would like to narrow down my perspective. When I refer to community groups, I am speaking only about those voluntary organizations who come together to affect the lives of their community or country: people who deal with issues of environment, with issues of justice. I know them well because I have found much of my own community within these groups.

These community groups have been essentially the extra-parliamentary opposition in this country for a good number of years. As communities, we took over this role when we saw that the traditional parliamentary opposition was fading more and more into obscurity, when we found that the moment someone in opposition became government, their outlook on life changed profoundly. In addition, many of the real issues seemed to get only bland responses, if any, from the traditional parliamentary opposition. Of course they support human rights, of course they love nature, and so much for that. As a result, it is the extraparliamentary opposition that provides the building blocks of democracy.

Who and What Is the New Technology For?

These community groups try, again and again, to cope with democracy in a technological society. Any time new technologies emerge, whether it relates to the workplace, to issues of war and peace or justice, or to the field we are discussing today—information and structuring of a discourse—it is the community that raises the questions. "What can these new technologies do in our work of furthering democracy? What effect will they have on the process? What do these technologies prevent us from doing?"

Community groups have asked these questions in their approaches to city planning and environmental issues, and it is important that we ask them again. "What does that new technology do, what does it prevent us from doing, and most importantly, what don't we do any more because the new technology is in place?" With these questions in mind, I am going to address that technology, specifically the electronic networks under discussion here, not so much in terms of how it has come about, but in terms of what it really signifies for me personally.

Vertical Communication

What is actually going on? I find this question very difficult. It is like a film on top of a film on top of a film. You don't always see clearly what is going on. As community groups, we talk about constituency. Think of those constituencies as building blocks of democracy. Genuine democracy cannot and does not work if there are disenfranchised constituencies.

Allow me to give you a very simple picture. Imagine the world is like a cake. Imagine that you slice it into the customary slices by making vertical cuts. Each slice of that cake can signify a constituency, located geographically as a segment of the larger cake. Each individual slice is influenced more by its immediate neighbours than by parts of the cake that might be quite far away. In many ways, our communities have organized themselves, by history and by necessity, around those vertical slices of cake. These slices are our parliamentary constituencies. Here is the slice where the member from Kicking Horse Pass resides. We know where our cities, our school boards, and our larger communities are. Historically, much of the communication in the vertical slices has been vertical communication: up and down between the bottom and the top, between those who reside in the icing and those who are the small crumbs on the bottom. Our reference to "trickle-down" effects comes from a vertical slice model. When we deal with our members of Parliament and our school boards, when we think of constituencies, however sophisticated we get, we are working through this historical image of a vertical cut.

The Expansion of Horizontal Communication

Technology is a means to mediate the relationship between space and time. What technology has done in the world increasingly is to make horizontal cuts in that cake. Now you talk not only up and down but across barriers horizontally. We see the extent to which the world has been sliced horizontally and how horizontal communication has begun to take precedence over vertical communication. Horizontal communication, not only of thoughts but also of actual movement, takes many different forms. In the past, while slow, the horizontal movement of people was reasonably straightforward. Now, as those who work with refugees and immigrants will know, the horizontal movement of people is very difficult, even with the great horizontal slicing that has given us air traffic. On the other hand, the horizontal movement of money is incredibly easy. It used to be difficult to take money even from Canada to the U.K., but now you can speculate on currency from your desk or your computer with ease. It takes less time to move money from New York to Tokyo than it takes the clock to move the stock-market opening time, and stock markets play on the time difference. Horizontal slicing allows a great deal of movement, and it is differentially specified as to who moves what. Trade and travel are eased through horizontal slicing. You might wear a shirt or a pair of shoes made in China. On the other hand, the packaging for that pair of shoes, which was also made in China, becomes your local garbage. Your taxes have to pay to get rid of it.

There is a peculiar intermixing in a world that is both vertically and horizontally sliced. The legislation and regulation that govern horizontal movements and things that move horizontally are very loose, even though they involve issues that we have to face. If a nuclear reactor malfunctions somewhere in the world, the pollution is distributed horizontally. You face it in your drinking water and your soil, and you have no recourse whatsoever in terms of mitigation, responsibility, or accountability because it came to you from an unidentifiable (or occasionally even identified) source through an uncontrollable horizontal movement.

The Internet: Access and Advocacy

The difference between vertical and horizontal traffic affects us profoundly as we deal with community groups, with access, and with advocacy. The Internet is one of those inventions that can work both vertically and horizontally. You can connect with everybody. Wouldn't it be nice if we could gather the relevant information we want for our work through that horizontal slicing of our world, and then use it vertically in our communities? If you are interested in clean energy or early childhood education, you might think that there is an enormous amount of usefulness in a horizontal gathering of the best and most detailed insights on the subject. You could use all this information vertically when you go to those who deal with implementing energy or education and say, "Look, this is the very best the world has to offer in terms of knowledge and insight. Let's go with it." If I said that to you, you would reply, "You must be dreaming. The world just doesn't work like that." Of course the world works very differently. There are two important provisos for gathering information horizontally and applying it vertically. One is that you are not alone; there are the others who also run around horizontally and vertically. The second concerns the place and nature of what we call information.

Knowledge versus Action

I go back fifty years, to the celebrations at the end of the Second World War. The liberation of the concentration camps in the final months of the war was a tremendous and profound shock to the world. When this became evident in the aftermath of the war, the Germans were asked, "What was your responsibility?" In the Germany of my childhood, the standard response was, "We didn't know." We didn't know—sometimes it was true, sometimes not, but the response "We didn't know" that the Germans used as their explanation and their excuse for consent to tyranny meant, "Had we known, we would surely have done something about it."

Now, fifty years later, it is no longer possible for people to say, with any credibility, "We didn't know," about a similar disaster, holocaust, or negation of human rights, assuming that had they known, something would have been done. Lack of knowledge as an explanation or excuse may have had a part in historical descriptions of the holocaust, but today all of us know a great many things that would require immediate intervention on the part of any person of conscience. Whether it is an environmental disaster, whether it is Rwanda, whether it is a civil rights violation in one of many countries, whether it is the increasing number of unemployed in our own country, whether it is the homeless we see on our way to work, it isn't as though we don't know.

Mathematicians nicely distinguish between necessary and sufficient conditions. There is a horrible realization that, while knowledge of factual information may be a necessary condition for action—as we talk about democracy in civic action—it is unfortunately not a sufficient one. What is needed for an effective mitigation and a revision of the conditions of which we have knowledge are channels to power that are not blocked and a responsive agency of power that can and will make the changes.

And as you deliberate the access to information on the information highway, be it factual information or the experience of like-minded people in other parts of the world, do please remember that knowledge may, in fact, be a less necessary condition than the one sufficient condition: access to power. In the end, knowledge, as one of my colleagues once wrote, has something to do with power and survival, and we are all, he added, in the business of both.

We cannot rest with the knowledge that we might gain in terms of information if we do not have a realistic grasp as to what could and would modify the conditions we are addressing. Again, being chronologically challenged, I have been in this game for too long, written too many briefs, been on too many delegations to address committees in Ottawa, to be sanguine about saying, "The poor dears need more knowledge. If they only knew what I know, the world would be a better place to live." One begins most of these civic journeys with the idea that those in power are well-intentioned and ill-informed, but I am sorry to say that many of us have learned that those in power are very well informed but ill-intentioned. They have no intention of doing what I might consider the right and appropriate thing.

When to Take a "Dim View"

We must, then, look at another source and another need for knowledge: the knowledge of "Why things that seem appropriate, useful, honourable, and decent do not get done." Our action, as community groups, of gathering that initial information is only the first act of a play. The real problem for any community group is to answer the question, "What do you do after you have taken a dim view?" This question is particularly difficult to answer in the area of access to the information highway. Our concern is not about gathering knowledge but rather about structures of power and responsibility. From my own experience, I should caution you about the misuse of information. I don't mean disinformation or wrong information. First of all, I will ask, "How much information do you really need before you take a dim view?"

I was once part of a small group standing in front of the president of our university, arguing that the university should divest itself from commercial investments in white South Africa. The university president said that the issue needed to be studied, and that he always had to look at both sides of a problem. I got very angry and said, "Could you please explain to me what is the other side of justice?" This has some bearing on the pressure that is sometimes put on community groups to study a question further. There are many things that may require further study, but there is also a tactic that I call "occupational therapy for the opposition," where community groups are sent off to do some more pushups on the Internet. You need to be mindful that information and the need for information can also be used as a means to delay the call for action.

Irrelevant Information

The other area of misuse of information is irrelevant information. There is an enormous amount of information that has nothing to do with anything. This information is a sort of civic landfill, and you ought not to go into the landfill business. If your aim is to change conditions, you need a certain amount of information, but not more. After that, you need to address the questions, "Why does nothing happen? Why do proposals that seem fairly reasonable, workable, and sensible never get beyond the lip-service stage?" The answers to these questions call for a different sort of knowledge: the knowledge of the structure of power. I have come to the realization that people, groups, or governments make the decisions that make sense to them, even if they look totally hare-brained to me. My task is to figure out the constellation of forces, the pushes and pulls that add up to that hare-brained decision-making. Then we can move to the next iteration and say, "What can we do about this balance of push and pull that seems to result in totally non-constructive decisions?"

Knowledge and Wrong Actions

This brings us to the experience that some of us have had and continue to have: that of a breed of people and politicians who do make decisions that may be morally and even nationally wrong, in the full knowledge that these decisions are wrong. It is difficult not only to think of ways in which we can counteract, clarify, or document such decisions, but also to communicate with intelligent people who, in the absolute clarity of their critical faculties, do what they know is wrong because of other narrow interests. It is one of the most disconcerting experiences. But don't gloss over it, don't hide it, don't excuse it. It's part of the landscape.

If you take this sort of information to the Internet, you might well find other people who have had experience with similar

undertones of power. But you are also in a public medium; you
are flagged and visible. The Internet is not just your private mul-
tiple telephone system; it is one of the most infiltrated and infil-
tratable highways in the world. In a way, it is much more serious
than what happens when governments claim that they consult
with community groups. You go to them and you give them all
your fine thoughts, and then you find they are mapping the terrain in order to find strategies to get around all those lumps and
hills. The purpose of the consultation was primarily to avoid trouble, rather than to do the right thing.

A quotation from Peter Drucker recently caught my attention: "If there isn't dissent, we would not know where the problems are." I said to my husband, "If there isn't dissent, we wouldn't
know *who* the problems are." I think we have to keep this in mind.
I recommend *The Electronic Eye*, a book by David Lyon[1] that deals
with the whole range of electronic technologies and their potential, along with their great and frequently used potential for surveillance, infiltration, and containment of individual freedom.

Every Tool Shapes the Task

You may ask, "What should we do? We live in this world. The
Internet obviously has great potential. How should an organization conduct itself?" First of all, I think we have to remember that
every tool shapes the task. When you get a new tool, it affects your
task. It might be a trivial tool in the kitchen; if someone gives you
one of those machines that slice and dice, you suddenly find yourself slicing and dicing instead of using your old recipes. Does anyone here know what an electronic microscope does to a research
group? Suddenly everything has to be observed at two thousand
magnifications because you now have this expensive beast.

Be mindful of how tools shape your tasks. You will only find
out when you learn about the tool. Learn about the Internet, but
keep your head clear and refer back to your goals. What, in the
best of all worlds, do you want to do? Do any of the applications
of your new electronic microscope bring you closer to your goal?
When do you need to go back to traditional tools: talking to people face to face, meeting with groups, organizing a potluck? Can

you recognize the moment when the intangibles of the potluck far outweigh the elegance of an electronic message? Because in the end, what we are all concerned about is people.

The Notion of the Common Good

What I most fear about the current developments is not the infiltration of the Internet. My first and profound fear is the restructuring of work that electronic media technology brings. We should not forget that more and more people have no meaningful work, and that this is particularly difficult for young people. My second fear is that when the community and individuals begin to really get hooked on the Internet, using it and enjoying the virtual communities they create, we are shifted away from what is probably our most treasured possession: the notion of the common good.

If you want to grow a cactus from seed or have sightings of the Virgin Mary, you will find people who have grown cacti or had visions of the Virgin on the Internet. This is nice, but the optimizing of the private creates a fragmentation that runs parallel to the fiscal privatization that takes away from the public space. We might think that cyberspace is a public space. But let's think about oceans. The oceans used to be a world resource that didn't belong to anyone. So everybody dumped their garbage in the sea. The potential of cyberspace as a global dump is quite substantial.

My central concern is, "What has happened to the notion of the common good?" If we, as members of a community, really think in terms of a common good, there is a limit to the interest of particular sectors. We cannot just leave labour to worry about structural unemployment. Labour needs to worry about the environment, and the environmentalists need to worry about unemployment. We all have to worry about justice. Does this mean we have to read every piece of miscellaneous information we can find on the Internet? Does this mean we have to reassess and define our common agenda? What will assure a civilized life? People can grow cacti or see the Virgin Mary as much as they wish, but it cannot be done at the expense of the time and effort that it takes to have a society that essentially promotes justice both to people and to the environment. I don't think any one of us knows, at this point, whether the information highway is a help or a hindrance. But it's not a trivial issue.

Note

1   David Lyon, *The Electronic Eye: The Rise of Surveillance Society* (Minneapolis: University of Minnesota Press, 1994).

BEYOND THE HYPE: THINKING ABOUT THE INFORMATION HIGHWAY

Address given as part of the Social Science Federation of Canada's Breakfast on the Hill series, Ottawa, 6 December 1995; published in Leadership in Health Services, *vol. 5, no. 4 (July–August 1996), pp. 14–17.*

STRUCTURES AND relationships have always fascinated me. My background is physics and, within physics, in crystallography: this has allowed me to study the relationship between structure and property, the ways in which parts of a whole reinforce or weaken each other's attributes. I have always been interested, for the same reason, in the impact of technology on the social, political, and human situation. Technology, in my definition, is essentially practice: the means by which we do things. Many of the human tasks of providing shelter, food, guidance, and order have not changed throughout history; but the means by which we provide food, shelter, health, and housing have changed profoundly. Advances in technology can involve not only machinery or electronics but also knowledge, organization, planning, and management.

Recently we have heard a great deal about a new technology: the "information highway." My definition for this highway is a broad one: it is a technology for exchanging information and, at the same time, an inextricable part of the exchange of goods and even people.

Technologies tend to involve issues of time and space. Just imagine what writing has done: it separates the message from the messenger. Moses was able to write down the law so that "the law" could be carried physically as a document; moreover, it could outlast Moses. By separating the message from the messenger, writing, and later audio and visual recording, added an important dimension to civilization. Yet while a preserved and disembodied message can transcend time and space, writing also introduces a degree of rigidity in pronouncements. Written transmission of traditional knowledge tends to be much sterner and less flexible than the orally transferred experience.

We should also remember that all modern technologies involve specialization—a particular kind of division of labour that has gained ground rapidly since the Industrial Revolution. Industrial production works efficiently because a skilled task is broken into a large number of steps, each needing only limited skills. At the same time, a new group of people is needed to supervise and take charge of the production as a whole, to plan it, and to see that all the steps fit together.

Here we see the other face of technology: its systems character and its adaptability. The relationships between working and planning, devised to serve the technology of industrial production, have been adopted by completely different sectors. The emphasis on planning and management now predominates throughout the world. Yet although we hear a lot from the planners, we hear too little about the "plannees," the people who are planned for, those upon whose co-operation the working of the plan depends. You can plan until the cows come home, but what you really need is the collaboration and the consent of the plannee. The neglect of plannees is an outgrowth of the type of technological thinking that regards every issue as a production problem. Since the tools that are used will affect the task, we should not be surprised when people are then treated as if they were pieces of equipment in a production process.

Many technologies have subtle yet profound social and political effects. As just one example: imagine a First Nations group who have run their affairs by consensus, who have taken pride in their way of coming to agreement on what should be done, who meet regularly and give themselves time to make these decisions by collectively drawing upon their shared values. One day they acquire a fax machine. Now someone sits in the band office and responds to the fax messages. The fax machine does not ask profound questions about the meaning of community. The fax machine sends disconnected little messages, asking, "Are these the right agenda items? Who will come to the meeting? Clarify point seven in the budget." Who answers each of these questions? The person in the office, of course; after all, they are just trivial questions. Yet, lo and behold, these trivial questions—which someone who may play only a minor role in the community answers in good faith—add up to fundamental decisions. By the time the elders meet, everything has essentially been decided: by the choice of items in the budget, by the agenda, and by the collective effect of twenty things that individually never looked like decisions. Such is life in a technological society.

The ability to separate message from messenger, sound from speaker, and picture from depicted, together with the speed with which information is transferred, has created a reality in which the manipulation of space and time has become one of the driving forces behind a new and complex way of doing things. We need to think about that reality and what it means for us as citizens, as a country, as a community, and as a culture. Collectively and individually, and in light of broader implications, we need to think about how much of society is determined by a different way of doing things, by the dictates of new technologies.

My model for understanding the world and the impact of new technologies is quite simple: imagine the world as a round cake. Imagine further that the cake has been cut into wedge-shaped slices. Each slice is a vertical thing: it has a top, a bottom, and stuff distributed within it. Imagine that each slice represents the social structure of a community. Whether you are a crumb or a raisin, your existence is defined by where you lie within the slice. We can even sense the notion of "upward mobility" in this image: the crumbs are on the bottom, the raisins further up, and if you are really lucky, you may be the icing on the top.

Historically, people interacted mostly up and down within one slice. Thoughts, ideas, and families moved up and down in essentially the same physical community. With this came the habit of defining people by their distance from your slice: an adjacent slice shares more with your community than a slice on the opposite side of the cake. Those people are what Maritimers call "from away." The sense of community is traditionally linked to physical space, to location and distance. Even today, unless we live among the jet set, each of us lives within the boundaries of our vertical slice. This is where we elect our member of Parliament, send our children to school, and where our garbage is disposed of. It is where much of the life and work of our community takes place.

Since early times people have also travelled. Sometimes they travelled to faraway places and returned with new ideas and new things. Because of this, the next traveller might find the voyage easier and, as transportation technologies improved, people, goods, and ideas began to travel more readily. Geographic and cultural boundaries became less rigid, and a world that had been defined by vertical slices began to change: it developed viable, horizontal layers. These horizontal layers have continued to grow in variety and importance. In conjunction with new electronic ways of doing things, we can observe a type of inversion—a reversal of what is seen as normal and what is regarded as unusual that frequently accompanies the introduction of new technologies. The concepts of space and of a local community begin to blur. People begin to consider it normal to move freely across the horizontal slice, viewing events in foreign lands from their living room, chatting on the phone, and exchanging ideas across the world as easily as they had done within their own community. Yet they talk less to their neighbours, and they know less of what goes on close by.

Before modern technologies, horizontal movement was restricted only by one's own ingenuity, strength, and resources. Goods moved more slowly than individuals. However, the complex body of law and conventions developed over time to constrain vertical roles, and mobility began to be transferred to selected movements across the horizontal layer. Today the movement of people across the world, other than individual round trips, is heavily restricted. Canada's immigration policy is an example. If you are a simple person in Taiwan and you want to come to Canada, you will find it exceedingly difficult even though the route is fully developed. If you are a simple shirt in Taiwan and want to come to Canada, you might have to wait your turn but you will get here. And if you are money in Taiwan and want to come to Canada, you'll be here tomorrow morning, if not tonight.

In spite of these observations, we have to realize that most of the laws that govern our daily lives are based on the vertical model of the world. Countries and their governments have borders.

Government and law—the instruments by which societies regulate themselves to produce some sort of order and establish a relationship between action and consequence—are devised and tested on the basis of a vertical model of society. At the same time, people are increasingly affected by the horizontal movement of new information, new images, goods, services, and money. Profits and losses that arise from activities based on horizontal movement have a profound effect upon the vertical community, but such horizontal activities operate on different and sometimes contradictory premises. This situation presents a new set of problems.

We encounter this type of problem in the case of taxation, for example. The tax rate imposed upon the individual is a function of the vertical slice: it is determined by a government with authority over those living within a country, a province, or a city. On the other hand, the tax rate that the same government can impose upon businesses is limited by horizontal considerations. A business that doesn't like the tax levels where it happens to be can pack up its patents, machinery, money, and information and go elsewhere. All of these things move easily and horizontally; only the people are left behind. As a result, the tax burden that a community can impose upon business is limited and is determined by international factors, while the burden upon individual citizens who are locked into the community is completely determined by the government in power. This technologically-based separation of business and community has created new and unresolved social tensions.

As the importance of the horizontal layer grows, boundaries between slices erode. Many slices start to crumble at the edges. But as communities begin to succumb to the predominance of the horizontal, we also see the development of what I call the "hard slice" within the slice—the reflexive rise of regionalism and nationalism. Canada has an example in Quebec. Europe has Bosnia. The answer to this tension will not come from an either/or decision. The quest by either side to "win" is automatically a losing proposition. The sooner we see this, the better, because what is required is a search for balance. Resolution will come through decisions that recognize that there are good and valid aspects of both the horizontal layers and the vertical slices and the activities that take place within them.

What is needed in order to restore this balance between vertical and horizontal is reinforcement of our communities. This might be done by giving vertical activities priority—in terms of emotion, talents, resources, people, and money—over activities in the horizontal layer. Local institutions can replace aspects of much larger ones: for example, a credit union can fulfil most of the functions of a national bank and will better reflect the wishes of the local community. Yet the horizontal and vertical are not mutually exclusive; it would be wrong to think about competing our way to a balance. The answer lies partly in recognizing the right of others and their institutions to exist and be content within the structure they have created.

What can help us find and work towards such a balance? I can think of four things. The first is clarity. We have to understand the workings of the world around us, to the best of our ability. We must resist intentional befuddlement and simple solutions. If I succeed here only in prompting you to think about the issues I have raised, and to wrestle with a broad understanding of the world, I will be quite happy.

The second is history. People have struggled repeatedly with the problems that come with change, and historically they have come out in a reasonably civilized way at the other end. This struggle is a very Canadian thing, and I think that we have had much better results than we realize or acknowledge.

Thirdly, we can draw on our increasing understanding of ecology and the complex relationships and balance of roles that make up the dynamics of nature. Human beings are part of nature: not only each of us as individuals, but societies as a whole. If we understand this we can recognize that, in order to be viable, our societies must incorporate an ecology of institutions, an ecology of diversities, and that these priorities also apply to our use of technology. Ecology affects not only individuals and their families but also, if I may use the word, our entire species. As a species, I think we have overlooked the ecology, the history, and the usefulness of our social institutions.

At the moment, we are witnessing a grievous attack on the structure of social institutions. We have to remember that these institutions evolved to serve particular purposes. A bank is not a church; a university is neither a bank nor a church nor a place of business. There are rightful tasks in a society for those who conduct business, for those who invest money, for those who produce places where learning and teaching are possible, and for those who run the courts and enforcement of law. These are each different tasks, but at the moment one of the greatest dangers to social peace and justice lies in curtailing or changing the mandates of social institutions that serve a particular purpose in the ecology of our country. We are badly advised to have one standard for all such institutions. We can only impose such a uniform standard when we have lost sight of the ecological balances within our society. We go into a great spin when we hear that peregrine falcons are becoming extinct, and rightly so. But we should also be worried when there is a threat to community services for the elderly or to the church that gets a bit of money to bring them together for lunch once a week. Our social institutions play a vital role in our social ecology. And since these institutions are about communities, they are very much affected by the erosion of vertical cohesion, by the crumbling of every slice in the cake. We must not let measures that facilitate a horizontal social function kill a vertical one.

This brings us to my fourth aid in establishing balance, one that I think is quite important. We must begin to think about what community and government are all about. One of my friends in the school system used to say that parents want their children, as they proceed through their education, to become personally happy and publicly useful. I have always thought that that was a wonderful way of encapsulating the life of a community. A community has to be a place where people can be happy—not at all times, but at times—and where they can be publicly useful—not at all times, but at many times.

The structural changes in our society that result from the tensions between horizontal and vertical functions, between business and community, are making it difficult for people—especially young people—to be both personally happy and publicly useful. Yet those two things are linked together as part of our nature: we cannot be forever personally happy without being publicly useful, nor publicly useful when we are personally miserable. Each component is important, and we must establish and protect the social means to provide opportunities for both. Without them, the human spirit withers and communities erode; the cake becomes a heap of crumbs.

WILL WOMEN CHANGE TECHNOLOGY OR WILL TECHNOLOGY CHANGE WOMEN?

Published in Knowledge Reconsidered: A Feminist Overview *(Ottawa: Canadian Research Institute for the Advancement of Women, 1984), pp. 81–90.*

THIS PAPER IS dedicated to the memory of my friend Kathleen Green Savan (1910–1981), whose life showed how one can cheerfully and constructively work as a pacifist and a feminist. I am indebted to Frieda Forman of the OISE Women's Resources Centre and Kathy Ochs of the Colorado School of Mines for guiding my reading, and to Monica Franklin for thoughtful and critical discussions.

Introduction

Whether we like it or not, we live in a technological society, a society that is moulded and operated according to technological principles and practices. It seems to me imperative that we, as feminists, concern ourselves with the structure and nature of technology in order to see how the values and goals of a technological society might advance or delay the goals of the feminist world that women aspire to create.[1]

This paper is intended as one contribution to a general ongoing discussion, giving some suggestions for future action and research. Although I have worked and taught in the area of the social and political impact of technology, this paper is not motivated by questions of scholarship. My main reason for making the case for a serious feminist critique of technology comes out of my concern for the fate of my women students. I taught in an engineering faculty for about fifteen years, and interacted with women students throughout this period. Early on, young women were actively discouraged from studying subjects in science or engineering, often well before they reached university. Later they were tolerated, and now they are persuasively urged to choose lifetime careers in these fields. Within this development I have done my share of encouraging and assisting, and thus I felt proud when I saw at the graduation of our 1983 class that the women, approximately 10 per cent of the graduates within the faculty, took 37 per cent of the top scholastic honours.

Still, I worry—I worry about what happens to the students as women, just as I wonder what will happen to the feminist hopes and expectations that accompany the entry into the labour force of larger numbers of scientifically well-trained and high-technology literate women.

The Technological Order

To clarify my concern, let me look first of all at technology in general, that is, technology as a social and political phenomenon of the late twentieth century. It is well to remember that there has been a significant increase—actually a real quantum jump—in the social and political impact of technology during the last two or three decades, just at the time that feminist analysis began to provide a new and different illumination of our social reality. Nevertheless, women's voices are not yet sufficiently prominent in the intellectual analysis of the phenomenon of technology per se. Women scholars have analyzed specific technologies.[2] They have dealt with the contributions of women to innovation and invention throughout history,[3] with the future of the technological society,[4] or with the impact on women of specific technologies such as computerization and automation. The last area is, of course, the central subject of recent concerns and interventions.[5] But when we look for a systematic feminist viewpoint on the historical meaning of technology, its modern evolution, and its dynamics, there are at present no women's names in the textbooks placed alongside the names of Lewis Mumford, E.F. Schumacher, or Jacques Ellul, or alongside technological optimists such as Harvey Brooks or Emmanuel Mesthene. Such contributions are still to come.[6]

In terms of the thrust of this paper, the discussions of technology per se are essentially based on the work of Jacques Ellul.[7] In my opinion his conceptual framework of the technological system offers the most hopeful basis for a broad ongoing analysis.[8]

Ellul defines *la technique* (unfortunately translated into English as "technology") as the totality of the operational knowledge, practices, procedures, and devices used to accomplish certain tasks in society. Specific and prescribed ways of doing things—that is, techniques—have, of course, existed as long as members of society have worked and learned together. But only in the post-eighteenth-century Western world have these techniques created an environment of their own. This environment, which Ellul calls the technological milieu, has its own values and standards, such as efficiency (regardless of what is being done efficiently), speed, and reproducibility. In the post–Second World War era the grasp of the technological milieu has extended into social space at an accelerated rate; today it is the dominating global environment in which our generation lives and in which we educate our children and their children. Ellul's analysis can help us to avoid regarding machines and devices as the essence of technological development. They are but tools of technological processes of organization and of control.

Often it is not emphasized sufficiently that, although mechanics and devices were the most visible instruments of industrialization and centralization, many administrative, legal, and social-control techniques have played an equally decisive part in the formation of the technological world order. This order can best be described as a technological system, using the word "system" in its academic meaning to denote that changes in one part of the system (for example, a faster switching mechanism or a better material) inevitably influence and affect all other parts of the system.[9] Thus techniques can no longer be dealt with in isolation from each other or one at a time. Women, it should be noted, would speak of a "web" rather than a "system" to illustrate the inherent interrelatedness of actions and events, a concept that, for women, is much older than the technical concept of system.[10]

To arrive at a critical analysis of the technological system and its values, a firm vantage point and a value base outside the system are needed. For Jacques Ellul this vantage point is his religious faith. For us, irrespective of our religious beliefs, it could be our common commitment to the values of a feminist non-hierarchical society.

From such a perspective we would see clearly that techniques are not only collections of means for achieving something, but at the same time means of preventing something else from occurring. The exclusion function of techniques, and the explicit foreclosure of future options, should be emphasized much more than they have been in the past, whenever we discuss the nature of contemporary technology. In many cases, it is as important to know what cannot be done anymore because a certain technology is put in place as it is to know what the technology actually achieves.

The conceptual analysis of the modern technological system shows how it encroaches upon and becomes a replacement of the old social order, which is essentially the traditional white male hierarchical power structure. Modern advanced technology continues and extends it. For women it is particularly important to understand this relationship and to recognize the process of grafting technology onto a system of traditional power.

Thus the social and political impact of technology must be viewed with these reference points in mind. It is then easy to understand why technical innovations rarely eliminate oppression and poverty, but tend to displace the centre of such injustices. One can see why technological changes by themselves do not produce more freedom, but often result in different and frequently more stringent constraints, though sometimes for different groups of people.

Though we recognize that much of the present technological system amplifies the power structure onto which it is grafted, this need not remain so. Technology in and of itself exhibits its own dynamics. It is up to us, as feminists, to come to an independent understanding of these dynamics and, in the clarity of our own vision, to use this knowledge to fashion a web of life that is intrinsically human.

Values in the Technological Order versus Values in the Women's World

To sharpen our perspective, we may now want to compare the values and attributes of the technological order with those of the world of women. The fact that the technological order possesses values that are intrinsic to it and quite unassociated with any specific context has been shown by many observers.[11] Just as one example of technological virtue per se, we may take again the virtue of efficiency (regardless of what is being done efficiently).

1   In the technological order, tasks are fragmented, specified, and prescribed, whether they are executed by humans or machines. The tasks are predictable, non-random, fully scheduled, and carried out without reference to context.

2   Tasks in the women's world arise in contexts out of specific needs and are thus defined. These tasks are, more often than not, flexible, unpredictable, non-specific, and integrated. They are unschedulable and there is a high degree of randomness both in the reality and in the expectations.

3   The technological order, narrowly specialized, offers little scope for improvision. The strict categorization of tasks and procedures, as well as the interchangeability of people and devices, leaves no room for spontaneity. The functioning of the technological order depends on the integration of hierarchical structures of increasing complexity. Planning and scheduling are absolutely essential. Authority is derived from access to and control of the various levels and interfaces of the structure.

4   The women's world, on the other hand, is to a large measure unplannable. It is horizontally structured and full of the unexpected, the "who would have thought." Diversity of skills is valued, as are personal loyalty and a sense of continuity. The world of women puts great stock in experience; experience is seen to be transferable to new, unforeseen, or unforeseeable tasks. Inventiveness, spontaneity, and improvisation are highly valued too.

5   On the other hand, the technological system stresses efficiency; it demands innovation and constant change. It has little use for experience and particularly for unrelated experience. The technological order is an environment that emphasizes personal achievement and quantifies it like machine output. Loyalty and continuity are usually incompatible with the

constant push for innovation. The often ill-defined notion of productivity, developed as a figure of merit for specific mechanical processes, is increasingly applied, like "brownie points," to wide and diverse sectors of society.

6   One may want to contrast this notion of productivity—churning something out at the lowest cost whether anyone needs that something or not—with the notion of "copeability," the ability to deal and cope adequately with a variety of circumstances. Copeability is a quality much valued and respected in the women's world.

7   Finally, as Berit As and I have pointed out frequently, the technological order is geared to maximizing gain; the strategies of the women's world are more often than not aimed at minimizing disaster.

As feminist insights provide fresh and more detailed pictures of the women's world,[12] we begin to appreciate the basic contradictions between women's values and the operational principles of the technological order, an order that we must regard as the current evolutionary successor of the traditional male hierarchical power structure.

These contradictions can be felt particularly acutely by young women who are now encouraged and urged to enter applied sciences, technology, and computer-related fields. I agree fully with the position taken by Margaret Fulton, Heather Menzies, and many others: women must have the education and technical literacy that will allow them access to decision-making and to meaningful work in the continually evolving technological society. But women will also have to survive as human beings, as creative, spontaneous, and cheerful persons. And, as I said before, it is here that I worry.

The Immigration Analogy

Maybe I should explain at this point that I came to relate the problems experienced by women in the technological world, and their responses, to the experiences of immigrants in a new country. Engineering students at the University of Toronto, like those of other Canadian universities, put out a student newspaper, the *Toike*. Like its brother publications, the *Toike* is essentially a filthy, sexist, and racist rag, often quite offensive. Ever since I have been a member of the faculty, I have taken part in campaigns to eliminate the offensiveness of the *Toike*, if not the *Toike* altogether. The result of these campaigns has always been the same: as the protests mounted, the *Toike* tuned down, only to pop up again after a while.

During the most recent campaign, initiated largely by women's groups on the campus, we tried to involve women engineering students in our endeavours. Several of these students were officers of the Engineering Society, the student body responsible for the *Toike*. Our encounters with these women were revealing and actually quite sad. They assured us that they were not offended at all by the sexist or racist jokes or cartoons; they thought many of them were really quite funny and that, after all, "boys will be boys." It was painful for me to see how most, though not all of them, were trying so hard to become part of the "tribe" that they were losing their own identity, their common sense, and their judgment.

After this experience I began to question my own assumptions and reactions. What did I expect to find? These girls had worked hard to be admitted into engineering and were working hard to remain there. Everybody, including myself, made a big fuss when they succeeded; surely, I could not expect them to be critical of their new milieu, just as I could not expect new immigrants, who are working hard to establish themselves, to vote against the government that allowed their entry, whatever the election issue might be.

Without wishing to carry the immigration analogy too far, I can say that it helped me to understand some of the interactions I observed. It also helped me to refocus my own responses and expectations. I now see why some women who have entered the technological order cope with adjustment to the new milieu and their new loyalties by denying their origins. They seek conformity in language and habit, absorb the new culture, and defend the new system without necessarily understanding it. For others, the cultural and emotional isolation brought about by immigration can result in a vague feeling of malaise. This often leads to feelings of, "I can't cope," "Why can't I feel at home here?" and a lot of self-blame. It must be recognized that it is not incompetence, lack of ability or stamina, but rather the breaking of the ties with a natural community that is at the bottom of this malaise. What is needed is affirmation that community can be established, ties can be strengthened and reinforced, loneliness can be admitted and collectively overcome.

But we should not be surprised if few women achieve positions of influence in the technological system while remaining active feminists. After all, how many practising pacifists, civil libertarians, or genuine socialists—not to speak of true Christians—currently occupy seats of power? Values that propel people to emigrate, such as resistance to oppression, love of freedom of speech, thought, and religious practice, opposition to war service, etc., were never the values that facilitate success in new countries. Thus it would be more than naive to think that the world will automatically be a better place once a woman becomes president of IBM or Exxon.

In the light of these thoughts, it seems unfair and ill-advised to put the major burden of changing the present system on those women who seek entry into it in search of advancement. *But change there must be.* Humanity will simply not survive the current technological order with its escalating human oppression, ecological destructiveness, and global militarism.[13]

What then are we to do? If women want to change the technological order in any significant way it is vital for us to strengthen the bonding among ourselves and to understand the structure and the dynamics of technology much better than we do now.

Maybe we should think of the work ahead as two interrelated tasks: (i) the struggle for community, and (ii) the struggle for clarity.

The Need for Community

Going back to the immigration analogy, we may want to learn from those who kept their culture alive, from the Jews, the Mennonites, the Japanese, or the Chinese. In all cases strength has come from common faith, common language, and common traditions, and from all those who gave much of their lives to keep the common culture alive. This has never been an easy or straightforward task. Many of us have experienced the conflict of values within immigrant families and the frequent resentments of the first-generation immigrants when they are reminded of their roots. Often it is only members of the second generation who rediscover the values and traditions of their past.

It is therefore important for us to remember and stress all the positive aspects of women's culture, to celebrate the creativity, the joys, the achievements, and the resourcefulness that women have shown in the past. Not all women's history is oppression and hardship. If we want to strengthen the feeling of belonging to a common culture, it must be strengthened among *all* women. There should be no overemphasis of "success," but rather a non-judgmental, non-pressuring support of all women by all women.

Specifically we should try to include women in the technical professions in women's activities. It seems to me often counter-productive to segregate women into different groups according to their employment. While specific work-related problems can only be tackled in this mode, the occupational clustering tends to obscure the basic structural and value-related community of all women. Groups can be too easily pushed towards working against each other if we are segregated by profession, age, denomination, or class.[14] The ongoing struggle for community cannot be left to intellectual exercises. Panel discussions and books are helpful, but it is friendship, understanding, and support that will, in the end, make the difference between assimilation and the presence of an enriching culture.

The Need for Clarity

There is a great need for a real and deep feminist understanding of the nature of technology. Most of all we have to approach this task by asking new and different questions. Before speaking about the different problem areas that could be addressed in future research, I want to spend a few moments on the question of *feminist* research itself.

Is there feminist research, particularly in the field of science and technology? Yes, I do believe so. It is the choice and definition of a problem that is the core of all research. There, women do have a different voice in their definition of problems and context, as, for instance, Carol Gilligan's research has illustrated so clearly.[15]

Unfortunately very few scholars, men or women, are at present in a position to define their own research projects on their own terms. At best, research in Canada today is a considered response to the granting mechanisms of various agencies and foundations; at worst, research studies can become a service purchased by a particular constituency for a particular use. Thus, in most cases, the research problem is either given or stated externally. One of the functions of organizations such as the Canadian Research Institute for the Advancement of Women surely is to press for research funds that CRIAW could administer, and to offer to funding agencies suggestions, plans, and projects for feminist research. Thus, while there is the possibility of feminist research, the reality of research funding is making its execution difficult.

Having defined a problem, possibly from a feminist perspective, what about *research methods*? Feminist research should be rigorous but not rigid. There is a genuine need for new methodological contributions, particularly when joining "hard" and "soft" research strategies in technical studies such as environmental assessments. There is the need to get away from the fascination with numbers and the overemphasis on quantifiable variables, as Linda Christiansen-Ruffman has shown.[16]

One example of a potentially useful and creative research technique is the strategy of "imaging." Instead of projecting current trends into the future and thus forecasting a development along a time line, the researcher may place herself into a technical or social setting in the future and "project back" the resources and constraints required to get from the present to that future ordering. This is an interesting and important alternative that could be explored in further detail.

In the field of assessing the social impact of technology, we are lacking research strategies that, while using mathematical modelling or technical simulation, are able to integrate these techniques to create new techniques that can truly record value judgments and differences in social perspectives. There are few successful attempts, for instance, to assess the impact of a technology both from the receiving end and from the administering end of the same research project.[17]

Let us turn now to *themes of research*. First and foremost, I see the need for a feminist critique of modern technology, aimed at a deep and thorough knowledge of the nature of technology and a real understanding of the criteria for structurally different technologies. Within this framework there are specific areas that need attention. One I have called "machine demography." It came as a surprise to me when I was chairing a Science Council of Canada study on "Canada as a Conserver Society" that, while population demography is an existing field of scholarship (with global statistics of birth rate and death rate, population densities, and demographic policies), there is no machine demography.[18]

One could define, in the simplest terms, a machine as a device that uses energy to do work. I was amazed to realize that there are no data on how many of these machines are presently supported by the world's communities, or on what the cost and benefits of this support are. There has never been a machines census, nor do we have anywhere integrated information on the financial, environmental, and social costs and benefits of our machine population.

It is not that the information on which such research could be based does not exist. It could be generated from published trade, production, export, and registration data. But somebody has to ask the appropriate questions. And at present such questions are not being asked in a way that would compel the accumulation, evaluation, and study of the pertinent information. A good interdisciplinary team of economists, engineers, statisticians, etc., on a budget of one or two cruise missiles per year (one of them costs approximately $2,000,000) would go a long way towards filling this gap in our knowledge.

Another field in which work, particularly from the feminist and humanist perspectives, is needed is the area of integration, centralization, and scale. Our connoisseurs in computer sciences, system design and logic are surely equipped to search into the different ways of systems integration. Is it possible to devise integrated systems that do not end up in hierarchical structures? What are the attributes of systems that can be integrated non-hierarchically? Is there a size limit to the subset and to the total system?

In practical terms, is there a "good" network design, and how does the purpose of the network—for instance, support, information sharing, action-coordinating versus control, constraint, and limitation of function—relate to the system's design? There are structures that are designed to incapacitate people; how do women recognize these structures before getting caught up in them?

There are other dimensions of the intrusion of the technological order and its thinking on our individual and collective consciousness. The fragmentation of work that accompanies the current practice of science and technology allows an unprecedented denial of personal responsibility. It is hard to find anyone who admits to making nuclear bombs or designing cruise missiles. All anybody ever designs are gears or devices. A scientist working on new explosives, when speaking about his work, told me that he was working on "highly energetic crystals." One could ask whether there are ways of organizing a technical production so as to keep the purpose of the work and the responsibility for it clearly in everyone's mind. I certainly would like to know something about that.

Earlier in this paper I mentioned the foreclosing effect of technologies; others have drawn attention to the de-skilling of workers, which often accompanies the introduction of a new technology. We should remember that among the skills that are lost or not developed are not only technical and manual abilities but also the skills of listening, of developing compromise, and of fostering co-operation and improvisation.

As a technological system extends deeper and deeper into society, the following questions will arise: How and where do new skills evolve? Normally, it is out of the encounters with the unforeseen, out of the need to cope with the unplanned and unplannable, that novel skills and different ways of doing things emerge. What can one say about a society that confines more and more people to more and more narrowly prescribed activities? Is this confinement the root of the violence emerging in modern societies? Are there technologies that do not curtail our creativity and initiative? Should we not search?

Those who are critical of the social impact of modern technology are often accused of rejecting technology as such, and with it the benefits that flow from it. It should be clear from the foregoing that this is not my position. I am not speaking about a lack of technology, but rather I am speaking about potentially *different* technologies. Just as those who reject unhealthy food are not in favour of starvation but are looking for a new diet, I am looking for technologies with a different voice and structure.

There are benefits to suggesting new research, but I think my central concern is clear. There are areas of research in the sciences and in technology that deserve urgent attention, particularly from feminists. Such work would help our search for clarity, the clarity of vision and knowledge that must be part of our ongoing action and education.

It is only through compassion and understanding that we can move forward towards a society in which women, men, and children are, as Camus puts it, "neither victims nor executioners."

Notes

1   In this paper my use of terms such as "feminist world" and "women's values" is generic in the sense that historians and anthropologists have used the words "mankind" or "man" as generic terms that automatically include women. I use the term "women's world" generically to refer to the world governed by the values and principles coming out of women's experience but including all men and women who subscribe to these values and live accordingly.

2   One example is Mary Kaldor's work on military technology in *The Baroque Arsenal* (London: Hill and Wang, 1981).

3   See Judith A. McGaw, "Women and the History of American Technology," *Signs,* vol. 7 (1982), pp. 798–828; and Martha Moore Trescott, ed., *Dynamos and Virgins Revisited: Women and Technological Change in History* (Metuchen, N.J.: Scarecrow Press, 1979).

4   Margrit Eichler and Hilda Scott, eds., "Women in Futures Research," special issue of *Women's Studies International Quarterly,* vol. 4, no. 1 (1981); and Joan Rothschild, ed., "Women, Technology and Innovations," special issue of *Women's Studies International Quarterly,* vol. 4, no. 3 (1981).

5   Heather Menzies, *Computers on the Job: Surviving Canada's Microcomputer Revolution* (Toronto: Lorimer, 1982). See also recent publications of Saskatchewan Labour and the Science Council of Canada,

including: Saskatchewan Labour, *The Future Is Now: Women and the Computer Age*, Conference Proceedings, Regina, November 1982; Science Council of Canada, *Who Turns the Wheel?* Proceedings of a Workshop on the Science Education of Women in Canada, Ottawa, February 1981.

6   Joan Rothschild, ed., *Machina ex Dea: Feminist Perspectives on Technology* (New York: Pergamon, 1983).

7   Jacques Ellul, *Le système technicien* (Paris: Calmann-Levy, 1977); English translation, *The Technological System*, trans. Joachim Neugroschel (New York: Continuum, 1980).

8   W.H. Vanderburg, ed., *Perspectives on Our Age: Jacques Ellul Speaks on His Work and Life* (Toronto: CBC Merchandising, 1981).

9   L. von Bertalanffy, *General System Theory* (New York: George Braziller, 1968).

10 Pam McAllister, ed., *Reweaving the Web of Life: Feminism and Nonviolence* (Philadelphia: New Society Publishers, 1982).

11 Philip L. Bereano, *Technology as a Social and Political Phenomenon* (New York: John Wiley, 1976).

12 Anne Wilson Schaef, *Women's Reality* (Minneapolis: Winston Press, 1981).

13 Ursula M. Franklin, "Women and Militarism," *Status*, February 1983, p. 4. See also pp. 100–03 here.

14 Jessie Barnard, *The Female World* (London: Free Press, Collier Macmillan, 1981); see in particular the chapter on "fault lines."

15 Carol Gilligan, *In a Different Voice: Psychological Theory and Women's Development* (Cambridge, Mass.: Harvard University Press, 1982).

16 Linda Christiansen-Ruffman, "Biases within Feminism: The Either/Or Syndrome," paper presented at the annual conference of CRIAW, Ottawa, November 1982.

17 T. Berger, *Northern Frontiers, Northern Homeland: The Report of the Mackenzie Valley Pipeline Inquiry*, 2 vols., 1977.

18 Ursula Franklin, "Where Are the Machine Demographers?" *Science Forum*, vol. 9, no. 3 (June 1976).

STORMY WEATHER: REFLECTIONS ON VIOLENCE AS AN ENVIRONMENT

Talk given to Women in Educational Administration in Ontario, Toronto; published in In Women's Voices: Journal of Women in Educational Administration in Ontario, *vol. 1 (1994).*

A T TIMES I FIND it hard to know how to speak about violence— be it personal, structural, or institutional violence—and how to work towards eliminating those conditions and mindsets that precipitate violent responses. It seems that there is all around us an environment that favours the loud over the quiet, the fast over the slow, the violent over the non-violent. Although there are obvious variations in intensity, this environment appears to be global rather than local; it has become the dominant climate of our time.

But how are we to understand and grapple with human climates and emotional environments in an age of changing social and political structures? A look at some of the models used in peace research might be of help in this task.

For this, we need to go back to the 1930s and 1940s and the work of Lewis Fry Richardson, a British pacifist and highly skilled meteorologist. Richardson realized that the problems of war and peace, of fear and the arms race, could be illuminated and addressed using the concepts and methodology of weather observation and prediction. He saw the advance and retreat of air masses, the predictable force and direction of storms and turbulances, occurring in patterns that were similar to the development of social strife, war, and political conflict. The past decades have seen many applications of Richardson's work in peace research, but to the best of my knowledge, his weather analogies have not been used to analyze social environments.

Let us look for a moment at an atmospheric model of our own social environment. Using such a model, we can interpret the social and political climate that we experience each day as a region of severe turbulence resulting from the clashing of two massive weather fronts (or value systems): the old order and the new order.

The "weather map" in Figure 1 illustrates the basic elements of the situation: the "old order" on the upper left is impinging on the "new order" coming up from the lower right. Where these two profoundly different climates meet, we see a highly turbulent "transition zone"—a stormy environment in which there is no discernible "steady state" and little climate predictability. In terms of their respective attributes, the differences between the old order and the new order are stark and striking.

The Old Order and the New Order

Historically, the old established social order has been based on hierarchies, where rank and standing conferred authority and rights, responsibilities and rewards. Within larger and smaller hierarchical structures the place and role of men, women, and children, of various groups, ages, and backgrounds, were fixed and invariant. All were expected to see their station in society as God-given and to live within the constraints of a hierarchical order that was essentially institutionalized dominance. The old expression that people ought to "know their place" summarizes the old order situation well. Conforming to allocated role was considered normal; non-conformity was therefore usually regarded as either madness or treason.

The new order, to which we are committed, is based on the principle of the equality of all human beings. This means that all people are equally unique, that the fate and well-being of everyone must be of equal importance in all considerations, that nobody is born to be either master or servant.

Within the new order women, who for so long have been assigned social roles and political places, are free to choose their own paths. The preferred structures of the new order are non-hierarchical: rank is a job description rather than an indication of social standing. In the new order there is no predetermined place or social role for any person or group. Diversity is normal and cherished.

Figure 1 The Stormy Weather Map

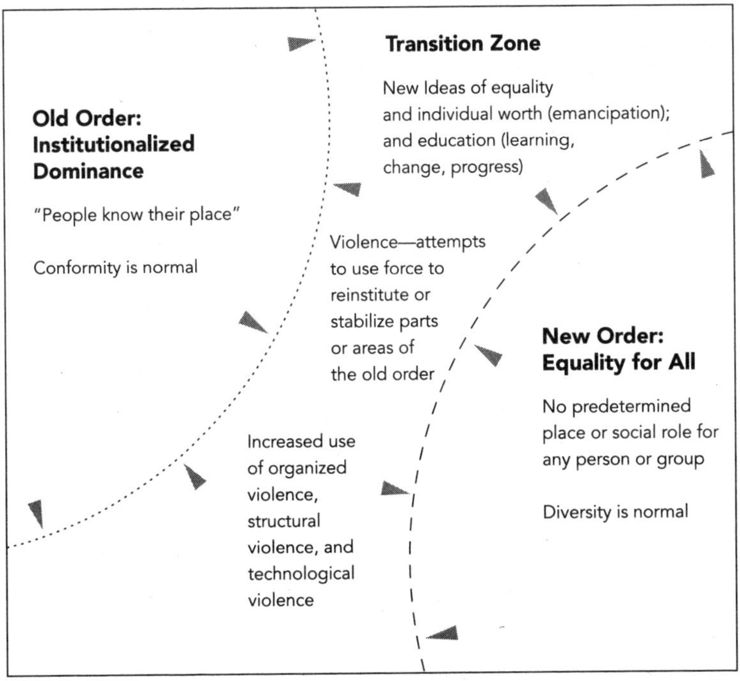

Transition Zone

Old Order:
Institutionalized
Dominance

New Ideas of equality
and individual worth (emancipation);
and education (learning,
change, progress)

"People know their place"

Conformity is normal

Violence—attempts
to use force to
reinstitute or
stabilize parts
or areas of
the old order

New Order:
Equality for All

No predetermined
place or social role for
any person or group

Increased use
of organized
violence,
structural
violence, and
technological
violence

Diversity is normal

The Thrust into the Old Order

The erosion and eventual breakdown of most of the old order have been part of a long historical process. What we need to remember most about this process is that it was *ideas* that produced the erosion: ideas of justice, equity, and human worth. Of these ideas, I want to recall two forceful blasts of fresh air thrust into the climate of the old order.

One came with the message of the Reformation, proclaiming that before God all people are equal. God's grace and love are directly accessible to each person, without the need for intermediaries. The profoundly revolutionary nature of this understanding was immediately clear, and slowly but surely its social and political implications permeated and eroded the old order. It became increasingly difficult to overlook the nagging question precipitated by the religious insight of the Reformation: "Why is it that those who are equal before God are not equal before men?" The old order had no answer to this question; only a new order could adequately address the moral and religious dimensions of equality.

The second thrust of outside air currents entered the old order climate through the ideas and practices of education. In terms of the stability of the old order, the potential of education proved to be as revolutionary as that of the notion of equality. The credo of education—the conviction that through teaching and learning, knowledge and competence could be accessible to all—turned into a powerful social and political force, since the power of the old order rested in large measure on the restriction of knowledge and vital information to certain classes and castes. The struggle to gain access to education has always been part of the struggle to overcome the old order. Conversely, the resistance to opening up educational institutions to women, for instance, is an indication of attempts to prolong the life of certain areas of the old order.

The Turbulent Transition Zone

With the weather map in mind, it is not difficult to see that we live and work in a transition zone: the old order is no longer viable, but the new order is not yet securely established. This turbulence, the unsettled and unsettling climate conditions, can be also understood as part of the clash of two weather fronts. But why is the environment not just unsettled and disturbed, but violent?

The term "violence," as used in this discussion, can be defined as the use of force to establish or maintain otherwise dysfunctional relations of power and authority.[1] I feel that this definition holds for physical, verbal, or economic violence, and that it can be applied in most places where violence occurs.

The reliance on force to settle conflicts on matters of power and authority is in part a legacy of the hierarchical past; however, it is also in part an indication of the lack of legitimacy and justice of the positions that violence tries to enforce. In this light it is clear that violence, more often than not, is an attempt to delay the coming of the new order. It is by no means the only attempt, but it is certainly the most destructive one.

Living and Working in a Violent Environment

It is my hope that the climate model of our present environment might help us to cope with the problems of violence more effectively and constructively. Let us firmly keep in mind that violence most often involves the use of force to establish and maintain unjust and unsustainable power relations: men over women, adults over children, large countries over small ones . . . Some of these power relations may have been accepted in the old order, but they are no longer legitimate; the use of force to maintain them is unacceptable.

Violence, clearly, is resourcelessness; it is the brutal response of those who see force as their only approach to conflict. Nonviolence, in contrast, is resourcefulness; it is the cultivation of and the reliance on a broad range of approaches to conflict resolution.

Many of the tasks of trying to prevent violence or to deal with situations in which violence has occurred will involve local resourcefulness, but the overall context must never be hidden. Everything we do should hasten the coming of the new order and shorten the transition zone. Our actions must make clear that the old order is no longer viable, that full equality will come, that there is nothing to fear from this historical change, and that it is pointless to delay it. Even in situations where we have been unable to prevent violence, it is necessary to articulate our standards and principles and reaffirm that violence is not a normal human reaction, it is an unacceptable response to change. Other responses can be developed.

Violence cannot be condoned or excused.

Violence is pointless; it will not yield the desired results.

Violence is illegal.

Violence has no place in the new order.

Images of the New Order

Weather maps may help us to understand the context of the stormy environment that we experience in the inevitable transition from the old order to the new order. But no map can provide us with images of the new order; these images can come only from our work and our hopes. Let me, then, conclude these reflections with my favourite image of the new order. Its peaceful world would bring a society that might work somewhat like a potluck supper, where everyone contributes and everyone receives, and where a diversity of offerings is essential. In such a world there would be no one who could not contribute their. work and care, and no one who could not count on receiving nourishment and friendship. I hold this vision with firm confidence.

Note

1   The following verse by John K. Rooke appeared in *The Blasted Pine: An Anthology of Satire, Invective and Disrespectful Verse, Chiefly by Canadian Writers*, ed. F.R.Scott and A.J.M. Smith, rev. and enlarged ed. (Toronto: Macmillan, 1967), p.134. Rooke's poem was first published in *The Canadian Forum*, February 1940.

> *Please don't believe the use of force*
> *Is how we change the social course;*
> *The use of force, you surely know,*
> *Is how we keep the status quo.*

COMMEMORATION FOR THE MONTREAL
MASSACRE VICTIMS

Address given at a commemorative service, University of Toronto, 19 January 1990, for the fourteen women murdered at l'École polytechnique, Montreal, on December 6, 1989; also read to the Senate by Roy Firth, 21 February 1990, as part of the request for a Senate Committee inquiry into violence against women; and published in "Violence against Women," a special issue of Canadian Woman Studies / Les cahiers de la femme, *vol. 11, no. 4 (Summer 1991), p. 9.*

THE EVENTS IN Montreal certainly and surely upset all of us deeply. As someone who has taught for the last two decades in the Faculty of Applied Science and Engineering and who has tried to encourage young women to enter our profession, as someone who is a pacifist and a feminist, the events in Montreal deeply trouble me. They trouble me because any one of these young women could have been one of my students, could have been someone I encouraged by saying, "Look, you can do it. It's a tough turf alright, but there are others. Nothing will change if we aren't there."

But these fourteen women are not there anymore. And many say that what happened to them was an act of a madman, something more or less like a random printing error that had nothing to do with anything except the state of Marc Lepine's mind. I'm one of those who say, yes, it was the act of a madman, but it is not unrelated to what is going on around us. That people get mad may happen in any society, any place, every place. But how people get mad, how that escalation from prejudice, to hate, to violence occurs, what and who is hated, and how it is expressed, is not unrelated to the world around us. When a madman uses easily available weapons and easily available prejudices, it is not totally his own problem that will go away when he does. At another time, it could have been Jews who were lined up, it could have been black people, but in Montreal it was women—women in an engineering faculty—killed by somebody who wanted to be an engineer.

In remembrance, what is it that we are called upon to reflect? We remember the fourteen students in Montreal. But we also remember that they were abandoned. Our memory should not block out the fact that Marc Lepine, at one of his killing stations, went into a classroom in which there were men and women. He asked them to separate into two groups, and when this didn't happen, he fired a shot to the ceiling. Then it did happen. The men left. Fourteen women were killed, and Marc Lepine could leave this classroom. It is not as much a question of how he got in, as how he got *out*. In our memory and reflection we have to include the fact that these women were abandoned by their fellow students. We must face it.

We men and women have to ask: "What does it take to make solidarity real? Is one shot to the ceiling or its verbal equivalent enough to abandon the victims?" You may wish to think on what you would have done, and perhaps even what you are doing in less lethal situations. Is a joke enough to condone harassment? There's a lot to be reflected upon. Many of the comments after the massacre were comments on what was called a "senseless killing." Are there killings that are not senseless? Are there sensible killings? Are there people who can be abandoned? If reflection shows that all killing is senseless, we may ask why, then, do we have tools of killing around since we agree that all killing is senseless. We may wish for a second to reflect on how we, as a community, would have felt if the identical massacre had taken place in a bank, in a post office, perhaps, heaven forbid, in a hotel where the young women were prostitutes. How would we react?

We speak on occasion with fair ease about everyone being brothers and sisters. Perhaps, finally, I could urge you, in memory of our young colleagues, to reflect on what it means that someone is your sister, someone is a member of the human family. That doesn't mean you have to like or love her, but it does mean you have to respect her presence. She has the right to be there on her own terms, not just by gracious permission of the dominant culture, not only as long as she keeps her mouth shut and goes through the prescribed hoops, but because we are members of one family, and each of us has an inalienable right to be, and to fulfil our potential. And if the grief we feel, the remembrance we must continue, and the reflections we have to share, bring us into a world in which it is not empty rhetoric to speak of each other as brothers and sisters, then, I think, the memory of the students in Montreal will serve us well.

LEGITIMATE EXPECTATIONS

Address given at the 15th Annual General Meeting of the Council of Canadians, Toronto, when Ursula Franklin accepted the Council's Distinguished Canadian Award, 4 November 2000; published in Canadian Perspectives, Winter 2001, *pp. 5–6.*

WHERE WE STAND in the world and where we look determine our point of view: what is in the foreground, what is in the background, what is big, and what is small. The existence of the Council of Canadians over the past fifteen years has meant, first of all, a Canadian standpoint. It is amazing that we cannot take this standpoint for granted. We might think that the job of government should be to run the country as if Canadians—all Canadians—mattered. The Council of Canadians was created out of the realization that we could no longer rely on the Government of Canada to provide this standpoint. Of all the accomplishments for which the Council can take credit, the non-negotiable presence of a Canadian standpoint is absolutely prime.

Of course, Canada is part of the world, as is every other country and community. But what this Canadian standpoint brings is a sense of priority, a sense of proportion, and a sense of obligation. In the social ecology of the country and of the world, that's what matters. Globalization, on the other hand, is essentially the denial of the standpoint of any community, of any country. In the view of those who advocate globalization there is only one standpoint: profit. Profit is big and in the foreground. The rest—care for people, care for nature, and if globalization becomes the universal standpoint, care for the not-for-profit sector—vanishes. Globalization is many things to many people, but it is important to recognize that, above all, globalization is the denial of any standpoint other than profit.

The dictionary defines the word "council" as an assembly of persons called together for consultation, deliberation, and discussion; to this, I would add action. By consultation, I do not mean the process that the government and industry occasionally practice on us: one has the feeling they give their officials earplugs and danger pay and let them loose for two days to listen to what citizens have to say. What I mean by consultation is a process of gathering together the best wisdom from the best corners so that we can begin to move from consultation to action. This is the beginning of citizen politics, wherever citizens try to shape their own lives and the life of their community.

Citizen politics begins with consultation and questions. "What are the laws? What are the limits to power? What are the job descriptions of those with whom we interact as communities?" But there are also, in that gathering of citizens for deliberation and discussion, some expectations. As Canadians, we have expectations of each other as citizens and of those who are supposed to run the country. There is in law something called the doctrine of legitimate expectations—I'm not making this up—which is on occasion used in land claims and civil disputes. The doctrine of legitimate expectations basically says that when two parties enter into an agreement, there is a legitimate expectation that each party will move towards—not away from—what the agreement is about. While on many occasions the question of legitimate expectations has ended up in our typically Canadian constitutional spaghetti, it is nevertheless an important part of a normative political landscape.

We have the right to some legitimate expectations. And while the legal mileage of this doctrine may be limited, both the moral and the pedagogical mileage are significant. As citizens the least we can expect is reciprocity between those who govern and those who are being governed. If we are expected to abide by the law and to conform to the expectations put upon us, including paying our taxes and putting out our garbage, then we should at least have a similar legitimate expectation of what Canadians are assured of under the rubric of "peace, order, and good government."

I would hold that, along with our gradual change in standpoint, we have, in fact, lost the institution of government. I hold that at this point in history Canadians are not governed but administered. We are administered on behalf of powers that do not have our standpoint, that are not in fact concerned about the well-being of Canadians. Instead of laws we find frameworks; we find ourselves designated not as citizens, but as stakeholders.

Instead of the legitimate expectations of governance, we must deal with a somewhat colonial administration.

Citizen politics begins with the assumption that one is governed, and goes on to ensure that one is governed well. This assumption was still valid when I entered citizen politics three decades ago. Yet we find—for example, in the debates on the Multilateral Agreement on Investment (MAI) and everything that has flowed from them—that the greatest difficulty Canadians face is that we do not have a government. For the work ahead, whether it is concentrated on the environment or education, on health care or the extent to which the public sphere remains an essential part of Canadian life, the central need is for good government.

There is no substitute for good government. I find myself saying this over and over again, like a long-playing record. I do not wish to live in a society in which the only standpoint is profit and everything else is other people's business. I really would like to retire and play with my grandchildren rather than be reminded that this week, when elections are taking place on all levels, the government of Ontario has passed a bill allowing private universities—and I have no way to stop it. I may, of course, not teach there. I might not send my children or grandchildren there. But that will be irrelevant when the General Agreement on Trade in Services (GATS), which threatens to open more public systems to private competition, begins to unfold. I am fed up with having to agitate around details of government when the very principle of government is in dispute. But I also take great joy and comfort from the groundswell of young people who say, "We too do not wish to live in a world in which there is no standpoint other than profit."

So, what is ahead? I think it is clear that, as Canadians, we need to articulate our legitimate expectations for good government. We have to say that there is a reciprocity to be respected, and that we are not inclined to talk about lawlessness at the bottom of society until we have talked about lawlessness at the top. We already possess enough knowledge to point those who want to get tough on crime in the right direction.

We need, I suggest, three things. The first is clarity. We cannot fall for the jargon, we cannot go for what I call "the censorship of stuffing," in which our newspapers give us thirty pages of totally irrelevant information and three lines about what really matters. We have to recognize those three lines as a contribution to clarity, and share them as an antidote to censorship. We must be clear that many of the political issues in which we as citizens may have to intervene have a common root, which, in short, is the denial of any standpoint other than profit.

Along with clarity comes solidarity: the recognition that this is not our private problem, and that if it is to be solved, we cannot accept a private solution. Justice is indivisible: there cannot be justice or prosperity for some if there is not justice and equitable prosperity for all.

The third component is integrity. Integrity has two meanings. One is that of honesty (and the Council has been impeccably honest in the face of so little honesty). The other meaning of integrity is "undivided" or "whole." This meaning is also part of the way forward, since it links us to solidarity, and we can rejoice that we are not alone. We are part of an integral whole, in the same way that Canada is part of the world. It also means that what is acceptable to us as good government must not do harm to others. We cannot sacrifice the welfare of the whole—be it the earth or the country—for the benefit of a few. Knowing this, we can move forward with integrity and a clear vision, together.

WHAT IS A GREEN ENERGY POLICY, AND WHAT WOULD WE HAVE IF WE HAD ONE?

Keynote address to the Green Energy Conference, hosted by the Canadian Coalition for Nuclear Responsibility, École de technologie supérieure, Montreal, 15 September 1989.

I WAS PARTICULARLY grateful to hear the presentations of our First Nations friends last night. They were incredibly moving, and there's little else that anyone could add to what they said to us. In the middle of their presentation, it came to me how horribly lopsided and unjust this world is. These people have to come to us, and say to *us* in *our* language, "We are dying." What sort of a world is this? Do we really want it? And so, when I talk about the subject of this conference—"A Green Energy Policy"—it is in a sense a vehicle to say, "What is going on is unconscionable!" Most of us have spent our lives trying to say so in word and deed.

Doing the Right Thing

This morning, I'd like to look at the question of energy, but mostly, I want to explore with you what it is that makes it so difficult to do what is obviously practical, right, and necessary. Why is it that we all have to grow old and not do the things that we really would like to accomplish in the endless struggle to do what is possible, what is common sense, what is just, and what is right? In addition to dealing with urgent matters of practical necessity— and they are there—we have to jointly step back and say, "What are the root causes that we must address so that our children and grandchildren will not also grow old trying to do what is practical, what is just, what is right, and what is doable?"

The title I gave Gordon Edwards for my talk was, "What is a green energy policy, and what would we *have* if we had one?" Being sensitive to language (as it becomes a Quebecker) Gordon revised it to read "what would we *do* if we had one?" I think these are two separate subjects, and I hope to comment on both. The reason that I took some liberties with the English language was to clarify the point that if we were to have a green energy policy, it would be the result of establishing a set of priorities that are drastically different from those that determine energy policy today. In an ironic sense, if we *had* a green energy policy, we wouldn't *need* it because we would have already sorted out what matters from what is peripheral. We would have sorted out our own and our community's sense of past and future.

The Concept of Energy

The concept of energy is not normal political currency. Energy is a concept that you use when you have a four-year-old who is driving you around the bend and you say, "I wish I had your energy!" Energy is something that we get from friendship. We recharge our energy through work and worship, friendship and joy. But energy in political terms is new.

Even in physics, energy is a reasonably recent term. There was a great kerfuffle in the mid-nineteenth century when the law of conservation of energy was discovered and formulated, because scientists literally didn't know what they were talking about. They were quite haughty and beastly to each other, each questioning the others' competence if not sanity. In the end it turned out, all were right and all were wrong, as they were disputing terms such as force, work, and power; eventually everyone realized how all these concepts are related to energy, which is the capacity to do work.

In political discussions, however, talking about energy can become a kind of camouflage: we talk about work, about force, and primarily about power—in a political as well as a physical sense. One of the real obstacles to sanity is not recognizing the direct link between the physical properties and utility of power sources such as fossil fuels and electricity and power in the political sense. If we think in such ambiguous categories, we can see why we differ so much both in terms of *what* ought to be done and *how* it ought to be done. Energy is basically the currency of the technological society. It is the wherewithal to do things. If we think of energy as money, it makes sense to say, "Don't waste it. Spend it intelligently. Don't fall for the schemes of con men. Don't buy on credit if you don't know what you are doing." And most importantly—"Don't leave bad debts." That is, or should be, the hallmark of a sane energy policy.

Canada as a Conserver Society

As most of you know, I was involved with the Science Council of Canada study "Canada as a Conserver Society." We knew from the beginning that the recommendations would not likely be accepted by the government of the day, so we designed the study in such a way that the process would be public; whatever happened to the recommendations, the process would, in and of itself, be a contribution to discussions of and possible solutions to the problem. We published a magazine called *Conserver Society Notes*, where we talked about the practice, about what it means to live in a conserver society. In terms of printings and copies distributed, our 1977 report was the most successful Science Council study to date. It is now out of print, and I think it was probably shredded; however, the recommendations are still there, as is the definition of a conserver society, to which I will return.

The report addressed the issue of what would Canada be like if we made a serious attempt to become a conserver society rather than a consumer society: to be mindful of limited resources, mindful of the future, and mindful of the world around us. What would it be like? The answer, of course, is that we would have to make changes, but that these changes are perfectly doable and are in no way something to be afraid of.

You may ask, as others have done, "What happened to that study?" Well, a lot of things happened. The most interesting observation is that reactions to the study split into three strata: ordinary people, institutions, and professionals. On level one, I think the study made a real and useful contribution. Ordinary people responded as individuals; they learned, they changed their lifestyles, and they tried new and different ways of doing things. Information from the study entered our thoughts and our discourse. The study was a success on level three as well. Architects, engineers, and other professionals who deal with the technological society made private decisions to incorporate at least some of the concepts to a certain extent. Some professions changed drastically.

Architects, builders, engineers, all made contributions. In my own field of metallurgy we now use processes that are much less polluting and far more energy-efficient. There is new technology (in the hard sense of the word) available to do what one could and should do. However, the momentum got stuck and reversed on the middle level: the institutions that have the power to change regulations, specifications, spending, and research priorities, to make overall changes that individuals or professionals can't do alone.

Institutional Intransigence

The institutions were totally unmovable. There was no change in the price structure. We still pay (in all provinces except Quebec) more for using less electricity. There are many endeavours where wasteful consumption is financially advantageous. There has been no significant change in the tax structure that doesn't make people feel like fools if they conserve. There has been no significant change in specifications structures. And so we are faced with this layer of institutional intransigence. This is the level we must address, and this intransigence has made the situation much more difficult today than it was in 1975.

Many people who begin to work on common problems that need to be addressed through government or public institutions such as Ontario Hydro or Hydro Québec believe that governments are ill-informed but well-intentioned, and that if we bring them good and logical facts, they will modify their behaviour. Through our work, however, many of us have been forced to come to the opposite conclusion: that governments are *well-informed* but *ill*-intentioned. If this is indeed the case, we don't have to give them more facts, but probably more kicks. However sad it may seem, sooner or later we have to face up to the likelihood of ill intentions on the level of those we elect to govern. I have reached this conclusion as a result of the resistance that we have encountered that prevents implementation of even the most obvious measures. Technology is one of the main factors in this intransigence.[1]

Government, or Management?

Governing the technological society is quite different from governing a non-technological society. Current governments around the world excel in a style that developed historically: in essence, we aren't governed—we are *managed*. If you think of government as an attempt at mediating powers (as it was dreamt of, and as it is still described in school books and when we go to vote), if you believe that a government is like a benign traffic cop seeing that nobody gets into a collision, and that the small are protected from the arrogance of the rich, be they corporate or individual, then you'd better think again.

All this, in my private opinion, has become crap. We aren't governed. There is no one to mediate powers for the benefit of all. We are managed. We are treated as workers—not even shareholders, but workers—in a reasonably small corporation, operating under a much larger corporate conglomerate. The style is that of corporate management. Head office tells you what to do. If you don't like it, get yourself another job.

The German poet Bertolt Brecht returned to East Germany after the war. During a clampdown by the East German government following a number of popular demands, the writer's union issued a leaflet stating that the government was extremely disappointed that so many writers and intellectuals had taken part in and spearheaded this movement. In response, Brecht wrote a lovely poem entitled "Die Lösung" ("The Solution")[2] regretting the government's disappointment and suggesting that perhaps they should elect themselves another people.

I think that we are being managed, and that we need to understand that fact. If this is the style, then our response should be as those who are being managed. We should insist on a few things. For example, we need to have a job description for the chief executive officer. In a corporation, a CEO has authority to do certain things, but there are other things he can't do. (I say "he" because it's usually a man.) We need such a job description for the prime minister. What can a prime minister of Canada do or not do? Now we have no such thing. Are we to simply assume that the prime minister will do the right thing? My foot! If we are managed, we must adopt the well-developed techniques of those who are in that position.

Nature, or Environment?

I want to share with you also my increasing unease about the use of the word "environment." It is somewhat reminiscent of what we went through when people began to talk about peace, and the American president named some of his favourite missiles "Peacemakers." So I don't talk about peace anymore: I talk about pacifism. We need to be very clear that something similar might be happening to what was originally a perfectly good notion: the natural environment. "Environment" is becoming a techno-centred and ego-centred concept. It seems as if everything around us is just an infrastructure of some sort. It isn't what we used to call Nature! We don't talk about Nature anymore. We talk about the environment instead, perhaps because it seems as if we can manipulate it. It is seen as an infrastructure, like air conditioning, lighting, or paint, that can be adjusted if it doesn't work. We need to start talking about Nature again, because Nature is an independent force, an independent power.

If I had one wish, it would be that the Government of Canada would look at nature as a power in the same sense that they regard the United States as a power. Every time they turn around they say, "Oh, the Americans may not like this. They will retaliate." Why don't we apply the same logic to Nature? Why can't we see that we are not dealing with a passive environment that we can adjust with parameters such as lighting levels and air flow? We are dealing with an independent power, and that independent power is retaliating. Much of Nature's retaliation strikes the defenceless: our friends in the North, our children, people who get sick. This is the retaliation we see, the response for our failure to treat Nature as a power that is not in our pocket.

If I had one wish that could really be fulfilled, it would be that the corporate and governmental big shots would understand that we are talking not about an "environment" but about Nature. We are talking about an independent power. If they are scared at the prospect of offending Maggie Thatcher or the United States, they should also be scared at the prospect of Nature's retaliation.

As we use the word environment, we can be more critical. We can encourage our fellow citizens to be mindful of the fact that we cannot manipulate the natural environment the way we manipulate the built-up environment of our cities. These two environments are very different. If we had a green energy policy, it would be like a foreign affairs policy. It would mean that we negotiate and that we listen, that we monitor and we talk, that we know the territory and respect the activities of that powerful partner in whose house we all live.

Sustaining Development or Developing Sustainability?

This brings me to my last point, which follows quite logically and is almost self-evident. I have great reservations about the concept of "sustainable development." There is rightness in it, if we want to sustain a livable environment. But it implies that we just want to tinker with things a little so we can carry on as before. To me, this is the equivalent of accepting arms control rather than demanding disarmament.

Many people understand sustainability as making things a little less lethal, but otherwise doing little else. Just as in the case of arms control, this sort of activity can tie up a lot of good people and prevent them from doing better things, such as looking at root causes. Why is all this going on? Like arms control, sustainable development can also be a first step to something better, but please be cautious about it. It can turn into what I call "occupational therapy for the opposition," keeping good people indefinitely busy, indefinitely poor, and indefinitely barred from seeing the broader spectrum. Don't reject sustainable development, but be critical.

Green Energy

Let me now return to the green energy policy. The question of acid rain is something that directly affects people. I want to stress that the problems of atmospheric pollution and even global warming do not come solely from CO_2. Sulfur oxides and nitric oxides also contribute to acid rain; methane gas and CFCs contribute to the greenhouse effect. We should also not forget that the ionization caused by the presence of radioactive pollution in the atmosphere can also trigger undesirable climate changes. Indeed there is a lot of pollution from nuclear power plants, especially in light of all the radioactive garbage that is produced. Don't let anyone tell you that nuclear energy is benign. In a piece on yet another report on Canada's energy options, *Maclean's* magazine states that apart from the problem of waste disposal, nuclear energy is benign. To me, this is like saying to Mrs. Lincoln, after Abraham Lincoln's assassination in the theatre, "So, apart from that, how did you enjoy the play?"

We are currently in the process of a selling job on nuclear power. If the job is successful, the result will be a significant increase in radioactive contaminants added to the existing atmospheric pollutants now plaguing us. Problems of radioactive contamination will be added to those of global warming, acid rain, and smog, and we will still have the unsolved problem of disposing of reactor and uranium mining wastes. I think the nuclear option is out.

If we were to have a green energy policy, what would we do? Our answers to questions would be different. We would say no to nuclear power, we would say no to energy megaprojects. And we would say no to exports that require the sort of thing that is happening to our good friend James Bay. We would shift our vocabulary. We would no longer say "What gain? What costs?" but "Whose gain? Whose costs?" We would see that the recommendations of *Canada as a Conserver Society* be implemented.

People or Technology?

Most of all, we would insist that there be a reversal in a seemingly global policy assumption that technology is the answer and that people are the source of problems. If you look at what is going on now, most governments and most technologies are essentially anti-people. We need to reverse this state of affairs. We need to say that people are the source of solutions and that perhaps technology is a source of problems.

If we had a green energy policy the number one priority would be to bring people back into the picture, not just as consumers, but as participants. There is an enormous amount that individuals can contribute to the whole area of energy and monitoring. (And I don't just mean that if Grandma would only turn off the bathroom light the world would be a better place to live.) People are exceedingly fine experimenters. For instance, air pollution can be monitored using ordinary garden plants. After all, some plants are very sensitive to particular elements in the air. If my plants don't grow, it may just be that I'm not looking after them properly. But if everyone on the street plants the same species, we will be able to see where the pockets of pollution are: how close they are to bus stops, how far they extend from the road. School kids can make a map of the area and monitor the acidity of the water and the rain with simple strips of litmus paper. There is a great deal of potential in people working not individually but together as groups in the workplace and at school. It needs to be done and it needs to be taken seriously.

My notion that we are managed rather than governed requires that in the course of our daily lives we have to work towards one important goal: a genuine renegotiation of the social contract. We are told that in a democratic society we have both rights and obligations. Fine. Let us return to the considerations raised when there was a real debate over the question of what the individual owes the community and what the community owes the individual. It is my contention that technology has totally changed the picture and that we must renegotiate that social contract from scratch. "What are the rights of government? What are the limits of these rights?"

Last night the question that was foremost in my mind was this: "Who has given anyone the right to intrude in the life of the Native peoples of Canada's north?" A satisfactory answer to that question requires us, as a community, to say not only what powers individuals give to the government, but also what expectations a citizen can rightfully have. It is like negotiating on the labour front, not for hours of work and pay, but for limits to how much we can be pushed around. When we talk about energy, there is a great deal to say, but the limit to political power is an issue we must address. Along with everything else that we can and should do in the course of our daily lives, our one important goal is a genuine renegotiation of the social contract.

Notes

1 For a detailed examination of technology issues, see Ursula M. Franklin, *The Real World of Technology* (Toronto: Anansi, 1999).
2 Bertolt Brecht: "Die Lösung" (1953)

> *Nach dem Aufstand des 17. Juni*
> *Ließ der Sekretär des Schriftstellerverbands*
> *In der Stalinallee Flugblätter verteilen*
> *Auf denen zu lesen war, daß das Volk*
> *Das Vertrauen der Regierung verscherzt habe*
> *Und es nur durch verdoppelte Arbeit*
> *Zurückerobern könne. Wäre es da*
> *Nicht doch einfacher, die Regierung*
> *Löste das Volk auf und*
> *Wählte ein anderes?*

> "The Solution"
> *After the uprising of the 17th June*
> *The Secretary of the Writers' Union*
> *Had leaflets distributed in the Stalinalee*
> *Stating that the people*
> *Had forfeited the confidence of the government*
> *And could win it back only*
> *By redoubled efforts. Would it not be easier*
> *In that case for the government*
> *To dissolve the people*
> *And elect another?*

Brecht's poem is in *Bertolt Brecht, Ausgewählte Gedichte* (Frankfurt am Main: Suhrkamp Verlag, 1964), p. 71. The English translation is from *Bertolt Brecht: Poems 1913–1956*, ed. John Willett and Ralph Manheim, with the co-operation of Erich Fried (New York: Routledge, 1987), p. 440.

CITIZEN POLITICS – NEW DIMENSIONS TO OLD PROBLEMS: REFLECTIONS FOR JANE JACOBS

Published in Ideas That Matter: The Worlds of Jane Jacobs, *edited by Max Allen (Owen Sound, Ont.: Ginger Press, 1997), pp. 191–95.*

IT IS A GREAT PLEASURE and privilege to offer these reflections on citizen politics to Jane Jacobs on this festive occasion. As we celebrate "Ideas That Matter," Jane knows, as I do, that the final value of any idea lies in those actions towards human betterment that the idea has stimulated. The greatest compliment that anyone can pay Jane is to take her seriously and to base actions and policies on the ideas and principles she has so ably articulated.

I would like to recall some changes in the dynamics and context of citizen politics as I have perceived them in the course of the past twenty-five years or so.

Let me begin with some definitions and assumptions. When I speak about citizen politics I refer to the collective activities of citizens undertaken to effect specific changes in governmental practices or regulations. Citizen politics is usually issue-oriented and aimed at intervention in matters of immediate relevance to the participants. Citizen politics tends to be direct and transparent.

There are, I feel, certain real differences between party politics and citizen politics. Members of political parties are normally bound together by a common system of political beliefs. Whether conservative, socialist, or libertarian, party members share their visions of desirable social structures and institutions. Politics is then focused on advancing these visions, rather than on addressing specific social or economic situations. Citizen politics, on the other hand, is usually precipitated not by philosophical arguments or long-range plans, but by immediate needs.

The focus of citizen politics is on practical approaches to common problems, which can range from peace to local traffic congestion. Citizen politics encourages groupings of participants that cut across traditional social boundaries such as party politics, class, age, and religion. Yet there are some common assumptions underlying all citizen politics, regardless of the specific issues addressed.

Citizens taking part in such activities assume that governance is legitimate and necessary. They organize not to overthrow government as an institution but to improve it, whether those in power like it or not. Thus "good government" is the overall purpose of citizen politics, and specific issues become occasions for involvement and critique. Good government is defined in its civic context: It must result in fair, just, accountable, and transparent practices.

Another assumption on which citizen politics rests is the existence of a public sphere, an environment of physical, social, and cultural amenities that is ours to own and govern, to care for, and to use in common. More often than not it is the quality and diversity of the public sphere that indicates the degree of goodness of the particular government.

Let me now turn to this city and to some aspects of citizen politics in Toronto, activities that have drawn much strength from Jane's ideas and from her guidance. My own growing involvement in civic affairs followed what is likely a generic learning experience, shared by many of my neighbours. One begins the journey by minding one's own business. Being a good neighbour means having no noisy parties, saying good morning at the bus stop, shovelling one's sidewalk, and putting out the garbage at the right time and in the right place. One pays taxes or rent when due, votes, and feeds the neighbour's cat when asked. One assumes that the city is run for the benefit of its residents and things are more or less in hand. That's Phase 1.

Then something happens. Suddenly it stinks when the wind blows from a certain direction, through-traffic increases, someone's dog is hit by a car, high-rise buildings appear and old houses are demolished, the local park becomes dust-covered and noisy. Neighbours start talking, people in the street get together. "Someone ought to do something about this, this is not right, what's going on here anyway?" Phase 2 has begun: learning about the reality of the city, meeting more knowledgeable neighbours, local councillors and trustees, discovering a sometimes dormant residents association, visiting city bureaucrats. Phase 2 often ends with the realization that it is either too late for locals to intervene or that it is said to be really a very complex issue.

Phase 3 begins with questions. How can one intercede before it is too late? How can one cut through the apparent complexity of issues? Fortunately for the newcomer, others have tackled such questions before. Toronto has a fine tradition of civic involvement through neighbourhood associations and through boards and advisory groups working with elected officials. When I began to be interested in local politics in the late 1960s, I saw with much admiration the past work and the ongoing influence on Toronto civic politics of the Association of Women Electors (AWE).

Since 1937 the AWE had consistently observed and recorded the meetings of city council, its main committees, and the boards of education. The AWE instituted local all-candidates meetings, and Association records and briefs have become trusted sources of reliable and far-sighted information. The Association was also a seedbed of civic talent and involvement. Civic leaders such as Mrs. Nordheimer (as she was always known—no first-name business for her), Jean Newman, and June Rowlands were among the active members. The work of the AWE was carried out entirely by volunteers.

Phase 3, then, has many of the attributes of an apprenticeship. One learns the craft of citizenship from its practitioners. One reads—if necessary between the lines—with new understanding. One observes more astutely and begins to participate in various activities.

Phase 4 entails action on the basis of what has been learned from the observation of civic realities. For me, there was much to be learned. Soon after I had become a member of the Deer Park Residents Association—and later one of its directors—I came to understand one particular reality of the city that I had not seen clearly before. The city, I realized, is by its very nature both a habitat and a resource base. It is the habitat in which we settle, work, and bring up our families, but it is also implicitly a resource base for all those who provide goods and services for a large concentration of people. Those exploiting the resource look for unimpeded access to all of it. They desire a minimum of constraints on their activities, planning, and scope. Those concerned with the habitat aspects, on the other hand, look to the city and its plan-ning regulations for protection of the habitat. They feel the need for through-traffic control and the protection of green space; they want assurance of sunlight, local shopping, and enforceable limits to noise and pollution.

Democratic city politics has to mediate the dynamics of these often conflicting interests in situations of unevenly distributed power. Sometimes it has worked well, sometimes not. Increasingly the city's planning activities became the fulcrum of municipal politics and the focus of citizen intervention. The Planning Board became the place to voice neighbourhood concerns and to watch for emerging issues.

The early 1970s saw several new and powerful players on the civic stage, and local citizens had to acquaint themselves with these new actors and their scripts. Developers appeared with increasing frequency and power; one had to learn that "the devel-oper" is not something to be purchased by the bottle in a photo store and used to bring out images on a film (though many devel-opers seem to come with their own fixers) but a type of transient entrepreneur, mainly in building and construction. .

Neither landlord nor occupant, the intrinsically transient nature of the developer rattled the civic scene. The customary civic fallback on tenure and permanency—the "you will experi-ence the consequences of your actions in front of all of us"—had no meaning for those who develop, sell, and leave; thus law and custom were ill-equipped to deal with this phenomenon and could not assign ongoing civic responsibilities to developers.

The increasing scale and scope of development proposals and their impacts on the urban habitat also brought an increasing complexity and sophistication to their discussion and assessment, bringing yet another actor to the civic stage: experts turned up more and more frequently with facts and figures, graphs and slides in hand. Frequently the expert was "from away." In fact, it often seemed as if the value of the expertise increased with the physical distance of the expert from the problems under discussion.

I think that facts—defined as the sum of the verifiable and pertinent information that can be brought to a particular situa-tion—have much less bearing on decision-making than is usually assumed or proclaimed. A situation that may in the end call for citizen intervention develops, I suggest, in the following steps. A course of action is worked out to satisfy the needs and opportunities of distribution and redistribution of political or financial power. Facts to rationalize and justify this course are then selected from the plethora of available information. "Research" may be commissioned to strengthen particular aspects, and in due time a proposal for legislation, for changes in land use, for development or public policy emerges. This proposal is subsequently presented to the citizens on the basis that the facts of the situation necessitate the proposed course of action. If there is any opportunity for debate or challenge, those who question the proposal have to counter "the facts." A debate on the legitimacy of the intent of the proposal is usually impossible.

Thus the citizen is drawn into the game of out-experting the proponent's experts, which is a costly and time-consuming activity that may embroider the problem beautifully but does little to change policy or power. Yet there is a place for counterfacts in citizen politics. They will come into the picture when other pressures—political or financial—have changed the power situation sufficiently to justify a change in what is being proposed. Now the counterfacts can become the authoritative rationale for changes without requiring an admission of pressure.

It is my struggle to understand the place of facts in citizen politics that has made me appreciate so profoundly the approach that Jane has taken in her *Systems of Survival*, where she places the conceptual roots of human interactions in the centre of her social analysis. I would like to thank her here again for this particular facet of her contributions.

Back now to citizen politics and planning in Toronto. In the 1970s active citizen politics grew, often focused on planning, with access by citizens to expertise and to the city's neighbourhood planners. At the same time, that decade and the next also saw structural changes in the processes of citizen intervention, reflecting the powerful tug of the resource base on the habitat. The round-the-clock presence of trucks and cars in every part of the city may serve to illustrate the successful encroachment of the resource base on the habitat. The city was increasingly managed as a place of commerce, not as a place for all to live peacefully.

In general, these changes in approach and priorities tended to move the decision-making processes away from citizens by increasing time and political distance between the intervention and its resolution. The changes also increased the costs of intervention for citizen groups. Indicative of the trend was the increased role of lawyers in the presentation and defence of development, rezoning, and environmental assessment applications before city council, its committees, and appointed boards.

There was a time when neighbourhood groups could troop down to the Ontario Municipal Board (OMB) when a matter of concern to them was before the Board, and state their views plainly and simply. They could answer questions in a respectful but unfussy setting, assured of being taken seriously. The arrival of lawyers changed the atmosphere drastically. The developers' high-priced hired help introduced a more adversarial and formalistic atmosphere into the proceedings. Citizens began to feel that they were not up to the type of cross-questioning and procedural argumentation, and opted for legal rather than personal representation. All of this extended time and cost tipped the scales of justice against citizen politics. Equally aggravating was a shift of the effective decision-making up to higher political levels. Such shifts occurred by utilizing the venues of appeal. What was once the de facto decision of city council or its committees could now be reassessed at the OMB and further appealed to the provincial cabinet.

Meanwhile the geographical boundaries of the habitat and the resource base had increased substantially. At the same time— looking now at the broader national climate—the public good and its care were being de-emphasized in favour of the glories of private enterprise. Nevertheless, in the early 1990s many Ontario citizens like myself felt that there was still hope and scope for useful citizen participation. The work of commissions, such as the Commission on Planning and Development Reform in Ontario, chaired by John Sewell, or the GTA Task Force under Anne Golden would cut through the baroqueness of the planning processes and provide clearer and simpler procedures of local governance, making citizen politics, with its emphasis on fairness and transparency, a renewed option for those committed to a civilized urban habitat.

"Fat Chance," say I in retrospect. The provincial Tories' slash-and-burn approach to local government and citizen representation has turned this hope into a mirage in the desert. While the events of the past two decades can be interpreted as a series of procedural shock absorbers and dirt deflectors placed in the path of citizen interventions on civic issues, the present provincial government is attempting to do something much more fundamental and drastic. As I see it, they are trying, through structural changes, to permanently decouple citizens from local politics and, using their legislative majority, turn local government into local administration.

Fortunately it takes two to tango—and many of the citizens of Ontario, Jane prominently among them, have refused to dance to the premier's tune. Citizen politics, with its traditional commitment to transparency and good government, has rapidly refocused during the past two years. It found its collective voice in new alliances that centred on local democracy as it applies to areas such as neighbourhood representation, education, health, and environmental protection.

This upswell of collective citizen response has been an amazing process. The intensity of the movement, its persistence and resourcefulness, as well as its novel structural features, brings new dimensions to the realm of citizen politics. We are still in the thick of it all and it is much too early to evaluate or sum up the new experience. But let me mention some attributes of the new developments that, I feel, warrant the notion of new dimensions to the process of citizen politics. Again I write as participant, not as an outside observer. I am trying my best to contribute to the survival of genuine democracy and passionately hope for it, so don't expect any "on the one hand, on the other hand" exposé of Ontario politics from me.

When I was first drawn into the circle of the Citizens For Local Democracy (c4LD to all), I was impressed by its openness and inclusiveness; there was an urgent task to be done, beginning with opposition to Bill 103 on municipal governance and earlier legislation on social assistance. Everyone concerned with the issues was welcome to participate in the deliberations and in the work, contributing in whatever way they chose. The amazing release of civic energy, resourcefulness, and co-operation was greatly helped, I feel, by the informality of the movement and the many different and spontaneous ways in which citizens made contact with each other. They used the oldest of community responses to common danger—the open meeting in the church (the Monday-night meetings at Metropolitan United Church regularly drew as many as 1,200 people)—and at the same time, the newest—e-mail lists, equally open, a well-designed website, and a telephone hot line—all became integral parts of C4LD.

In many ways this development broke the old rhythm of citizen politics. The speed and extent of electronic communications curtailed (if not eliminated) the information monopoly of the provincial government and the mainstream print media, and opened up the scope for citizen response. Texts of bills and submissions, notices of meetings and events, comments and insights became almost instantaneously available both at C4LD meetings and on the Internet, not only in Toronto but also throughout the province.

Even more remarkable to me is the broad range of citizen participants and their contributions. Since the electronic links between citizens engaged in a common task are decoupled from the traditional time-space requirements (that is, you don't have to be in the appointed place at the appointed time to make your case and listen to the others), they offer new dimensions to citizen politics. Those hesitant to speak in public because of age, class, or accent are less encumbered on e-mail. Those unable to attend meetings at a given time or location can still do so on the Net. For better or worse, there is no charisma or hypnotism on e-mail. None need feel persuaded against their will. Yet, in the mix of the old and new ways that has evolved in C4LD there is community and synchronicity in meetings and events, while the asynchronicity of the Internet broadens and invigorates the pool of citizens from which the community can draw.

Thus there are, I feel, new dimensions to citizen politics, dimensions that might increase the scope and effectiveness of our interventions, provided that the new mix of approaches retains its openness and transparency. And so I stand between hope and fear. My hope is rooted in my belief in the resourcefulness of the human spirit. Yet I fear the ascent of a global techno-feudalism, being mindful that what is happening to us in Ontario is embedded in larger global dynamics. The power and scope of most national governments are changing dramatically. Multinational trade activities and national laws to facilitate them seem to be turning the globe into one giant commercial resource base, while denying a decent and appropriate habitat to many of the world's citizens.

At the same time, more and more citizens throughout the world, particularly those who have been disenfranchised in the past, are struggling for their right to participate in shaping the future. It is as if more and more hands are attempting to get a grip on the steering wheel, while the ship of state that they want to guide is on automatic pilot. The course is pre-set somewhere else. Jane, closing these reflections, I cannot offer you predictions, but only these lines from Adrienne Rich:

> *my heart is moved by all I cannot save:*
> *so much has been destroyed,*
> *I have cast my lot with those*
> *who age after age, perversely,*
> *with no extraordinary power*
> *reconstitute the world.*[1]

Note

1   Adrienne Rich, *The Dream of a Common Language: Poems 1974–77* (New York: Norton, 1978).

CITIZEN POLITICS: ADVOCACY IN THE URBAN HABITAT

Address given as the third annual William Kilbourn Memorial Lecture, presented by Heritage Toronto, Ontario Heritage Foundation, and The Toronto Star, 5 October 1998.

LET ME THANK you, first of all, for your kind introduction and for the invitation to give this lecture. Those who invited me are, of course, not responsible for what I am going to say. In this half-hour that I have been given to speak to you, I would like to touch on three strands of thought, all related to the work and legacy of Bill Kilbourn: I want to reflect on some basic attributes of the city, any city. Then I would like to define and characterize "citizen politics," both as a concept and as an activity. I will suggest to you that citizen politics differs significantly from the politics of political parties and that this difference is very important for our civic life. Finally, I need to point out that the past two years have revealed the fragile legal and constitutional basis of our citizen politics. There are consequences of this new evidence and conclusions that we will have to draw from recent experiences.

When we think about cities in the way, for instance, that Jane Jacobs does—and I feel profoundly honoured by her presence here tonight—it becomes clear that cities, as aggregations of a large number of people in a small area, fulfil two separate social functions. The very fact that lots of people live in close proximity results in a pool of talent, but also in a pool of needs and opportunities for business, commerce, art, and enterprise, all attempting to serve the inhabitants and be served by them. This makes the city a resource base par excellence. At the same time, the city is a habitat, it is the place where many of us live, where we raise our families, bury our parents, and live out our lives. Today the majority of Canadians live in cities.

Almost twenty years ago, when I was a member of the Yonge–St. Clair Task Force, I wrote a brief to the Toronto Planning Board on behalf of our residents association. This brief, entitled "The Resource Base and the Habitat," pointed out that the two functions of the city often imply contradictory planning requirements and demands. The view of what is a desirable level and character of public planning varies greatly, depending on whether the city is seen as a mining site or as a place to live. Land use, density restriction, traffic patterns, and green space require- ments have very different consequences for those interested in the resource aspects vis-à-vis those seeking what Kilbourn called "a livable city." The genius of good city politics lies in the ability to mediate these conflicting demands. Advocacy on behalf of the habitat function is usually left to the local inhabitants. Toronto has had a long and noble tradition of citizen participation in the gov- ernance of the city, both through its directly elected representa- tives, such as Bill Kilbourn, and through civic associations.

For me, it is the political aims and practices of such civic asso- ciations, be they residents' associations or home-and-school groups, that define "citizen politics" and its characteristics. Political parties and their local representations, such as riding associations, normally try to change the personalities and political philosophies of those in power. Citizen politics, on the other hand, is directed not towards taking over local government but to watching over it and, through intervention, rendering the governance of the city more accountable, transparent, and fair. In my contribution to *Ideas That Matter*,[1] a recent book honouring Jane Jacobs, I sketched some of the ways in which citizens become involved in local pol- itics because of their concern over the quality of local governance. In many cases citizens are reluctant to become civically engaged, but eventually do so because the cost of non-intervention, the consequences of doing nothing, become less acceptable than the giving of time and energy to citizen politics.

And so one intervenes and takes part in fact-gathering, budget critiquing, committee-watching, and meeting with coun- cillors and bureaucrats. Over the years citizen politics has devel- oped a large collection of tools, legal instruments, and processes in order to bring habitat considerations and values into city gover- nance. Bill Kilbourn did much to encourage and nurture such civic feedback activities. He understood well the need of citizens to illuminate, balance, and, if necessary, rectify civic decision- making mechanisms without wanting to replace them.

It is important to stress that the practices of citizen politics as defined here rest on two assumptions that must be shared by those who are governed and those who hold public office or administer public affairs: the first is that local government is legitimate and necessary; the second is that those affected by legislative or administrative decisions can expect their views and needs to be part of the decision-making process. Regarding the first assumption, citizens usually don't doubt the need for public administration of the city along certain rules of conduct. They want to know what the rules are, who sets them, and whether they are enforced fairly, transparently, and competently. Their concern is "good government." Citizens will be only too happy to go back to watering their petunias if they have the assurance and evidence of good and reasonably competent government. I must say, in passing, that in my experience, onlookers tend to overrate the entertainment value of citizen politics: I have yet to meet anyone who has become an addict of meetings of the Committee of Adjustment.

Turning to the second assumption at the root of citizen politics, we hold that in a democratic society those who inhabit the habitat have a rightful say in how the habitat is structured and run. This implies that, however awkward citizen intervention may appear to decision-makers, citizens have the right to be heard. And "to be heard" does not mean that submissions are received to be turned into legislative compost, but that arguments are dealt with on the basis of their merit in an open and clear manner and an adequate time frame.

Please don't assume that I am making this all up. In law there is something called the "doctrine of legitimate expectation."[2] This doctrine is evoked internationally in discussions regarding compliance with treaties, but it is also used nationally. To quote a relevant paragraph: "The expectation which is protected by the court is not the person's or group's expectation of the benefit of the interest which is at stake but the expectation of being afforded some form of process before that interest is being affected.... Legitimate expectations can also lead to the affording of more substantial procedures than might otherwise be necessary or the enforcement of a particular regime of procedures generally deployed in the decision-making process in issue."[3]

This is the point I want to stress: much of Toronto's traditional citizen politics has been based on these two assumptions: the right to good government, and the citizens' legitimate expectations that their views be heard and taken into account before decisions affecting their habitat are made. These legitimate expectations are considered a part of the entitlement of citizenship and not a matter of digression, grace, or favour. Bill Kilbourn, I am sure, would have readily agreed that these assumptions are appropriate and workable. Yet, in the few years since Bill's death, we have had to wonder whether these assumptions are indeed still shared between those who are being governed and those who hold public office.

The experience of citizen interventions regarding recent Ontario legislation, such as the amalgamation bill (Bill 103), the changes to the education act (Bill 160) and, as I will show in a moment, the results of the citizens' legal challenge, lead me to question seriously the ability of citizens to engage meaningfully in the processes that affect and shape this city. By "meaningful engagement" you will understand I do not mean separating one's garbage properly or volunteering to help children in the neighbourhood after-school programs. I am speaking of participation in civic decision-making. I am speaking of being part of the voice of the community, a voice that is heard before decisions affecting the community are made. I am speaking of a meaningful engagement during which views and arguments are presented and plans are modified so that the final decisions are negotiated rather than dictated.

When the amalgamation bill was introduced, those of us who opposed both the scheme and the bill took out our tool kits and went to work. We got the facts and developed the critique, we wrote briefs and signed petitions, we visited city councillors, MPPs and MPs, we found experts and prominent citizens to lead public discussions. In the referendum that followed, more than 75 per cent—and there was an amazingly high turnout—voted against amalgamation. Yet the bill passed.

Out of the struggle against amalgamation arose a popular movement of spectacular breadth and imagination, matched only by a spectacular lack of effect that all its efforts had. Most of us stood breathlessly in the face of the disregard of the citizens' legitimate expectations. We had expected, in one way or another, to be able to influence the drastic changes that were to alter our habitat so profoundly. We went through hearings where nothing was heard, we made submissions that appeared not to be received.

I was particularly concerned with the legitimate expectation of being represented in the legislature by our elected representatives, and I recall a public meeting when I was on the platform with Isabel Bassett, the minister of citizenship, culture and recreation. It was at the time between the referendum and the final vote on Bill 103. At the meeting I suggested to Mrs. Bassett that, as the elected representative of a riding that had voted overwhelmingly against amalgamation, she was obligated to take this into account in her vote on the bill. She did not. And I say this not in terms of judgment or criticism, I say it in profound and desperate sorrow. As every member of the Conservative Party approved the amalgamation bill (and all other government bills) in a clause-by-clause vote, doing so in spite of the opposing views of constituents, something died. Their action left citizens confused and perplexed as to who represents what, and, more significantly, it left the democratic process severely bruised.

Torontonians then did what good citizens in a democratic society tend to do when they feel their rights are affronted: as the last resort, they turn to the courts for help. Within a few days of the passage of Bill 103, several legal challenges were filed by the affected municipalities and by a group of citizens concerning the content and the process of the legislation. Regardless of the legal focus of each challenge, in lay language all were based on the same question: "Surely there is something in law that can protect citizens when they are suddenly and drastically cut off from influencing decisions that affect them profoundly." They were, after all, accustomed to more consultative ways of being governed. While no one cited "legitimate expectations," it was the disregard for the legitimate expectations regarding process and substance that so offended citizens, not only in Metropolitan Toronto, but all over Ontario.

I cannot in this lecture describe in detail the points made in the legal challenges, the response of the province, and the position of the court. This has been done by Beth Moore Milroy, the director of Ryerson's School of Urban Regional Planning, in a paper entitled "The Constitution and the Canadian City: The Case of Toronto's Amalgamation."[4] This paper is an important contribution to current civic discussions. It illuminates the basis in law, or the lack thereof, on which citizen politics can be based. It is important for us to remember that the legal challenges were lost on all counts. Let me share with you a few sentences in a section of Milroy's paper headed "What Was Learned": "Toronto citizens had to learn or re-learn that though a piece of legislation affecting cities may be highhanded or ill-conceived, once passed by the Provincial Legislature it is the law—like it or not. What it entails may be stupid, it may be irresponsible but it is legal."[5] This is pretty scary stuff for someone like me whose childhood was spent under the shadow of the Nürnberg Laws, which were perfectly legal and yet compliance with them led to genocide and crimes against humanity. My own experience has given me a clear sense of the difference between law and justice, a difference that we all, as citizens, need to be mindful of.

As an instrument of citizen politics, the legal challenge did not work. The law let us down. It confirmed that cities are creatures of the province and the province can turn the city into a tool for its purposes, with or without the consent of the inhabitants. The habitat has no voice. Let me read another few sentences of Milroy's discussion: "Residents have no constitutional right to a vision for their city. The province's vision for the new city was utilitarian. There is no recognition of the metropolitan region's multiculturalism, of its arts, the quality of its neighbourhoods, or its civic activism which makes it the kind of place it is. The citizens had a very different, non-utilitarian vision of their city."[6] This passage is particularly relevant tonight as Heritage Toronto honours the preservation of and the respect for Toronto's unique culture.

In the wake of the constitutional challenge, then, it is clear: the habitat has no legal voice and those who advocate on its behalf are supposed to stand aside when push comes to shove. To me, this is unacceptable, as I am sure it would have been for Bill Kilbourn. I am not prepared to acquiesce when the consultative processes of decision-making that I consider part of my legitimate expectation of citizenship are ignored or turned into instruments of public anger management.

Where does all this leave us? I want to suggest, as part of my conclusions, that some of the emphasis of citizen politics has to change. We need to be concerned about *structures* as much as with *substance* as we intervene, be it in small neighbourhood issues, be it in big issues like the disaster of homelessness that will be the focus of citizen action in the days and weeks to come. From now on we need to design our activities so that we not only deal with the issue at hand, but also reform or replace the structures of responsibility and accountability that are more often than not creating the issues in the first place. We need legitimate civic instruments that do not again leave us with the care for the habitat and without a legal voice.

I recognize the intertwining of the resource base and the habitat in the making of a good city. But we need a governance of the city structured "as if habitat mattered," to paraphrase Fritz Schumacher, the author of *Small Is Beautiful*. Citizens do not struggle for good communities and open neighbourhoods in order to provide "curb appeal" for tourists or investors. They inhabit the communities, the habitat is theirs. Advocacy in the urban habitat now turns into advocacy for the urban habitat. The struggle has begun to reclaim or to fashion anew the legal and structural instruments that can enable citizens to deal with the uncivil use of civil power.

Notes

1 Jane Jacobs, *Ideas That Matter: The Worlds of Jane Jacobs*, ed. Max Allen (Owen Sound, Ont.: Ginger Press, 1997).
2 See *The Canadian Encyclopedic Digest*, 3rd ed., Ontario, April 1996, pp. 213–18, 384–86.
3 Ibid., p. 215, no. 73.
4 Beth Moore Milroy, "Toronto's Legal Challenge to Amalgamation," in *Urban Affairs: Back on the Policy Agenda*, ed. Caroline Andrew, K.A. Graham, and Susan D. Phillips (Montreal and Kingston: McGill-Queen's University Press, 2002).
5 Ibid., p. 173.
6 Ibid., p. 175.

PLANNING AND THE RELIGIOUS MIND: "DER MENSCH DENKT, GOTT LENKT"

Published in Reclaiming Democracy: The Social Justice and Political Economy of Gregory Baum and Kari Polanyi Levitt, *ed.
Marguerite Mendell (Montreal: McGill-Queen's University Press, 2005).*

P LEASE ALLOW ME to begin with my thanks. Being asked to
contribute to this book is a privilege and an expression of
friendship that I appreciate deeply. The invitation has also given
me the impetus to revisit the issue of planning and think about
the inherent ambiguities in its foundation and practice, which
have troubled me for many years.[1]

The thoughts offered in this paper rest on a few assumptions.
One of them is that there are two attributes that seem to differentiate between secular and religious views and value systems.
(Certainly, there are more than two distinguishing attributes, but
these two will suffice for the task at hand.) The religious mind is
informed by the knowledge that power is not merely the aggre-
gation of human might (the German *Macht* shows so nicely the
link to *machen*, the ability to make or to create). All religions stress
that there are powers above and beyond human knowledge and
interventions. Furthermore, while secular approaches reckon time
in terms of the lifetime of individuals or governments, religious
faith involves a very different sense of time—and with it a different scale of obligation and stewardship. Next I need to delineate
the particular realm of planning that I wish to address because I
want to focus on modern planning.

There have always been prophecies and predictions of the
future, based on experiences and observations of the past.[2] The
type of planning I want to look at here involves deliberate and
organized attempts—plans—to structure and design future commercial, social, and political developments. Such private and public planning activities are relatively recent phenomena, made
possible, and at times necessary, by the technological and political
changes brought about by and since the Industrial Revolution.

The Industrial Revolution brought new methods of production and factories that utilized new divisions of labour and new prescriptive technologies. These technologies in turn required new and different levels of co-ordination, planning, and management. The prescriptive technologies and their structures spread well beyond the manufacturing industries, profoundly changing all social and political relations.[3] In the wake of these developments, many social images and metaphors changed. Notions of production, of input-output and efficiency, came first to supplement and then to substitute for the traditional images of shared experience drawn from nature: metaphors of seed and growth, soil and sea, of bearing fruit and facing decay. The new images conveyed the increasing sense of mastery and control that production technologies, and the new sciences that complemented them, gave to certain people and institutions.

Thus, with the success of industrial manufacturing came the justification of an increasingly secular view of time and power, as well as the acceptance of planning and management as a legitimate commercial and political activity. After the First World War, more and more of the life of a Western nation began to be seen as a production activity, and to be regulated or planned accordingly. The acceptance of the GNP (Gross National Product) as an important indicator of a nation's well-being symbolizes this mindset. The present economic and political situation of nations, including the effects of globalization, must be seen as both intended and unintentional planning outcomes.[4] In retrospect one may forget how many good and deeply moral people saw efficient and well-planned industrial production as a potential instrument for social justice and human betterment. Some of the best minds of the time enthusiastically urged enlightened planning.[5]

Throughout the first half of the twentieth century and beyond, the scope of and the approach to planning activities appear to be discussed mainly in terms of "who plans for whom." While aims and planning parameters might vary greatly among, say, planning for corporate expansion, national security, public health, or land use, the planning process itself—that is, the laying down of conditions, procedures, and instruments for structuring both present and future endeavours—remained essentially prescriptive, in the sense of industrial production.[6] Thus, even highly motivated and enlightened planners came perilously close to playing God—claiming dominion over the future by attempting to plan it, to "fix it up."

Kenneth Boulding[7] pointed out that while plans and planners are readily accepted, little attention is given to the *plannees*, those who have to conform to the plans of others—like it or not. Yet, the success of any and all plans depends significantly on the co-operation and consent of the plannees; the downfall of many plans can be traced to the resistance and creative avoidance schemes of reluctant or unwilling plannees.

Planning, we should not forget, has not always been a good word in Western political discourse. While corporate planning and budgeting were regarded as prudent activities, public and state planning were for a long time synonymous with political coercion and ideological brainwashing. Soviet-style five-year plans were criticized not only as inefficient and simplistic but also as intrinsically oppressive and thus unacceptable tools of a democratic society. We all remember George Orwell's images of conformity as he tried to illustrate the human consequences of being captive plannees.[8] Nevertheless, since the discussions of the 1930s, which were strongly influenced by the events of the Great Depression, thinkers such as Gunnar Myrdal have regarded public planning and an increased public sphere as essential components of progressive social policies.[9] But it was war that provided the great justification and extension of planning and its tools. Once "total war" became the umbrella that covered a country's directives and plans, attempts at non-compliance by plannees could be readily dismissed as treason.[10] The political and psychological environment of war, with its opportunities to commandeer human and material resources and direct their deployment, led to the development and use of new techniques of management and control in the countries at war. The field of operational research (or operations research) may serve as an illustration of the war structure in planning practices.

It is worthwhile to go back to the accounts of one of the field's most foremost British practitioners, P.M.S. Blackett, the 1948 Nobel Laureate in Physics. In *Studies of War* he describes the emergence of the science of systemic planning and assessment of war activities.[11] The cool, scientific analysis and evaluation of military operations, together with the single-minded focus on the destructive powers of war, forged a set of powerful planning tools; the new quantitative approaches to the efficiency of operations were startling even to the military. In 1953 Blackett presented his reflections on the problems studied by means of operational research. In his paper, he speaks about his wartime assessment of the "dehousing by bombing of the German working class population" and of his mathematical predictions of the number of civilian casualties resulting from British bombing raids on German cities. He comments, sounding somewhat disappointed, that "the actual number of German civilians killed in 1941 was 200 per month, just one half of my estimate."[12] Rereading Blackett's account today of the debates regarding the bombing of purely civilian targets for the sole purpose of demoralizing the enemy population is interesting in this connection. The discussion shows clearly that those advisers to Whitehall who objected to the practice—at the time or later—did so because "it did not work." It did not seem to trouble them that the practice was immoral and illegal; the important facet was that it was inefficient and wasteful of resources. This they demonstrated quantitatively in units of tons of bombs per person killed. It seems as if the commandment "Thou shalt not kill" had been replaced by the dictum "Thou shalt not kill inefficiently."[13]

With these uncommonly transparent arguments, Blackett introduced operational research as a new and sophisticated planning tool, well-suited to assess the means of war in terms of their quantitative effectiveness. By the end of the war, operational research was regarded as a positive and important new development in the field of planning and management. Blackett foresaw clearly the subsequent growth of operational research. He wrote in 1948: "Operational Research, the technique of the scientific analysis of operations of war, particularly as developed in Great Britain during the last war, has been the subject of considerable amount of public discussion. The interest in these developments lies partly in the practical importance of the results achieved and partly in the feeling that similar methods might be applied with success to some of the urgent problems of the postwar world." Yet, not even Blackett could have foreseen the speed and enthusiasm with which this planning strategy was incorporated into postwar economic and social policy-making.[14] The imperative of planning for outcome by the most efficient, though not necessarily the most acceptable, means was smoothly transposed from war to a postwar period, which in turn quickly became a bipolar, Cold War world.

While during the Second World War most plannees accepted the constraints and interventionist measures of wartime planning "for the duration," many of the constraints—such as the quantification of activities, the emphasis of the measurable over the intangible—lasted long after the war, and the plannee remained to a large extent a servant of plans. While plans became primarily commercial, the strategies and tactics, including the disregard for plannees and for context, remained military. Thus the "war on poverty" hardly considered the views of the poor, and the "war on drugs" rarely dealt with the power plays and economics of the international drug trade.

As the massive transfer of military technologies to the private and public sector shaped the industrial world, the large-scale use of computers, the development and interlinking of huge data bases, began to turn planning into programming. Tools of unprecedented power became available to the global ruling apparatus and, it seems to me, are being used mainly to turn all of God's world into one giant production site. As citizens and as communities we are continually forced to be both planners and plannees, whether we like it or not. Who among us has not been part of drawing up yet another strategic plan? Who has not seen the narrowing of their personal and moral scope as a result of being a multidimensional plannee, a component part of many plans.

All of us are enmeshed, usually without our consent, in schemes of power and dominance, in attempts to predetermine the future. Most of these schemes do not work for any length of time, not even for the powerful, not even for the oppressor. The present, our daily life here and now, is, after all, the recent past's future, and in this light it is hard to think of any moral or religious justification for supporting current planning activities. This, then, is the moral and the practical "ouch nerve" of the enterprise of planning. Since all present planning (programming, modelling) involves the structuring of the future through technical and social design based on specifying desirable outcomes, in the production sense of the term, one has to face the question: "Is it morally defensible to participate in a process that 'creates' or arranges the future for others? Is such a process practically doable?" My own answer is "No" to both parts of the query.

I would now like to provide the reasons for my stance and suggest another approach to planning that might be more helpful. First, let me focus on the fundamental distinction between *organism* and *mechanism*, a Kantian distinction that Brian Goodwin restated beautifully in a recent book on modern biology:

> A mechanism is a functional unity in which the parts exist for one another in the performance of a particular function (think of the clock and the assembly of its pre-existing parts to serve a dynamic function, i.e., keeping time). An organism, on the other hand, is a functional and structural unity, in which the parts exist for and by means of each other, in the expression of a particular nature. This means that the parts of a particular organism—roots, leaves, flowers; eyes, heart, brain—are not made independently and then assembled as in a machine, but arise as a result of interactions within the organism.[15]

Clearly, society is an organism, and Gregory Baum has reminded us of Karl Polanyi's emphasis on the individual's need and right to be a functional part of society, contributing to its evolution.[16] The methods of industrial planning and management that were derived for the utilization of increasingly complex arrays of mechanisms may be inherently unsuitable to "manage" organisms. I hold this view, though I am aware of some of the sophisticated attempts to study complexity and self-organizing systems, as well as of the advances in large-scale computer modelling.[17] These refinements of planning and programming tools pose special problems for those concerned with justice and with the well-being of God's creation: the very sophistication of the instruments can hide the fact that they are still outcome-focused, still based on production thinking. Besides, the development of more and more fancy tools can prolong the temptation to regulate nature and society as if they were manageable mechanisms, while impeding their functioning as evolving organisms.

Let us reaffirm that society is a living organism and that organisms are characterized by their functioning—that is, how their components work together—and try to draw some conclusions from the mechanism-organism dichotomy. What if, for a moment, we were to stop being preoccupied with *what* is to be done, and worry instead about *how* things are done? In other words, switch the attention from ends to means, from product to process. Such a shift would recognize the lessons of our daily social reality: that, beyond the world of isolated mechanisms, "outcome" is not really programmable or predicable. (Kenneth Boulding has spoken about the "who-would-have-thought" theory of history.) This change of focus would remind us, too, how profoundly the *means* determine the *ends*: wars do not bring peace; unjust laws cannot advance justice.

A planning shift from ends to means could also facilitate negotiations between planners and plannees. If we could even begin a planning discourse, a discourse about structuring the future, by considerations of means, attention would move away from outcome-related details to the principles of life and community, a realm that does not constrain the religious mind of either the planner or the plannee but could utilize the insights that religious knowledge can provide. What if one were to look for consensus on the most unacceptable of means? What if one would prepare for a future in which killing is unacceptable as a means to any end, however desirable the "outcome" may appear? Since the commandment "Thou shalt not kill" must surely include the killing of spirit and body through deprivation and oppression, the unacceptability of means that kill could be an effective and universal "means test" for trade deals and for the support of both foreign and domestic policies. Why not consider, discuss, and teach the "means" option as an approach to planning?

Finally, I see a direct connection between my plea for considering means as a planning focus and the work of Gregory Baum. His emphasis on solidarity and on the inclusive nature of community has always been a reminder that the activity of each part of the social organism affects all other parts and is at the same time shaped by them. This implies for Baum a moral obligation towards "the other" as an autonomous partner in community, a partner to be respected and validated. Perhaps watching over the means that a society uses to accomplish its tasks is a useful way of meeting this obligation. Perhaps it can offer a mode of planning that might be not only practically realizable but also acceptable to the religious mind.

Notes

1   Ursula M. Franklin, "On Speaking Truth to Planning," *Friends Journal*, September (1978), pp. 6–9. See pp. 305–10 here.
2   Richard Lewinsohn, *Science, Prophecy and Prediction* (New York: Harper & Brothers, 1961).
3   Ursula M. Franklin, *The Real World of Technology* (Toronto: Anansi, 1999).
4   See, for instance, Fernand Braudel, *Afterthought on Material Civilization and Capitalism* (Baltimore: Johns Hopkins University Press, 1977); Michel Chossudovsky, *The Globalization of Poverty* (Atlantic Highlands, N.J.: Zen Books, 1997); William Greider, *One World, Ready or Not* (New York: Simon & Schuster, 1997); Eric Hobsbawm, *Age of Extremes* (London: Little, Brown, 1994).
5   John Desmond Bernal, *The Social Uses of Science* (London: Routledge, 1939). See also Maurice Goldsmith and Alan Mackay, eds., *The Science of Science: Essays on the Twenty-Fifth Anniversary of the Publication of "The Social Function of Science"* (Harmondsworth: Penguin, 1964).
6   Gunnar Myrdal, *Beyond the Welfare State: Economic Planning and Its International Implications* (New Haven, Conn. and London: Yale University Press, 1960); Gilles Dostaler, Diane Ethier, and Laurent Lepage, eds., *Gunnar Myrdal and His Work* (Montreal: Harvest House, 1992).
7   Kenneth E. Boulding, "Technology and the Changing Social Order," in David Popenoe, ed., *The Urban Industrial Frontier: Essays in Social Trends and Institutional Goals in Modern Communities* (New Brunswick, N.J.: Rutgers University Press, 1969); Kenneth E. Boulding, "Some Reflections on Planning: The Value of Uncertainty," *Technology Review*, November 1974, pp. 1–8.
8   George Orwell, *Nineteen Eighty-Four* (London: Secker & Warburg, 1949). See also J.D. Bernal, "The Assessment of Soviet Planning," in *Science in History*, 3rd ed., vol. 4, pp. 1183–93 (New York: Penguin, 1965).
9   Myrdal, *Beyond the Welfare State.*
10 For example, consider the treatment of conscientious objectors to war service. For a modern survey, see: Peter Brock, *Twentieth-Century*

Pacifism (New York: Van Nostrand Reinhold, 1970); Merja Pentikainen, ed., *The Right to Refuse Military Orders* (Geneva: International Peace Bureau, 1994).

11 P.M.S. Blackett, *Studies of War, Nuclear and Conventional* (New York: Hill & Wang, 1962), particularly part 2, "Operational Research."

12 Blacket, *Studies of War*, p. 169.

13 In the current war "plan," the attack on Iraq, "shock and awe," is presented as an enormous advance in military precision. The reality of this brutal war has U.S. war experts disturbed by unanticipated resistance and the failure of their "efficient" strategy. One reads these disturbing references by Franklin in a context we could not have predicted. [Editor's note.]

14 For archetypical examples, see, for instance: S. Beer, *Decision and Control: The Meaning of Operational Research and Cybernetics* (London and New York: Wiley, 1966); P. Whittle, *Optimization under Constraints* (London and New York: Wiley, 1971).

15 Brian Goodwin, *How the Leopard Changed Its Spots: The Evolution of Complexity* (New York: Simon & Schuster, 1994).

16 Gregory Baum, *Karl Polanyi on Ethics and Economics* (Montreal: McGill-Queen's University Press, 1996), p. 197.

17 See, for instance, *The Science and Praxis of Complexity* (Tokyo: United Nations University, 1985), particularly the papers by E. Morin, M. Zeleny, and G.P. Chapman.

ON SPEAKING TRUTH TO PLANNING

Talk given at Friends General Conference, Ithaca, New York, September 1978; published in Friends Journal, *1–15 (September 1978), pp. 6–8.*

THE TITLE OF MY talk is an acknowledgement of the debt of gratitude that I—like so many other Friends—carry. The American Friends Service Committee pamphlet *Speak Truth to Power* [1] has had a great influence on my thinking and on my work. For some time I have wondered whether, twenty-five years after the publication of *Speak Truth to Power*, it is time for Friends to take stock, to seek clarity, and then to speak truth to planning as a future-oriented application of power. It is my purpose here to encourage Friends to take a much more searching look at planning, and to think particularly about the underlying moral and ethical assumptions of planning activities.

For coming generations of historians, one of the characteristics of our time will likely be our preoccupation with the future. Universities offer courses on future studies, journals such as *Futures* or *The Futurist* are published in all major languages, and some of the most interesting contemporary thought—for example, Hazel Henderson's collection of essays entitled *Creating Alternative Futures*—is cast in the vein of future projections. Thinkers are not the only ones who use the future as if it were their own. Business also reaches ahead in unprecedented ways. Who but the fertile, commercial brains of the second half of the twentieth century would have thought of trading in futures: buying and selling rights to things, such as grain to be planted next year, that do not yet exist? The institutionalized possibility to profit now from the work of others in the future is a sign of our times, a mirror image of the consumer credit approach of "Buy now, pay later."

Future-determining activities are possible today because of the development of certain social and technological trends during the past three decades. Two types of trends are of interest here. The first is related to the character and scale of advanced technology. The second, largely as a consequence of the first, is the increase in planning and the resultant enforced increase in the predictability of the future.

Planning is the basic vehicle that our time uses to influence (if not determine) the future. This is nowhere, incidentally, more evident than in the development of weapon systems. What is planning? Webster's dictionary provides us with a nice, brisk definition: "to make a plan, to arrange beforehand." The question I have been wrestling with is this: to what extent should we, as Friends, attempt to plan and arrange things beforehand, not just privately for ourselves, but publicly for others in our community? As I will outline later, during the coming decade we will have to address the moral dimensions to these apparently technical activities. But first I want to say something about planning itself.

I realize, of course, that both the ability to plan and the need to arrange beforehand are integral parts of the technological society in which we live. After all, one of the striking features of technology is that it alters the relationship between cause and effect in both time and space. There are many ways in which technology can delay or speed up action and reaction. At times we rejoice in the shortening of distance that modern communications and travel can achieve, but we have learned of the lengthening effects in an even more drastic manner. The results of large-scale technological interventions can affect people and environments in times and places far removed from the point of the intervention. We can readily cite examples: it is not surprising that Sweden traces some of its air pollution to activities in Britain, or that the storage of radioactive wastes will place heavy burdens on those yet unborn. People have always inherited the successes as well as the problems of those who coped with life before them, but now a quantum jump has occurred in this process. The scale of interaction between the present and the future has greatly increased; effects of present decisions will be felt for longer times at greater distances than ever before, and these effects will be much more all-embracing.

In other words, presently available technologies are such that it is possible (likely for the first time in history) to lay down the plans for a future global society in a technologically almost self-fulfilling pattern. Resistance against this pattern will be very difficult, if only on purely structural grounds. For instance, when channels of information and communication are fixed, cross-communication and regrouping become impossible.

More than a decade ago, in *The New Industrial State*, John Kenneth Galbraith[2] pointed to the political consequences of the long reach of advanced technologies, and drew attention to the fact that when the industrial cycle of planning-investment-production-return becomes long and complex, there is a powerful incentive for industry to press for long-term political stability. Here stability means absence of change. Thus change, as an unplanned and unplannable phenomenon, becomes more and more difficult, regardless of the nature of change or the need for it. In addition to the effects of industrial technology on the rate and nature of political and social change, other responses to large-scale technology have emerged, notably in the field of public institutions and public processes. Attempts have been made to anticipate and possibly prevent the many detrimental effects of large-scale technology that are now blatantly evident throughout the world. We are witnessing the evolution of a variety of social processes designed for this purpose, ranging from citizens' interventions and public advocacy to environmental impact assessments, from public hearings to royal commissions. In Canada the best example of such an attempt may be the royal commission inquiring into the effects of a northern gas pipeline, headed by Thomas Berger. This investigation was carried out with competence and great integrity, but by its very mandate, even this inquiry could only study the possible effects of a pipeline. The question that that should have been asked—"Who has the right to arrange beforehand the conditions of life for others through irreversible acts of technological intervention?"—was beyond the commission's mandate.

It is not difficult to appreciate that today planning is frequently a strong tool of power. Those who have the power of enforcement usually plan quietly and effectively for the continuation of the status quo. Attempts of citizens around the world to force a more open and more accessible planning process are the rightful and democratic reaction to this condition. However, citizens, by their very intervention and participation, have given legitimacy to the planning process, just as the acceptance of alternatives has given legitimacy to the institution of compulsory military service. Thus it is clear that planning, in the widest sense of the word, has become an area in which different values within a society clash as different groups try to influence the shaping of the future.

The very process of planning—at least as it is carried out today—may not allow certain values to emerge at all. We must be clear, whichever side we are on, that the meaning of planning is to make the future more predictable by restricting choices, either for good or for evil. For Friends, choice is a religious exercise, not a more or less wilful or random activity. The way to choose, the mode of proceeding from a given situation, is a central expression of Quaker faith, totally open, and unplanned; to me it is the utter opposite of what the world around us is driven to doing.

This is where I find myself increasingly uneasy and in need of guidance. Many of my own activities during the past years have touched on or directly involved planning. This is probably not unusual for a Friend of scientific training and with an awareness of the social impact of science and technology. This has been an enriching experience and I have learned much from it, but even at the most thoughtful, conscientious, and prayerful moments, I could not quite suppress the question in the back of my mind: "Are you trying to play God?" I realized then that sooner or later we have to come to terms with one fact: as we try to respond to the technologies of our time, and as we try to guide and direct their use, we are attempting to influence the future, by the best of our own lights. Perhaps our lights are better than someone else's lights. But still, how far should we allow ourselves to carry on planning in the sense of "arranging things beforehand" for ourselves and for others? Are we not, by eliminating options and ways that could open, crippling for others the very processes that are central to the practice of our faith? To me, these questions require urgent and thoughtful consideration, because we are, as yet, quite far from an understanding of the extent of planning that can be morally justified, in contrast to any operational justification.

A few years ago, in a short paper titled "Some Reflections on Planning: The Value of Uncertainty,"[3] Kenneth Boulding pointed out that the world moves into the future through decisions, not through plans, and that plans are of importance only to the extent that they lead to decisions. This is a point well taken. I am concerned with planning as an activity carried out in the expectation that the plans will be implemented through appropriate decisions.

At this point, you may well say: "Okay, you've made your point; I can see that modern technology requires long-term planning, and that it also provides tools to do this effectively. I can see that decisions, made on the basis of such planning, will lay down much of the future in terms of physical and organizational structures. These can so thoroughly predetermine the major features of the future that they leave little room for meaningful options and true alternatives. I can see that the attempts by the few to fix up the future for the many are contrary to all that Friends believe about proceeding in the Light. They are contrary to Quaker faith, that the way will open for the leading of the Spirit at the time when the decision is needed. Planning for others without their knowledge and consent clearly violates their human rights. But what can we do? Planning will continue, with Friends, or without. Do you advocate that we withdraw from all participation in planning? Shall we opt out, go back to our meeting houses and deplore what is happening?"

My answer is, "Not quite." I do believe that there is a way out, just as there is a way out from the destructive use of power. *Speak Truth to Power* placed non-violence in the centre of Friends' approach to power. I have tried to show that planning is one of the arms of power, reaching into the future. How can we counter it except by the creative use of non-violence? I am convinced that it is possible to develop a non-violent approach to planning, and that this is, in fact, what is needed. There must be an approach and a mechanism for planning non-violently—that is, making plans that do not result in oppression, that do not violate the spiritual or political freedom of others.

Some of the groundwork for such an approach already exists. E.F. Schumacher frequently spoke of violent and non-violent technologies, and he made a clear distinction between product and process. He stressed the importance of *how* technologies produced their goods, rather than *what* they produced. Today, planning mainly specifies the product, taking "product" in the broadest sense of the word. For instance, we plan cities in terms of which buildings ought to go where, if only because we have no way of indicating explicitly how the city should function. On the other hand, the only thing that *matters* is how the city functions. Once we become attuned to the dichotomy of product vs. process, it becomes evident in much of planning. We can even understand why so many of the best-laid plans have not achieved their stated aims. Specifying product without specifying the process has frequently permitted unethical processes to take over and consequently subvert the aims by the means.

When it comes to process, Friends do have something to say, not only theologically but in terms of practical experience. Most of the work that Friends corporately engage in is related to correcting societal processes that have gone wrong. Over the years since the Vietnam War, the emphasis on "process" in Friends' work has increased: our concerns are not only with the criminal but also with the justice system, not only with the poor, but also with the economic conditions. There is surely, among Friends, a pool of experience and understanding regarding non-violent means that could be brought into the planning process.

I consider it a matter of real urgency that we, as Friends, address ourselves to the subject of planning. For this, it will be necessary to develop a non-violent planning strategy. This will require a much greater clarity about and a knowledge of oppressive and non-oppressive technologies, about ways of specifying process rather than product, and about means of constraining the mortgaging of the future. It is my hope that *Speak Truth to Power* will be followed by an application of the principles of non-violence to planning, so that we may now begin to speak truth to planning.

Notes

1   American Friends Service Committee, *Speak Truth to Power—A Quaker Search for Alternatives to Violence: A Study of International Conflict Prepared by the American Friends Service Committee* (Philadelphia: AFSC, 1955).

2   John Kenneth Galbraith, *The New Industrial State* (Boston: Houghton Mifflin, 1967).

3   Kenneth Boulding, "Some Reflections on Planning: The Value of Uncertainty," *Technology Review*, November 1974, pp. 1–8.

PART FOUR

TEACHING AND LEARNING

THE PEDAGOGY OF co-operation and peace has long been a preoccupation of pacifists, though the need to reassess accepted knowledge, to enlarge understanding, and to change social attitudes has been felt by many other people interested in social change. Thus the past decades have seen a broad spectrum of critiques of the content of formal education and of its institutions, as well as discussions of issues of accessibility.

Even within the framework of the technological society, inquiries into the state of teaching and learning have had diverse aims and motives—ranging from questioning the efficiency and utility of the teaching and learning enterprise itself to laying bare implicit assumptions, inherent biases, or the social injustices of established practices. Furthermore, modern communications technologies, in and of themselves, have drastically changed teaching and learning practices. While many of the papers and talks in the previous parts of this book have pedagogical overtones, the writings assembled here directly address teaching and learning as an activity per se.

Throughout my life I have genuinely enjoyed learning and teaching. But even as a novice researcher I was troubled by two facets of the field and career I loved: one was the near absence of women practitioners in science and mathematics; the other was the emphasis within the scientific enterprise on the acquisition and utilization of scientific knowledge for war and war preparations.

It became clear to me, as it did to other feminists and pacifists, that these two aspects of the scientific landscape were not unrelated. The hierarchical structures of society impose their ordering and priorities on many, if not all, social activities, including scientific research, notwithstanding the oft-proclaimed objectivity of science. The twin problems of the nature of scientific inquiry and the absence of women practitioners in the sciences are not merely questions posed by and for scientists. They are civic questions that bear on citizens' participation in decision-making—especially when such decisions involve new scientific and technical information.

Much of the work of the Science Council of Canada, in which I participated in the 1970s, was intended to clarify the scientific and technical components of political decisions that lay ahead for Canadians and their government. Through its reports to Parliament, the Council tried to facilitate clear and competent decision-making. Indeed, it was a great privilege for me to serve as a member of the Science Council and later of the National Research Council and the Natural Science and Engineering Research Council of Canada. These were years of intense learning for me; they sharpened my understanding of the many dimensions that differentiate "doing science" from "understanding science" or "using science." These experiences made it easier for me to step beyond my role as a practising scientist, and to teach and learn as an informed citizen, a feminist, and a pacifist. These years also convinced me that all citizens, but particularly those who want to challenge the status quo, need a sophisticated pedagogy, appropriately fashioned and taught within the full context of a technological society.

"Reflections on Science and the Citizen," a contribution to this emerging pedagogy, contains a critique of the role and place of technical experts in public discussions and consultations. The paper was written for *Planet under Stress: The Challenge of Global Change*, an authoritative discussion of the evidence of global climate change and its impacts and possible mitigations, published in 1990. For this book the Royal Society of Canada had solicited the best available scientific evidence in order to bring the relevant basic information to the general public. The book is a good example of the somewhat dated mode of civic teaching and learning. Increasingly, critiques of scientific findings and discussions of evidence *selected* versus evidence *ignored* became core arguments of political debates. Citizen groups presented *their* research, carried out by *their* scientists, to elected and appointed officials, as did my colleagues from the Voice of Women and I myself, on many occasions.

The feminist thrust of the new pedagogy is reflected in the discourse on women in science—women as teachers, learners, or subjects of study. I have always tried to emphasize that teaching, research, and scientific inquiries are social activities and that if a society is to move towards peace and greater social justice, we need corresponding moves in the priorities of education and research.

In Canada the Royal Commission on the Status of Women (1967) produced overwhelming evidence of the exclusion of women from many crucial areas of society, including the practice of science, law, and medicine. The debate that followed the publication of the Commission's findings moved quickly from "what's wrong with women?" through "what's wrong with the education of women?" to "does the structuring of present-day knowledge and research inherently include biases that militate against the full participation of women, over and above the prevailing biases of society itself?"

Focusing and encouraging these debates took up a lot of my time and energy, but it was an exciting and stimulating decade. Fresh modes of teaching and learning began to emerge, and feminist scholars, including myself, enjoyed enlarging circles of common interest and companionship. "The Second Scientist" illustrates the flavour of the general debate, while "The Sandbox and the Tools," part of a symposium on women and scholarship held by the Royal Society of Canada, reflects aspects of the debate within the academy. The formal as well as the informal aspects of teaching and learning were changing, and nowhere more than in mathematics and the sciences, where the climate of learning, individual mentoring, and awareness of context became part of the new pedagogy. This development had lasting impacts on those who taught and those who learned—as I tried to capture in the papers that follow. But were we successful—we, the feminists drawn together by the Royal Commission and its follow-up?

"Looking Forward, Looking Back" reflects my thoughts on the advances of women in engineering. Yet it is the changes in primary and secondary education into which I now put my hopes for the advancement of justice and peace. During the past ten years much of my work on behalf of the pedagogy of pacifism has focused on secondary education, mainly through my happy involvement in the Ursula Franklin Academy, a public high school in Toronto.

In "Personally Happy and Publicly Useful" I tried to outline my thoughts on the role of schools as part of the social fabric of this country. I also restated my rejection of the production model of education, so often used in policy-making, in favour of a garden model, so much more appropriate.

Fortunately, new generations of teachers and students, well-acquainted with concepts of equity, diversity, and justice, are now part of shaping the face of teaching and learning. *Teaching as Activism* is a fine collection of feminist and pacifist practices from some of this new generation; my prologue to their book concludes my reflections on teaching and learning in this reader.

REFLECTIONS ON SCIENCE AND THE CITIZEN

Published in Planet under Stress: The Challenge of Global Change, *ed. Constance Mungall and Digby J. McLaren for the Royal Society of Canada (Toronto: Oxford University Press, 1990), pp. 267–68.*

TWO FACETS OF what we call science may be worth reflecting upon here: one relates to the scientific method, the other to the notion of a scientific field or discipline and the work of its practitioners. Francis Bacon's new science, with its experiments, its requirements of internal consistency, and its aim of discovering universally applicable laws of nature, carried within itself the separation of knowledge from experience. The reductionism required to extract the general from the particular allowed an accelerated accumulation and spread of knowledge about the physical world. Thus the last two to three hundred years have seen an unprecedented growth of knowledge and information.

However, the shadow side of this historical development cannot be overlooked. First of all, there is the intrinsic lack of context in any general law that limits the law's usefulness as a sole guide to specific applications. Then there is the emphasis on abstract knowledge over concrete experience. This has dramatically lessened the confidence of people in the astuteness of their own senses. There are many today who prefer not to rely on their own direct experience, but look for "experts" to tell them what it is they sense, feel, or hear.

Secondly, in terms of the facets of science, one has to raise the question of what defines a scientific discipline and its practitioners. The answer to "What is physics?" has always been "Physics is what physicists do." The content of physics as teaching and research has changed greatly over the years. Much of what traditionally constituted physics at one time is now regarded as a domain of mechanical or electrical engineering or of applied science. But the discipline is still defined by the problem areas addressed by its practitioners, however restricted or extended those problem areas may be.

Defining a scientific discipline by the activities of its specialists gives such scientists a gatekeeper role. They will admit or reject both people and problems in an "us vs. them" or "inside vs. outside" mode. The exclusion verdict that "this is an interesting approach, but it really is not science/physics/biology . . ." is well known to all those who have tried to bring outside knowledge to inside reasoning.

The participation of concerned citizens in political decisions with significant technological or scientific components has been greatly impeded by these two facets of science. Often citizens bring direct experience to the discussion with experts only to find that this experience is undervalued or discarded entirely in favour of non-contextual and abstract information. Usually citizens are outsiders vis-à-vis specialists and experts, who tend to equate a particular career path with the possession of relevant knowledge.

Though, in my opinion, these hurdles are perceptual rather than real, the practical impediments to citizens' participation are very real indeed. There are, however, relatively simple ways to overcome them. One of the joys of my professional life has been my work with citizen groups on issues related to pollution, energy conservation, the arms race, and research priorities. Freed from the competitive shackles of the compulsory educational system, my neighbours, mostly women, learned easily and quickly. They were eager, helpful, and co-operative, and were always ready to share knowledge and resources. I have had no problems in explaining quite complex chemical and physical phenomena. These were retained and utilized not only in terms of facts that entail certain consequences but also in terms of the underlying chain of reasoning and evidence.

A number of these citizens have become able interveners at public hearings and in themselves are now resources for us. The key elements in the acquisition of scientific knowledge by citizens—knowledge that makes them responsible citizen scientists— include a strong motivation, a confidence in their own common sense, and a non-competitive atmosphere in which participants are both teachers and learners. This is not difficult to achieve.

As an academic, I have learned in this process of working with citizens' groups that the link between doing science and understanding science is much more tenuous than I had previously assumed. It is possible to understand science and its impact in considerable depth without actually doing science.

Conversely, doing science—that is, conducting successful research—does not necessarily imply that researchers have an understanding of what they are doing in a broader context. The task for the future, then, is to build knowledge and understanding among and between citizens and scientists to the extent that the distinction between the two groups vanishes and both become citizen scientists.

THE SECOND SCIENTIST

Published in a supplement to The Canadian Forum, *December 1985, pp. S3–4.*

IT IS MY FIRM conviction that women have contributions to make in all fields of scholarship, but particularly in science and technology. You may question this, knowing that the laws of nature, the rules that govern the microcosms of the organic and inorganic world, are applicable to all research, whether the projects are conceived by women or men. The very notion of the scientific method is based on the assumption that different experimenters will obtain the same results when conducting the same experiment at different times or in different places. This reproducibility is used to test the experimenter. If reproducible results cannot be obtained consistently, then the experimental set-up, not the science itself, is questioned.

However, reproducibility and internal consistency do not imply neutrality or objectivity. Long before any experiments are conducted, scientists are formulating the questions to which the experiments or studies are intended to provide answers and insights. Implicit in all scholarly activities is an original underlying choice. Some problems get attention, others are left unexamined. It is in this area of focus and problem definition that we find a significant difference in the approaches of men and women.

It is now quite clear that men and women do not perceive problems in the same way and frequently approach solutions in a different manner. Carol Gilligan, a Harvard researcher, has found that in problem-solving strategies, context is much more important to women than it is to men. The wish to look at a problem from a broad perspective, the desire to "walk around" the totality of a situation, develop an understanding for the context, and arrive at a strategy that is appropriate rather than universal, is characteristic of problem-solving by women, be it in small daily situations or large research designs. I see this desire to solve problems within a given context as the seedbed from which women, through their historical and collective experience, will make major contributions to many fields. In science and technology, this keen awareness of context has never been needed more urgently than at the present time.

Historically, the increased domination of modern industrial societies by the methods and mystiques of science and technology has greatly lessened the understanding and appreciation of context. In the past, much of the success of experimental science, particularly in mathematics and physics, came from reductionist research designs that restrict the number of intervening variables in an experiment in order to discover basic and functional relationships unimpeded by situational details. We owe much of our intellectual structures and much of our applied science to the results of this type of research. However, the strength and clarity of simple relationships sometimes hide limitations of the assumptions from which they were derived.

It is tempting to study problems in simple settings. Imagine investigating the cause of traffic accidents. It would be nice to be able to do it at 3 a.m. when there are fewer vehicles on the road; the experimental situation would be much less messy. However, the results of such studies would show, for instance, that speeding is a major cause of accidents. The obvious solution—reduction of speed—might be useful at 3 a.m. but would be irrelevant at rush hour. At 5 p.m., the very factors that had been eliminated in order to facilitate the research would be, in fact, dominating the picture. If this sounds like a far-fetched example, have a look at some reputable scientific and technical journals. They are full of studies in which extremely narrow experiments (for instance, the study of single-crystal properties at near zero temperatures) are interpreted in terms of immediate, "real life" applications. What I am trying to illustrate is that the joy of simple relationships is confined to simple experiments in the laboratory. Life itself is complex, messy, multifaceted, and inaccessible without a clear understanding of context.

The historical approach of reducing complexity to a large number of pseudo-independent actions and events has brought with it the increasing fragmentation of knowledge and an ever-narrowing focus of scientific and technological expertise. Both the workplace and the organization of production and administration bear the imprint of these changes. In many cases, the awareness of interactive processes has diminished as specialization and fragmentation have accelerated.

The inability of our society to deal with problems of complex systems and understand their nature and dynamics is evident in many ways. Look, for instance, at our powerlessness in dealing with acid rain or the problems of international peace. In many cases, it is the absence of a sense of context and the lack of a methodology for taking context and complexity into account that limit our ability to deal with problems characteristic of the industrial societies of today. The great impact of Rachel Carson's *Silent Spring* and Helen Caldicott's message depicted in the Terri Nash film *If You Love This Planet* lies in the fact that these women were able to set events in context, to show the impact and implications of actions that are normally looked upon as autonomous events, whether it is the use of pesticides or the build-up of nuclear weapons.

Think for a moment about another consequence of the fragmentation of our scientific world and its technology: fewer and fewer people are able to see and identify the totality of their work. A worker no longer builds cars, but instead makes interchangeable car parts or sub-assemblies, not knowing where, when, and how they will be incorporated into a functioning vehicle. This development explains why so many people are alienated from their work and why so many have lost a sense of personal responsibility for the jobs they do.

It is impossible to identify any one worker or group of workers who "make" nuclear bombs. Since one group may manufacture explosives, another may put together the shell, the switch, or the assembly, no one group of workers would feel responsible for the use to which the "fruits of their labour" will be put. The same problem of identification and responsibility applies to people who make intellectual contributions to devices used in anti-people activities and to people involved in studies that may be applied to the detriment of those investigated.

The ultimate illustrations of loss of context are found in recent technological megaprojects. Historically, we can look at the development of technology in terms of its two constituent types: work-related technology is designed to make the actual work easier for those who are engaged in it (examples include an electric typewriter); control-related technology is designed to influence the control of work, the worker, and the workplace. The major impact of modern high technology has been in its control-related application. Control-related technology deeply distorts workers' sense of context; human operators increasingly become part of a controlled chain of devices, robots to be manipulated by technology. People are increasingly deprived of their uniquely human abilities to relate, to make decisions, to execute judgment, to use common sense.

It is this technical ability to control, to co-ordinate, and to exclude that has created the basis for megaprojects. Large, single-purpose entities (such as the tar sands or nuclear power installations) are designed to work under very specific maximizing—or at least optimizing—conditions as large, totally controlled systems. They are the ultimate reductionist design. Everything that matters is controlled; nothing else matters. The megaproject is like a megaphone: a device with which the operator can project over everything and drown out smaller voices.

All megaprojects, though, are incredibly vulnerable and lack resistance. Every mistake becomes a megamistake, and in fact the economic usefulness of megaprojects is now in question. However, what is most in question is their social usefulness. Not only is complete control of all interactive factors rarely possible, but it is also undesirable. It is technological dictatorship.

This does not mean that a society cannot undertake big projects. But what we must realize is that magnification is not the only way of enlarging something. Multiplication and association of smaller units can also enlarge. Instead of having megaprojects, we could have multiprojects. Living systems can be very large and interconnected; they are multicellular rather than megacellular. Sometimes the megacellular—for instance, in the case of a tumor—leads to breakdown and destruction. Biological systems do not amplify, they resonate. Considerations of scale, size, and distribution within a total context are what must guide projects and megaprojects.

War is the megaproject to end all megaprojects. War and the preparations for war bear all the characteristics of the megaproject:

centralization, the cutting out of all interactive and interfering effects, the drowning out of all human voices. And, like other megaprojects, war and war preparation do not serve the purpose for which they were intended. In an age that knows nuclear weapons, the megaproject of war is totally pointless. Whatever needs there are, whatever problems exist, it is hopelessly inappropriate and suicidal to address them through the megaproject of war. What is called for, as with all megaprojects, is first of all a realistic assessment of problems and needs. Then we must work out the multifaceted multiprojects that can address those needs and problems in the context of global environments and human lives.

Contemporary technological societies are establishing an anti-people climate in which people are increasingly regarded as sources of problems, and technological devices as sources of solutions. The contribution I hope will come, in the future, from all people but particularly from women as they enter the fields of science and technology—be it as workers, teachers, or researchers—is the re-establishment of the centrality of human needs and of the human scale. There are ways of restructuring knowledge and awareness to emphasize interactive rather than isolating parameters. Ways can be found to make technology serve a multifaceted and flexible approach. What this task requires is thought and praxis to guide us with a clear human vision.

It is not difficult to understand why so many women put all their energy into restructuring that biggest megaproject, war. Women train all their lives to deal daily with the task of assessing problems and needs, always by taking account of the total context. I hope that women at universities and elsewhere will be cherished for their contributions as women, because it is from them that we will learn to look at problems and projects again in terms of an overall human context. We must be conscious of, and clear about, the tendency of megatechnology to evolve into a device for dehumanization. People must become once more a source of problem-setting and problem-solving. Women and men, people and technology, must work on co-operative projects of human size and context if we are to solve the pressing world problems of today and tomorrow.

THE SANDBOX AND THE TOOLS

An address presented at the symposium Women in Scholarship: One Step Forward, Two Steps Back, *University of Victoria, Victoria, British Columbia, 3 June 1990; published in* Transactions of the Royal Society of Canada, *series 1, vol. 1 (1990), pp. 43–46.*

A LLOW ME, as we look together at "Women in Scholarship," to step back for a moment in order to begin with a few definitions and general thoughts. Ruth Hubbard—her book *The Politics of Women's Biology* is a must—provides a helpful definition when speaking about scholarship and science that emphasizes the social nature of scholarship. She says that scholarship, particularly in the sciences, is essentially socially sanctioned fact-making. There is in society a process by which experimentation, study, and contemplation result in knowledge that after certain processes of vetting, society accepts as fact. It is important to realize that fact-making is a social process, and that much of the process of sanctioning the fact-makers has taken place within male society.

Who, for example, is entitled to make facts? Whose contemplation and whose work are then accepted as genuine facts? We know of course it is a limited group, a group that has privilege, status, and reward, a group to whom the state and all its citizens increasingly give the wherewithal for appropriate fact-making. There is, then, an agreed practice that we call the scientific method; there is an agreed form of consensus that we call peer review. And the fact-makers in that process more frequently than not begin to address questions that are the very ones that those who provide the wherewithal—from the ancient church to the modern state—have an interest in seeing asked and answered. In a social context, then, we have to ask whose questions are contemplated and for whose use are facts arrived at? We also have to ask, how does that process of fact-making advance? What happens when women attempt to acquire the tools and instrumentalities of fact-making and say, "Maybe we could make some facts too."

What happens then? Imagine a sandbox. There sit the boys with their tools, and they say to the girls: "Maybe you could come and help us make some facts and if you are nice you can use some of our tools. And if you are really nice and I am in a real hurry and have to make a lot of facts for a lot of people, I can show you how to use those tools." This, of course, is a situation that we all recognize. The conflict arises when the girls say, "Really, you know, we want to use our own tools. Maybe we want to make our own facts. Maybe we even want to have our own sandbox." What then? Some of the boys, who are crude and a bit demented, like Marc Lepine and others, just throw the girls out and say, "No, no, we don't want any girls around. The sandbox is getting crowded and some people may like your facts better than they like our facts and you might get some of the money for the new tools. We can't put up with that sort of thing." I think the challenge of feminist scholarship is in fact the struggle for the sandbox and the tools. That one can go around having a different process of fact-making, finding a different methodology, finding a different process of consensus and sanctioning, is indeed at the heart of feminist scholarship. Such a methodology would entail not necessarily asking fellow scholars for their opinions, but seeking the views of those who might be the users as well as the source of new insights. Might that not make sense? But is that what you experience?

Here then is, of course, a most potent issue in the sciences, realizing that science in and of itself (in a way again like law) is an attempt to separate knowledge from experience. That works in some cases better than in others, and in fields in which science is ill-advised to rely totally on the part of knowledge that can be separated from experience, the challenge of different methodologies, the challenge of feminist methodology, becomes threatening. Thus, what is before us when we contemplate women in scholarship is the question of how to navigate the spectrum that extends from teaching women the boys' tools so that they too can be part of that sandbox; to say yes, perhaps the world is such a complex place that indeed we need not only different tools but also different fact-makers, different sandboxes. It may be necessary to admit that traditional fact-making is limited, inadequate, and perhaps not even good for the fact-makers.

It seems that this is where we now are. The question of women in scholarship has to be addressed over the entire spectrum, from those who look for more women to be more or less streetproof to withstand the push and shove of the academy, all the way to those who say the most important thing for us is to understand why women, women's knowledge, and women's scholarship have had so little part in the academy and in the fact-making. Thus we have to look at a spectrum of possible research.

I want therefore to draw your attention first of all to the constraints on women's scholarship in the existing funding system. The questions that must be asked in order to receive research support go through a process of elimination that in my opinion often eliminates the most creative ideas. If there is anything that troubles me even more than discrimination in terms of people, it is the mortgage on the imagination that the granting system increasingly provides. Good, creative, imaginative thought, particularly among young scholars, is stifled before it is even developed into questions, through a put-down rationalization: "Who will ever fund this? Who will ever supervise a thesis like that? Who will ever give a scholarship?" If there is anything we need to do, it is not to centralize funding and the search for matching grants, but rather to have diversity, a seedbed for experimentation.

If I had money, one thing I would do is to have an annual conference on unfundable research. It would not involve all the unsuccessful projects from this year's grant competition. Rather this conference would be an invitation to imagine, to dream about the kinds of questions to which people retort after a good evening's discussion: "No way! Nobody will ever get money for that." It may take several years before people find their ideas sufficiently credible even to themselves, to be able to say, "Yes, I'll take that to next year's conference on unfundable research." This is more than a fanciful joke. I think it's really important to look at research in terms of fact-making and to ensure that it is not constrained to the obvious and that not all the fact-making becomes merely an amplification of existing knowledge.

I would also like to see the development of a very simple piece of research: an index of well-being of women on campuses, like the indexes for restaurants. For the first time, young women will have enough confidence to choose, to realize how important their presence is, rather than merely saying, "Thank God, I have a little niche here or a scholarship there." These women, after all, make the statistics that get their elders elected to the Royal Society of Canada, and so they might as well make good statistics for hospitable universities. I see no reason not to develop out of those thirty parameters produced by the Ontario Confederation of University Faculty Associations (OCUFA) a small set of indexes at the top of which I would place pay equity for senior women on the staff. It may be fine to be nice to young girls, but there is a mortgage of thirty years or more of neglect that I see in my pension. I would also add a number of indices, such as, are there people like Rose Sheinin in senior academic positions? Is there a harassment policy that is not just on paper? What about women's concerns in terms of the type of subject and the methods that are taught? Is there a real willingness to have interdisciplinary programs? Or are there, as I have found, appalling instances of young women petitioning *not* to have their extradisciplinary courses— not only in women's studies but also in certain fields of the humanities or theological studies—recorded on their transcripts for fear that no one would hire a woman engineer who had taken two courses in an unusual-looking curriculum? Is there a willingness at the university to be interested in odd combinations of scholarship and not burden the students, as many of my women students have been, with a requirement of doing two Masters theses if they opted for interdisciplinary studies? Let us soon have a publicly available index on well-being that can be revised (just as restaurant indexes are) so that young women can choose.

Finally, I think we need a good deal more recognition that women contribute to scholarship whether they are on the professorial staff, on the support staff, or are secretaries and librarians. I have often been asked, especially in the past, what it is like being the only woman in the department, the only woman in the faculty. I always answer, "I am not. There are lots of women. There have always been lots of women." So we have secretaries, lab technicians, and librarians, all of whom have lives of their own in scholarship as valid as ours. It is essential for us, especially for the senior women, to recognize this, to publish differently, to look at who contributed in a different manner. If women want to be part of scholarship, other than being men in skirts, they are required both to *be* different and to *do* things differently. One of the different things that I find essential is to abandon the notion of rank and with it the thought that one becomes more clever as one attains the rank of full professor.

THE REAL WORLD OF MATHEMATICS, SCIENCE, AND TECHNOLOGY EDUCATION

Address given during an invitational colloquium hosted by the Mathematics, Science and Technology Education Group of the Faculty of Education, Queen's University, Kingston, Ontario, 16–17 May 1991.

A SYMPOSIUM ON mathematics, science, and technology education is a very important undertaking, especially because it stresses education. Such education is urgently needed in today's world, which is so significantly shaped by mathematics, science, and technology.

To begin I would like to define what I mean by "education" and then speak about the models and metaphors that are used when people talk, write, and act in the domain of education. We need to look at the assumptions and processes that the models and metaphors implicitly and explicitly contain. At this conference I feel we should explore whether there is a specific thrust to mathematics, science, and technology education in the here and now, and be very practical about it. In other words, what will be different about our own activities next week, in terms of our day-to-day existence, because we have attended this conference?

Let me start with what I think about when I use the word "education." For me education is the enhancement of knowledge and understanding, and there is a strong and unbreakable link between the two. There seems little point in acquiring knowledge without understanding its meaning. Nor is it enough to gain a deep understanding of problems without gaining the appropriate knowledge to work for their solution. Thus knowledge and understanding are both necessary conditions for the process of education, but only when they are linked will the process bear fruit. Only in the balanced interplay of knowledge and understanding can we expect to achieve genuine education.

Fritz Schumacher, the author of *Small Is Beautiful*, once spoke about a pun embedded in his name. In German *schumacher* means the maker of shoes. But in order to do their work well, Schumacher reminded us, the shoemakers needed to know about feet and about the activities and lives of their customers—where the feet have to go and what loads the people carry. The knowledge of how to make good shoes is truly useful only when it is linked to the lives of those who are to wear the shoes. Schumacher's little meditation has always impressed me as a profound illustration of the link between knowledge and understanding, a link that is easily broken and difficult to restore.

Once we recognize the link between knowledge and understanding, we can also recognize that knowledge is not neutral, objective, or value-free. It is impossible to assume that science, technology, mathematics, or any other knowledge-seeking activity is neutral, because the search, selection, and construction of new knowledge begin with questions, and questions arise in a given setting. Questions make sense only in a particular social and political context.

In her book *The Politics of Women's Biology,* Ruth Hubbard, a recently retired Harvard biologist, points out that scientists are the socially sanctioned fact-makers. However, scientists constitute a small and homogeneous social group that in the past was almost entirely male, almost entirely white, and schooled in similar settings using similar or identical texts. Yet, because their insights and the results of their research become "facts," scientists shape the whole society. On the other hand, when those who work outside this in-group of scientists—such as women who nurse, cook, or garden— bring forward observations and insights, however well tested and verified, these contributions rarely achieve the status of facts.

I raise these issues to point out that the knowledge we try to convey and the understanding we try to build are often fragmented. The ways and means by which knowledge is accumulated and understanding is developed always structure the process of inquiry itself. Therefore it should come as no surprise that dominant views on gender, race, and ideology have profoundly influenced scientific questions and scientific facts. In other words, the teaching of science and technology will be truncated and incomplete if it does not include discussions about why certain problems are of interest and fundable at particular points in time while other questions don't seem to matter. We also need to make it clear that experimental science, in its reductionist and abstracting mode, is but one source of understanding of the world around us. For instance, ecological problems show very clearly the limitation of traditional science as a basis for understanding and acting on some of the world's most urgent tasks.

Let me turn now to the process of education itself and to the metaphors we use to describe and discuss it. We often think about education as a natural process with underlying patterns. The oldest and most commonly recognized pattern is that of growth. Historically the natural cycle of growth, bearing fruit, maturity, decline, and decay furnished metaphors for the interpretation of human and social activities. Anyone who has planted a garden or brought up children has come to understand that growth can be nurtured and encouraged, or it can be hindered and stunted, but growth cannot be commandeered. You can plant carrots in the appropriate soil, water them, and care for them, but you cannot force carrots to grow. Considerations of growth make it easier to accept the limitations of human intervention. However, I must make it quite clear at this point that bringing natural growth metaphors into our discussions of education does not mean accepting determinism. While carrots will be carrots, boys will not be boys in any but the most basic anatomical sense. What growth considerations do imply is recognition of and respect for the inner dynamics of development and maturation.

With the Industrial Revolution came a significantly different pattern of life: that of production. The new division of labour that took hold in seventeenth-century industrial Britain constituted a social invention of major consequence. In his treatise "The Wealth of England" (1662) William Petty pointed to the economic advantage of dividing the craft of making of watches into a number of distinct steps, each the responsibility of a separate worker. One person would fashion the watch dials, one the handles, another the springs or the cases. Not only was the making of a watch less time-consuming and costly, but also workers in this new prescriptive production system needed to be familiar only with the subtasks assigned to them. They could be more easily trained and more readily replaced. Successful production depended not only on clear prescription and specification of the subtasks but also on effective management and planning. Much of the control of the work moved from workers to managers and planners. As the production mode of organizing work and people spread throughout industry and through public and private administration, it furnished a powerful model for work and a new metaphor for social processes.

In today's society our image of life and education is shaped far more strongly by a production model than by a growth model. Educators should be aware of the impact of the production model on their responsibilities. They should note that the demands for more and more frequent testing and evaluation, for detailed marking schemes and curriculum specifications, are quality control considerations transferred from production to education. Such demands may set up serious conflicts with the insights flowing from a growth model of education. We cannot evade such conflicts, but we need to debate and mediate them.

Perhaps we should now step back from models and metaphors and ask: "In terms of social purpose what is the goal of education?" What would you answer? How does society benefit from having "educated" citizens? After all, in some discernible way, those who were "educated" by spending time in the appropriate institutions ought to be different from those who did not. Educators hope and often claim that educated persons will function more creatively, more productively, and more usefully within their society. Education is expected to show how acceptable contributions to the community at large can be made and what it means to be a responsible member of the larger collectivity. Assuming that these are the social goals of education, how does science and technology education fit into the picture? The core of our consideration of science and technology is not the question of *who* is being educated, but *why* and *how*.

While I am frequently critical of applications of science, in particular technologies, it would not occur to me to say to anyone, "Forget about mathematics or electronics—that stuff is for manipulative uses." On the contrary, I particularly advise those who are uneasy about a technology-dominated society to become competent enough not only to "read technology" but also to read between the lines, so that as citizens they can help to write a different technological text. But, as I see it, mathematics, science, and technology education has not yet found the vocabulary or the critical methodology that could be used for a textual analysis of science in the manner in which the use of language is analyzed today. If technological literacy is one of our aims, then such methods and discourses are urgently needed.

Another aspect of technological literacy requires attention. What textbooks are being used? What are our primers? I recall a conversation a number of years ago with a colleague who had just negotiated a large donation of computers for his institution with one of the big computer manufacturers. Since we respected each other, I could say to him, "Please, just stop for a moment, take a deep breath, and reflect. Think about the analogy between your computer gift and the gift of free Bibles." In the not so distant past many good people, for the honourable purpose of literacy and education, donated Bibles to teach "heathens" to read. When Bibles are used as primers, the process becomes more than simply learning how to read. The newly developed literacy brought with it an acculturation that often resulted in the loss of indigenous cultures. How different is the cultural programming of the computer from the cultural programming of the Bible? Should we not be asking, "How can we bring technological literacy to our students using our texts and primers without imposing undisclosed techno-values to the detriment or destruction of the students' own cultures and values?" This doesn't mean that we should not teach for fear of indoctrination, but rather that we need to use many primers and explicitly transparent programming, elucidate the purpose, strengths, and limitations of all devices or programs, and, most importantly, clarify the social assumptions that are embedded in every design.

It will take many pieces to complete the puzzle of how to educate in and for a world that is so decisively shaped by mathematics, science, and technology. We have some of those pieces now, but many others still need to be invented or developed. This reminds me of the joke about the school principal who solemnly addressed an assembly by noting, "I see many who are missing." I too see much that is still missing, and can only encourage all co-operative efforts—such as this symposium—to bring more pieces into the puzzle.

An analogy can help here. Imagine a society that is striving for universal literacy. Young children go to school to learn to read at an early age, but as they grow up their teachers are not satisfied that they can read and comprehend a text or follow a set of written instructions. The responsible educator sees to it that the ability to read between the lines becomes part of the quest for literacy, because literacy encompasses the ability not only to read and understand the written text, but also to be mindful of what has not been expressed, although possibly implied.

Will those who advocate greater technological literacy today teach their students to understand technical instructions, or will they teach them to read between the lines of what they experience of mathematics, science, and technology? Much benefit has come from the recent stress on "media literacy"—the ability to read and interpret mass media offerings in terms of their institutional and political context—but I think that we have not yet arrived at a similar level of "techno-literacy." There is not yet a public knowledge of mathematics, science, and technology that goes beyond the "gee-whiz" state. But such knowledge is needed to allow a critical understanding of some of the most powerful forces of our time.

There is, then, one more question for me to pose. "What do we do now, how should we proceed in our own daily work in the field of mathematics, science, and technology education?" To me it seems important to reaffirm, again and again, some basic tenets of the work. There is the need to reaffirm the primacy of people. Whatever we do, as we teach children or adults, we must enrich the learners; we must not cripple or incapacitate them. Thus, as technology becomes part of the education system—be it as teaching instruments or as tools for skills transfer—the impact on people must be conscientiously assessed. Are such tools enabling or disabling? Do they make individuals more resourceful, more self-reliant, stronger, and more versatile? Or do they constrain human potential? In particular, does the technological mediation of teaching and learning constrain the imagination?

Are words not contained in the "spell-checker" deemed as unacceptable vocabulary? Do they become unthinkable when a conventional expression is instantly at hand? Sometimes I muse about whether "jabberwocky" could have been created on a word processor and wonder whether "'twas brilig . . . " could come to mind in front of a blank screen. If we rely heavily on tools that normalize and standardize language, we should find extra time to explore non-standard language, to write poetry, to rhyme or compose nonsense verses.

Programming for learning must not become a cast that constrains imagination or creativity. If your leg is in a cast for a period of time, the muscles can atrophy; similarly, technological intervention in teaching and learning can hinder the leaps of the mind, and cause mental activities to atrophy. Machines often free us from routine and repetitive tasks—we are grateful not to have to do square roots or long division—but merely delegating such "simple" tasks to devices can deprive the young learner of the joys of mastery and the exploration of non-conventional solutions. In traditional schooling such learning occasions might occur naturally, but in technologically mediated teaching it takes special efforts to provide such opportunities.

This is particularly applicable to mathematics. Those of you who are connoisseurs of mathematics will know how one rejoices in what can only be called an "elegant solution." An elegant solution is not necessarily the solution of an advanced problem, and it is more than the correct solution of any problem. It is a solution achieved with the minimum of fuss and the maximum of ingenuity—elegant in its frugality, its approach, and its architecture. Even if we had the world's best programs to solve mathematical problems, I would contend that we must not, by their use in teaching, deny people the joy of finding their own elegant solution through a combination of intellectual curiosity and serendipity.

Sometimes I tell a story about Karl Friedrich Gauss (1797–1855), the great German mathematician. One day the younger children in the local one-room school were given the task of adding the numbers from one to one hundred on their slates while the teacher instructed the older students. This exercise was obviously designed to keep the kids busy for some time. When Gauss quickly came up with the correct answer, he was accused of having learned it from his older brother, who had done the same exercise the year before. Gauss, who was reportedly a somewhat withdrawn and sullen child, insisted that he had no help. The head-master asked Gauss how he had found the solution so fast. The child explained that all he had done was to add $100 + (99 + 1) + (98 + 2) +$ all the other blocks of 100 as well as the residual 50. Now, there is an elegant solution that anyone could have found, although nobody else did. Not all our students will turn out to be creative mathematicians, but the joy of the elegant solution, even to simple problems, ought not to be denied any learner, young or mature. If the use of the devices eliminates settings in which Gauss-type interventions are possible, then equivalent settings should be put in place before the devices become part of the curriculum.

I think that as the education system continues to incorporate technology into the teaching environment, the primacy of people must be affirmed and reaffirmed. Technology, whether a tool of teaching or a subject of instruction, must enrich learning and human growth, and it must not cripple or constrain either. This principle provides the measure for our ongoing critique.

Secondly, the joy of learning must not be stifled by the efficiency of teaching. No one should miss the excitement of the elegant solution, of seeing the hitherto unseen, of recognizing patterns in what appeared to be random—the sense of delight that I still have, after so many years of practice, when I look through a microscope.

Thirdly, we must affirm the resourcefulness and resilience of people, and build teaching and learning on these attributes. Technology, not of necessity but often by design or implementation, is essentially anti-people. This was already evident at the beginning of the Industrial Revolution, when factory owners dreamt of machines that would replace all workers. The workerless factory totally under the owners' control became the desirata, perpetuating the notion that people are sources of problems, while machines and devices offer modes of solution.

As teachers and as citizens we must be careful to recognize, celebrate, and utilize the resourcefulness and resilience of people. We must never lose the vision of education as a way for all teachers and learners alike to think and to be thoughtful. In this light education has always been a subversive activity. I urge you to keep it this way!

LETTER TO A GRADUATE STUDENT,
FROM URSULA FRANKLIN

Published in "The Legacy of Margaret Benston," *a special issue of* Canadian Woman Studies / Les cahiers de la femme, *vol. 13, no. 2 (Winter 1993), pp. 12–15.*

Dear Marcia,

A few months ago, you came to me to talk about your future. Should you, a feminist and a graduate student in science, embark on a doctoral program in a physics-related field? Is not the gulf between the goals of a scientist and the goals of a feminist too great to be bridged within one person who wants to live in peace with herself? We talked for a long time and I spoke a lot about my friend Maggie Benston and how her life and work illuminates your questions and helps to answer them. Yet, after you had left, I felt uneasy. Did my argument for not giving up on science make sense to you? Was I able to give you an idea of the nature of Maggie's pioneering contributions, and of Maggie herself, a vibrant woman and an original thinker and doer?

Now that this volume, "The Legacy of Margaret Benston," has been assembled, I want to return to our conversation. You will find clarification and elaboration of the ideas we touched on in many of the papers in this book. Perhaps we should now pick up on three strands that ran through our talk. You asked about Maggie as a person—what made her tick? Why did she have such a strong influence on people's understanding of the technological world around us? What does her life's contribution mean for young women like yourself?

For me, the uniqueness of Maggie lies largely in the unity of her life. She wasn't a scholar and academic on Monday, Wednesday, and Friday, a unionist on Tuesday and Thursday, a member of the women's movement on the weekend, and an environmentalist when on vacation. She was all of these, and more, simultaneously. All her activities were rooted in the same soil, each aspect of her life was linked to and informed by all other aspects of her being. The pattern-setting force in her life was her belief in the possibility and practicability of a feminist, egalitarian, and non-oppressive society. Whatever Maggie did, as well as what she did not do, must be understood as a direct consequence of this belief.

People have often commented on how few hang-ups Maggie seemed to have. As I recall, she did not spend much time agonizing about joining a particular demonstration or supporting a struggling solidarity group; her response was quickly derived from her general standpoint, the place where her life was anchored. Once her basic position—*that patriarchy or hierarchy is not an option*—had been taken, daily hang-ups faded into the background. Much strength flows from a fundamental decision not to accept the rules of an alien convention. There is the liberating effect of declared non-conformity, the joy of sharing and following one's own conviction, the lack of inner contradiction. A lot of creative energy becomes available when the internal conflicts have been eliminated. Indeed, I feel that the great influence that Maggie asserted on so many people springs directly from the qualities of her own life: its inner consistency, its openness and rootedness in a feminist vision. By the way, Marcia, don't overlook the trap here. In dress and lifestyle, demeanour and politics, Maggie stressed her ordinariness; she seemed just like everybody else. Don't let this fool you. Maggie was in many ways quite extraordinary and exceptional, not the least for her ability to integrate the ordinary and the extraordinary into one seamless life.

Perhaps we should talk about Maggie's contributions to feminist theory. We can speak about her feminist practice later, when we discuss what may lie ahead for you. Just remember that for Maggie, theory and practice were inextricably linked, and she would joyfully deny the existence of a tactical boundary between them. Her two major theoretical papers were the fruits of considerable search and research: "The Political Economy of Women's Liberation" (published in 1969) and "Feminism and the Critique of Scientific Method" (published in 1982).[1] I want to reflect on the seminal nature of "Feminism and the Critique of Scientific Method."

When this paper first appeared, Maggie had been at Simon Fraser University for fifteen years. At this time she held a cross-appointment in the departments of Chemistry and Computer

Science. On its initial publication, "Feminism and the Critique of the Scientific Method" did not have the same instantaneous impact as did "The Political Economy of Women's Liberation." This may have been due to the fact that at the time those involved in arguments about the structure of scientific knowledge did not consult books with titles such as *Feminism in Canada*. To the best of my knowledge, this paper was never translated into another language, although it became a central contribution to the debate on the nature of science and on the intrinsic limitations of the scientific method. You will be familiar with this rich discourse on the social and political structuring of knowledge, to which feminists have added so many fresh insights, and therefore you may ask about Maggie's place in all this.

For me, the importance of Maggie's work here is twofold. In the first place she explores, explains, and illuminates the notion of science in all its aspects. Secondly, she draws practical consequences from what she and others found, and she acts upon them in her own work. Like a good anatomist, Maggie first dissects the concepts and practices of science using the instruments of feminist and socialist analysis. She looks at science as a social and political structure and finds it wanting, in the same way that she found economic systems wanting when she critiqued the political economy of women's liberation. Maggie lays bare, for all to see, the postulates and assumptions, the methods of work, and the internal reasoning within the enterprise of science. This "pedagogy of understanding" is embedded in all of Maggie's work. A particularly telling paragraph listing four of the core assumptions of scientific practices will illustrate what I mean:

1   There exists an "objective" material reality separate from and independent of an observer. This reality is orderly.
2   The material world is knowable through rational inquiry and this knowledge is independent of the individual characteristics of the observer.
3   Knowledge of the material world is gained through measurement of natural phenomena: measurement in a scientific sense consists of quantification, i.e. reduction to some form of mathematical description.

4   The goal of scientific understanding is the ability to predict and control natural phenomena (this postulate often takes
the form of equating science with power).[2]

Interweaving her analysis with the insights of other feminist
scholars, notably Ruth Hubbard and Marian Lowe, Maggie then
exposes the double myth of the objectivity and neutrality of the
scientific method, pointing out the inherent limitations that the
methods of science place on the scope of any scientific inquiry.
The impact of reductionism—this preordaining of certain variables as being more important or indicative than others—
becomes the next focus of her pedagogy of understanding. In this
context she quotes Ruth Hubbard:

> Of necessity, we can tackle only the few limited aspects of
> nature of which we take sufficient notice that they arouse our
> interest or curiosity to the point where we examine them more
> closely. The scientific modes of thought and action therefore
> elevate some things and events to the rank of "facts," indeed of
> *scientific facts*, while being oblivious to the existence of others
> and actively relegating yet a third category to the foggy realms
> of suppositions or, worse yet, superstition.[3]

Ruth Hubbard later elaborated on the role of scientists as socially
sanctioned "fact-makers," and you will find more on this in her
book *The Politics of Women's Biology*.[4]

Other thoughts in "Feminism and the Critique of the Scientific Method" will also be of special interest to you, Marcia. In
terms of the impact of reductionism and bias in scientific practices, Maggie points to the notion of "side effects" and writes:

> In fact, there are no side effects, only effects. The definition of
> some of the results of the process under study as unimportant
> is done in terms of the intent of the investigator rather than the
> reality of the process. The "pill" is a good example—suppres-
> sion of ovulation is one of its effects, while another is a change
> in blood chemistry that may make blood clotting more likely.

A less distorted methodology would not dismiss this second
effect as lightly as present medical science does.[5]

Have you noticed, Marcia, that Maggie speaks throughout the
paper of "present science"? She explains her terminology in a
footnote: "I use the term 'present science' to refer to the methodology and practice of science *now*, since I believe that ultimately
feminist and other critiques will lead to a quite different conception of what science can be."[6] Maggie uses the term "present
technology" in the same manner. There are many indications
throughout the paper that Maggie was not giving up on science,
but instead was pressing for work on a different science. The final
section of the paper is actually headed "Towards a Different Science." Quoting Ruth Hubbard again, Maggie writes:

> As women and as feminists we must begin to deal with the sci-
> ence and technology that shape our lives and even our bodies.
> We have been the objects of bad science; now we must become
> the makers of a new one.
>
> What is needed in such a new science is, first of all, a sense
> of the limits of the appropriateness of reductionism and the
> development of a methodology which can deal with complex
> systems "that flow so smoothly and gradually or are so pro-
> foundly interwoven in their complexities that they cannot be
> broken up into measurable units without losing or changing
> their fundamental nature." Difficult as this may be in practice,
> its very adoption as a goal must mean a major change in scien-
> tific methodology.[7]

And this is precisely what Maggie did in all her own projects and
studies: she conducted scientific or technical studies using new
and different methodologies reflecting her own different values.
The fact that these studies had realistic goals and practical
results—be they new designs of computer networks or a novel
way of automating clerical work—should not camouflage the
emergence of radically different methodologies. Please, Marcia,
don't let the down-to-earth attributes of Maggie's projects blind

you to their *theoretical* importance; each one is an experience, testing the methodologies of a new contextual science.

Vividly imagining the new and cultivating constructive dreaming were important to Maggie. Did you know that she had a great deal of interest in science fiction and in utopias, particularly the feminist ones? She taught several courses on utopias, emphasizing their different sciences and knowledge structures and their novel social relationships. Her 1988 paper "Feminism and Systems Design: Questions of Control"[8] begins with reflections on Marge Piercy's utopian novel *Woman on the Edge of Time*.[9] For Maggie, science fiction and utopian writing provided a space where the social and the scientific imagination could meet and play. Had she lived longer, she might well have written in this genre too.

But now I must return to your initial question: Is there is a place for a young feminist in science?" My answer is clearly, "Yes," but you and other women should understand the political and social structure of present science and technology and try to equip yourselves to deal with this reality. However, this need for an understanding of the political and social structure of the enterprise in which one invests one's labour is not required only from those who prepare for work in science and technology. If you were to go into law or medicine, social work or architecture, the same questions about assumptions and paradigms would exist, although some disciplines might be more prepared to face such queries than is present science and its practitioners. Maggie certainly was not prepared to give up her participation in the practice of science or technology. In "Marxism, Science and Workers' Control," she states quite explicitly: "In general, I don't want to be understood as being 'anti-rational' or 'anti-science.' What I argue is that it is necessary to recognize the problems inherent in the present practice of science."[10] And, she could have added, do something about it.

Let me assure you, Marcia, that I know how constrained the choices for graduate students in terms of research subjects and supervisors have become in these tough times. Yet there are choices and they have to be made with care. Choose your supervisors, if you can, for their human qualities. You must be able to respect them, even when you have to disagree with them. To me, considerations of human substance are of greater importance than the selection of a subdiscipline.

Among the research areas open to you, choose, if at all possible, one that has been neglected because of the very biases that Maggie discussed. For instance, in the field of solid state physics we both know that the past fifty years of concentrated research have yielded a very complex and complete body of knowledge related to the interaction of solid inorganic material and radiation and currents of any kind. Without this body of knowledge, there would be no semiconductors, no microchips, no fibre optics, you name it. Now compare this situation with the small body of uncertain information regarding the interaction between living organic solids—blood, tissue, cells, bone—with the same currents and radiation. Isn't it amazing how little research effort and attention the organic materials have attracted?

Unquestionably, the experimental context is more complicated and "messy" for organic materials—that is, it is less amiable to reductionist simplification—but most problems look complicated and messy until one has a conceptual handle on them. You may also want to ask yourself whether the neglect of this research area could have a political component. The beneficiaries of the neglected subfield would likely be, in the main, "mere" people, while the present solid state knowledge has yielded enormous industrial and military benefits. Here is clearly an area of inquiry that is crying out for the new methodologies, for new forms of collaboration and data gathering. Try to associate yourself with those who worry about such neglected fields, as Maggie always did.

Let me also urge you not to forget how much joy the study of science can give. The world in which we live is rich and full of wonder and beauty, as Rachel Carson so often said. Can you recall the feeling of sheer joy you had when you grasped for the first time the underlying reasons for the regularity of the periodic table of elements or the nature of crystallographic transformations? I certainly can, and even now, some forty years after my Ph.D., I still find microscopic examinations of samples a wonderful and joyful activity.

The joy of mastery and understanding—not at all unique to scientific studies—the pleasure of seeing patterns emerging where none were seen before, the elegance of a fresh mathematical approach: all these treasures are there, and should not become invisible because they remain in the shadows cast by the overreach and overapplication of "present" science and technology.

Yes, you may say, all this is fine and good, but what about the "chilly climate"? Good question! I do acknowledge that the structurally, and at times personally unfriendly, environment deters young women from planning research careers in a scientific or technical field. Yet as a feminist, you are less vulnerable than young women who have no understanding of the social and political structures of science and technology, and who might still fall for the myth of the objectivity and neutrality of science and technology. You may think that I am joking, but let me give you my argument. First and foremost, don't check your feminism at the laboratory door; it is an important layer of the coat of inner security that will protect you from the chilly climate. Since your values will be questioned constantly—implicitly and explicitly—you will depend for your sanity on an ongoing rootedness in the women's community.

Take the time to keep involved in women's issues, and don't ever think of yourself as "the only woman in . . ." Likely you are not, just as I have never been. Wherever men work, there are also women working, usually for much lower pay. You may well be the only female doctoral student in a particular group, but what about the secretaries, the cleaning staff, the librarians, and the technicians? You may link up with them and gain their support and friendship. As you watch over the safety and well-being of others, your own will take care of itself and the chilly climate will warm up a bit.

Don't become petrified by rank! Only hierarchy pulls rank. As feminists, we see rank as the institutional equivalent of a postal code, not as a figure of merit. In other words, rank or title indicates people's sphere of work and responsibility; it does not, by definition, imply that they know more or know better than those of lower rank or title.

Remember also that what is morally wrong and unjust is, in the end, also dysfunctional—a point Maggie often made. All the advanced science and technology for war has not brought peace to anyone. All the advanced systems of oppression have not brought security to their owners. As a motto for her paper on technology as language, Maggie used a line from a postcard of the International Women's Tribune Centre: "If it's not appropriate for women, it's not appropriate"—a good phrase to remember.

Finally, when the going is tough, and you feel yourself surrounded by jerks, take an anthropological approach. Take field notes (I mean this in real and practical terms) and regard yourself as an explorer having come upon a strange tribe. Observe and describe the tribe's customs and attitudes with keen detachment, and consider publishing your field observations. It may help you and be of use to future travellers. I know from experience that the exercise works.

Please keep in touch and remember, you are not alone.

Your friend,
Ursula Franklin

Notes

1   Margaret Benston, "The Political Economy of Women's Liberation," *Monthly Review*, vol. 21, no. 4 (September 1969), pp. 13–27; "Feminism and the Critique of Scientific Method," in *Feminism in Canada*, rev. ed., ed. A. Miles and G. Finn (Montreal: Black Rose, 1989); "Feminism and Systems Design; Matters of Control," in *The Effects of Feminist Approaches on Research Methodologies*, ed. Winnie Tomm (Waterloo, Ont.: Wilfred Laurier University Press: 1989).
2   Benston, "Feminism and the Critique of Scientific Method," p. 63.
3   Ibid., p. 68.
4   Ruth Hubbard, *The Politics of Women's Biology* (New Brunswick, N.J.: Rutgers University Press, 1990).
5   Benston, "Feminism and the Critique of Scientific Method," p. 73.
6   Ibid., p. 62.
7   Ibid., p. 74.
8   Benston, "Feminism and Systems Design."
9   Marge Piercy, *Woman on the Edge of Time* (New York: Knopf, 1976).
10 Margaret Benston, "Marxism, Science and Worker's Control," in *Work and New Technologies: Other Perspectives*, ed. C. DeBresson, M.L. Benston, and J. Vorst (Toronto: Between the Lines, 1987).

LOOKING FORWARD, LOOKING BACK

Concluding address to the More Than Just Numbers conference, convened by the Canadian Committee on Women in Engineering, University of New Brunswick, Fredericton, 10 May 1995; published in More Than Just Numbers: Report of the Canadian Committee on Women in Engineering, *Fredericton, 1992.*

HAVING BEEN ASKED to look forward as well as to look back, I want to use the short time we have together to reflect on how we got to where we are now, so that we might see more clearly·the path ahead and find out what needs to be done next.

Before doing this, though, I would like to pay tribute to Monique [Frize] and the work she has done.[1] To me, it is not only important to honour what she has done, but—even more so—how she has done it. There has been a very special spirit of generosity that has flown through all of her work, work that culminated in this conference; it was also present in all phases of the process of the investigation she chaired. This combination of generosity and professional competence, which Monique has exhibited, is something very rare, and I would like to salute Monique here and say, "Monique, yours is a job well done and well to be continued." I am thankful that her professorship has been renewed to 1999 and I am sure she, as well as all of us, has a lot of urgent work ahead of her.

As a point of departure for this evening's reflections I would like to take you back to the murder on December 6, 1989, of the fourteen young women who were students at l'École polytechnique in Montreal. This event has become a benchmark for all of us, because so much changed in the wake of this tragedy, in terms of perceptions and interpretations of the climate and the realities of life for women in engineering. In light of the sudden, horrible realization of what happened in Montreal, it became possible—likely for the first time in Canada—to say, "This could have happened at our university, it could have happened in my class." There was a quantum leap in reality recognition across this country. I remember that my son, who, like most sons, did not appear to have much interest in what mother was doing, phoned Peter Gzowski's *Morningside* on CBC-Radio to share his feelings on hearing the news of the murders and Marc Lepine's hit list. He suddenly understood that, at another engineering school, it could have been his mother's name on the hit list.

The shock of the events was, of course, felt particularly strongly within the engineering profession, and out of this atmosphere of profound upset it became possible to act, to inquire, to map the reality of the lives of women in engineering. The resulting soul searching not only brought enquiries and the commission on whose recommendation we meet today. It also brought many of us the first opportunity to name and specify what has been going on. It became possible to speak publicly about the chilly climate, about bias, sexism, misogyny, and patriarchy. These concepts could be used and understood in the emerging discourse, a discourse that looked for ways and means of rectifying the unacceptable conditions in the study and work environments of women engineers.

The process of identifying the obstacles in the path of women in engineering yielded a number of significant results. It responded to the publicly expressed need of the engineering professions to see more clearly what was going on in their own house, and it allowed us to separate specific obstacles and suggest remedial measures. The report *More Than Just Numbers* not only provided recommendations based on statistics and well-documented evidence, but also insisted on benchmarks, tangible evidence of change and of accountability. The report clearly states that fixing a few things behind closed doors is not good enough. What women are pressing for has been, and is, equal participation in engineering opportunities and transparent processes of selection and decision-making in appointments and promotion. These insights link the struggle of women in engineering to the fundamental issues in the general struggle of women for equal opportunities everywhere. There is always the same concern for justice and the same concern about the lack of respect afforded to women and the often implicit downgrading of their abilities.

Some of you will recall the surprised tone of voice when someone, on learning of your field of study, would say, "Oh, you

are in engineering . . ." implying that this may be really too difficult for a nice girl like you. I remember well a funny incident that
happened not too long ago during the first week of term. I was
going into my office when I saw a young student, his arm full of
books, trying to negotiate the heavy double doors of the Wallberg
Building of the Faculty of Engineering at my university—obviously a first-year student making his way into the halls of the Faculty. I held the first door open for him, then the second door. He
thanked me politely and then asked, "Do you work here?" "Yes,"
I replied. "Are you a secretary?" "No. I'm a professor of metallurgy." "Holy cow!" was his instantaneous response, quick and
uncensored. It was a quite natural and uninhibited reaction, expressing disbelief and surprise at the possibility of a woman being
a professor of metallurgy.

Surely, I am not the only one here who remembers being the
sole woman in a class, remembering professors asking whether
you were not in the wrong lecture or lab. All such incidents illustrate our double grievance related both to the lack of justice and
the lack of respect for our potential that runs through all our lives
as women. Speaking specifically about engineering education, I
can say that the rectification of such grievances has been ap-
proached from two basic directions: one approach was systemic;
the other more case-specific and directly addressing women. I
used to call the latter "weightlifting for girls," and I have never
been very enthusiastic about it. Although I understand full well
the need to encourage young women to enter engineering and to
support them personally in every possible way, acculturating
women into engineering and hardening them against the chilly
climate may change the problematic aspects of the culture of
engineering less than one might think. That approach also puts
the prime burden of change on the disadvantaged, which is never
a very good idea.

Truly, it is not just a question of numbers; it is a question of
structural, institutional, and cultural changes, systemic changes
that must involve the elders of the engineering tribes as well as
the majority of traditional "average" male engineers. At this five-
year benchmark, we should recognize and celebrate the real and
significant changes that have taken place. The mindset that con-

sidered sexist student newspapers, crude initiation pranks, and "girly" pin-ups to be integral parts of the education of engineers is no longer publicly acceptable. While new codes of conduct have been issued, sexist language has been curtailed and criticized, and issues of gender sensitivity have been advanced, we know, and heard again this afternoon, how much more work needs to be done, especially in the area of gender sensitivity.

Central to the achievements of the past five years is the fact that the grievances of women in engineering have become real and tangible; they are not figments of our imagination but concrete issues about which something can and will be done. Certainly, some issues will reappear in different guises: the girly calendars may be passé, but pornography on the Internet and in the computer rooms is just coming at us, and with it the "boys will be boys" and anti-censorship arguments. I am confident, however, that each new reincarnation of sexism will find less acceptance and a clearer and faster rebuttal because the climate has changed.

You may well ask why, since I do see changes in the climate brought about by concerted attempts to address the grievances of women in engineering, I am still unenthusiastic about acculturating women into engineering. My reason is that I would like to make engineering fit for women, rather than women fit for engineering. I feel that the past exclusion of women from engineering has been bad for our profession. The exclusion of women has meant that some of the values that women traditionally bring to their tasks have been missing in the habits of work and thought in engineering.

I know that when some of my women students objected to the bad manners of their peers, to the put-downs of women and "artsies," they were told: "This is what engineering is like. You better get accustomed to it. If you can't hack it, go into early childhood education." My point, however, is that there is nothing wrong with women and their values, including those values that may make their professional advancement difficult. There is nothing wrong with caring, there is nothing wrong with *not* being aggressive and pushy. There is nothing wrong with expressing the hurt of being treated unjustly. What *is* wrong is the put-down, the insensitivity, and the lack of justice and respect—not women's response to it. And I, for one, do not want to see women engineers so "work-hardened"—to use a good metallurgical expression—that they lose their acute sensitivity and are unable to recognize discrimination or injustice when they or others meet it. Nothing is served if we become mere substitutes of our traditional male peers.

That's why I interceded this afternoon when someone suggested that in discussion of the mentoring program, we might not want to speak about nurturing, but about coaching. I did not like this suggestion because I don't think life is a football game; I don't think coaching *the* team to win *the* game helps anyone in the end.

Language is very important: language expresses our values and we should not be afraid to use words such as nurturing, concepts such as caring, including the willingness to, if necessary, take second place on occasion. Nurturing, caring, and helping are the very attributes that our society so desperately needs. There is no point for us to downplay them, even at the risk of our own advancement.

How then do we proceed from here, you will ask, as we come together to celebrate achievements and to express our gratitude to those who have helped to bring them about? For my answer, let me take you back to the central theme of my thoughts on "looking forward, looking back." When we deal with questions important to women in engineering, we are concerned with issues of justice and compassion. Our work is therefore embedded in the patterns of change within the larger society of which engineers are but one component. How we, as women in engineering, conduct the next steps on the road towards our professional equality can be of considerable help—or hindrance—to the advancement of our sisters in other fields.

Women are increasingly coming into positions of power and influence. I am profoundly convinced that the conduct of women in power must be guided and informed by the collective experience of women when they were powerless. In other words, none of us can forget women's experience of exclusion and discrimination and tolerate or use practices of bias, not only on the basis of gender, but also on the basis of religion, ethnic origin, or sexual orientation. We cannot condone generic put-downs of "others," just as we do not condone these tactics when they are applied to women as a group. The use of such a reciprocal yardstick may be one of the most important contributions that women, newly coming into positions of power and responsibility, can make.

Another concept, another relic of the patriarchal structures of hierarchy and power, also needs revisiting and reinterpretation: the concept of "rank." It is quite clear to me that women view rank differently from men. For us, rank is not a station in life or a figure of merit. Rank is the social equivalent of a postal code; it tells others where we work and where our territory can be found. We rejoice when one of our sisters gets a promotion, a new postal code, a larger area of responsibility, because of the greater contributions she may be able to make. But recognizing people's rank is not like grading eggs; a promotion does not imply that on July 1 someone who has been a "Grade A small" will become, by some administrative miracle, a "Grade A large." The human attributes of people do not change with a change of rank; they do not become better persons or better friends on promotion, nor do they become less valuable human beings if they are not promoted, if they have no rank to parade.

It is really important for women, as they move into positions of responsibility and power, not to be either frightened or hypnotized by rank. Each of us can help in the ongoing process of clarifying the notion of rank by extending our unchanging care and friendship both to those of our sisters who are promoted and those who are not.

Another facet of our discussion of rank and promotion should be mentioned here, lest someone think that rightful and unbiased promotion and advancement for women are now the rule. Earlier I mentioned that some of the problems, well known to women in engineering, can resurface in new guises. Thus one finds that the gatekeepers of the old order may move from objecting to potential colleagues on the basis of gender to questioning the legitimacy of their research interests. In other words, no one in his right mind will say anymore, "I don't like women in the department," but it is not uncommon for senior staff to insist that any new person hired has to continue the area of research that old Professor what's-his-name cultivated so faithfully over the past thirty years—effectively blocking the entry of anyone who might want to do different research in a different manner. Such gate-keeping regarding research fields happens and bears watching.

We need to be mindful of the danger posed by the present climate of cutbacks and retrenchments to the ongoing advancement of women in engineering. In this context it is again important to stress that women engineers are not mere substitutes or clones of their male peers. As women they bring different perspectives and experiences to their work. All considered, it is certainly not yet plain sailing for women engineers.

My concluding remarks are addressed primarily to the younger women in the audience. First of all, if you have been helped by your mentors, don't forget them now. They will be getting old and may need you as you have needed them. Secondly, don't forget your feminism and your solidarity with other women. Feminism is not an employment agency for women; feminism is a movement to change relations between people to more egalitarian, caring, and non-hierarchical patterns. Feminism provides a way of life that our society, I feel, desperately requires and that we need to practise.

Do remember that even if the Marc Lepines of the world no longer haunt the engineering faculties of this country, violence in most societies is rising, and this usually means violence against women and children. Don't be indifferent to their fate. Those of us who have the privilege of working in an environment in which verbal as well as physical violence has become unacceptable have to make sure that such environments do not remain exceptions but become the norm.

Finally, be careful and conscientious about the language you use and the images your words evoke. Language is terribly important; it is the vehicle of thought and concept, the medium of learning, and the reinforcement of images. Don't make violence appear normal by using the language of organized violence; why speak about "target audiences"? Surely you don't want to shoot your students or clients; you just want to reach those particularly interested. There are really no targets, no conquests, no strategic plans, no deadlines—only interested groups, changes of attitude and habit, plans, and due dates. There is no aiming at, only addressing and responding. There is also a need to watch sexism in the language of social and political discourse. Sexism has not yet disappeared: think of the different connotations of the terms "bagmen" and "bagladies." The society that we envisage and work for will care for the homeless—called bag ladies—and have no place for the manipulators of power—called bagmen.

With these thoughts that I have put before you for your reflection and use go my good wishes and my thanks for your attention.

Note

1   Professor Monique Frize, the conference chair, holds the first Canadian Chair for Women in Engineering. She inspired and carried out much of the groundwork that made it possible to hold this conference and to provide a national accounting. The More Than Just Numbers Conference was convened to document and discuss the progress of women in the engineering profession during the past five years. Those gathered included not only younger women, newly entering the field, but many of their senior women colleagues who had struggled for many years to assure a more equitable environment in engineering education and practice. There was a warm bond of friendship among all the women at the Conference.

PERSONALLY HAPPY AND
PUBLICLY USEFUL

Address given at the Canadian Education Association convention, Toronto, September 1997; published in Our Schools, Our Selves: A Magazine for Canadian Education Activists, *vol. 9, no. 4 (October 1998), pp. 81–96.*

I HAVE BEEN ASKED by the conference organizers to reflect on what it is that we should think about at the beginning of this conference, an important international gathering focusing on schools that will take a full week. You will be asked to consider how—at this point in the history of Ontario, of Canada, of the world—we should think about schools. Given this mandate, it seems important to deal with the real issues, and not be diverted by phantom matters raised to detract from the search for clarity and genuine understanding.

If we want to make concrete contributions, it is necessary to reflect on where we are and where we are going. To begin, let us remember that schools are social institutions. They are integral parts of their society, institutions that have evolved through time for one particular purpose: to equip the young to cope with the future, to provide them with attitudes and skills so that they may meet the demands and the needs of their society in the future. Schools have always been a place to acculturate the young into their community.

Control over schools has been contested throughout the history of this country, and every struggle around schools has involved this central mandate. Embedded in these struggles were always questions such as: Who needs which skills in our society? What is the future of the country going to be? Where will future leadership originate? Who is going to attend school? Boys alone, boys and girls together, the sons of the rich, the sons of the poor? Should they be educated together or separately? What skills do the sons of the rich require that the society may not wish to transfer to the daughters of the poor? How does any community preserve and transfer knowledge? What type of knowledge is worth preserving and transferring? Who is entitled to write the books from which the students will learn? Who is going to teach the students, who is going to influence them? Who are going to be the role models after whom they are expected to shape their lives?

It is not surprising, therefore, that there is political and social pushing and pulling around schools. The problems of acculturating the young to their future tasks and roles have been a consistent undercurrent in the power struggles around education. Even after acknowledging this context, though, other questions remain: Where is the starting line for this future? Is it at the end of the students' schooling or is it when they are mature citizens? Is it when they apply for their first job? When does their future, for which we educate them, actually begin?

One final question about public education deserves our most serious consideration: What are the obligations of the teachers to each and every student as a human being, not as a cog in a society, not as a member of a particular constituency or clan, of a family, class, or religious group, but as a unique individual? What are the obligations of teachers, of educators, of elders to a student purely as a creature with a mind, a conscience, with gifts, abilities, and needs?

Schools as social institutions often have had to mitigate with judgment and compassion the social forces around them. The perspectives of the educators have not always coincided with the popular opinion of the day. Others have felt, as we do today, that there are things which we ought to teach, even if they are not politically popular. The discipline of education has at its base a subversive component that I hope can be retained. It is this component that can bring critical skills, historical perspectives, and good solid reasoning to young minds. This is the component of teaching in which I delight.

Schools are, of course, not the only place where children learn. We know very well that in the best of all worlds schools should be the hub of a wheel, with each spoke leading to a different learning situation, be it on the playground, in the family, in the neighbourhood or the church, in the workplace, or in entertainment or travel. What any school hopes to do is to integrate these learning experiences, add to them and help the students to interpret them. We can see, however, how a student's world can drift out of balance if one spoke of the wheel—say, the entertainment spoke—culminates in the glorification of violence, while the school tries to teach conflict resolution, tolerance, and understanding. When such imbalances and contradictions occur, it is not necessarily the fault of the school.

If the school constitutes the hub and is designed to integrate and unify, then learning is well served only when the wheel is reasonably well balanced. Thus, when you discuss "school failures" later at your sessions, do remember that schools are social institutions and that they may be unable, unwilling, or unauthorized to integrate and make legitimate the failures and shortcomings of society. If within the society there are failures in compassion, knowledge, or tolerance, it is not the job of the schools to produce students who can comfortably fit in. On the contrary, the schools ought to draw attention to these failures and stress that they require correction.

In terms of our social ecology, it is essential—as it is in nature—that variety and diversity are maintained. Society needs a diverse ecology to be viable. I believe, to paraphrase Gertrude Stein, that a school is a school is a school, a bank is a bank, and a church is a church. But a school is not a business, a bank is not a church, and a church is not an entertainment centre. We will be in a grievous position if we forget our own ecology and promote social monoculture—the civic equivalent of giving up on a wide range of species and plants—and cultivate only what yields the day's profitable crop. We know from the experience of agriculture that monoculture is usually a poor ecological practice. Monocultures deplete the soil, so they require constant fertilizing and the crops will likely become susceptible to bugs and insects. The produce will clog the market and prevent other crops from being offered. To a society, monocultures of the mind are as unproductive as the monoculture of the soil. If schools are to remain social institutions for the benefit of the future, rather than becoming business enterprises focusing on the tangible benefits for some segments of society today, then there is a limit, purely from the point of view of social ecology, to which monocultures of the mind should be pursued.

In the same spirit there are limits to the wisdom of developing all-purpose hybrids of the mind: the "one-size-fits-all" brand. We may end up with the social equivalent of chequered flamingos or chickens that do not lay eggs but can sing. Please remember not only the nature of the school as a social institution, but also that in our social ecology, schools—just like banks, businesses, and churches—have their particular task.

The task of schools is the pursuit of education. You may ask, "Well then, what is education?" Education, I suggest, is a process of growth in knowledge and understanding, whether that is in the teacher or in the student, whether it is achieved formally or informally. I want to make a particular fuss about the two components being linked in an unbroken manner. As a society we cannot afford knowledge without understanding; you have all met those characters who know it all and understand nothing. But we also cannot afford understanding without knowledge; you have also met people who have a profound understanding of the problems they and others are facing, but do not have the knowledge, or the access to knowledge and power, to do anything about it.

What we try to do, in this enterprise of education, is to create an environment in which knowledge and understanding can grow, while taking great care that the link between the two components remains unbroken. It is important for me to emphasize this essential link between knowledge and understanding so strongly, because the acquisition of facts and the procurement of information has been so drastically changed by modern technologies. There are now many new and different ways in which facts, information, and knowledge can be transmitted and acquired, and this is good. But these developments affect one component of education much more than the other. It means that the pursuit of understanding, of the social learning that happens in school, must be emphasized and analyzed a great deal more than in the past.

As I prepared this talk I struggled to find a good way of illustrating the two types of basic activities that are involved in the process of learning in a group. One type is obvious or explicit learning: the transfer of known and sound information, such as that nine times three is twenty-seven. The other type is the non-obvious—implicit—learning that goes on in any classroom. Here

I am referring not to the fringe benefit of a discipline—the recognition that the study of mathematics also provides training in logic, or that the study of Latin can lead to a general understanding of grammar—but to the social learning, the learning about others, that takes place in the classroom.

Because of differences in learning pace and the needs of those in a class, the group setting provides learning opportunities for social skills: listening, tolerance, anger management, and inventiveness. A broad array of social learning goes on implicitly in the classroom, and so much of it is absolutely essential for students and their society. Yet in the past this type of learning was considered as implicit and of little importance because it came "by the way" as students learned whatever they had to learn.

As the process of transfer of information changes, as single students sit in front of single computers, one using a calculator, another using the Internet, these implicit learning opportunities can no longer be taken for granted. But the need for the skills acquired through implicit learning is greater than ever. Thus, the analysis of the non-obvious learning component, the naming and clarification of what the skills are that used to be included implicitly in school curricula, is becoming very important. Personally, I think we greatly underestimate the level and complexity of social learning that takes place "by the way" in the classroom.

I want to propose to you a Franklin variation of the lever rule. You may recall that little piece of elementary physics we all learned in school. The lever rule expresses the fact that if the length of a lever arm is increased, a given load can be lifted using a smaller force. This is the principle on which cranes and mechanical lifting devices are based. I remember the lever rule being drilled into me at school together with the fact that the energy required to lift the load does not change. We were told, over and over again, that whether you use a small force and a large lever or a large force and a small lever, you can never save on the work you have to do in order to lift the load. While the deeper insights of this lesson were probably lost on grade-school kids, the resonance and memory remained.

Using this image, today, I suggest a variation on the lever-rule theme. As you compress the obvious learning component by technological means, the time necessary to assure the acquisition of the non-obvious skills increases: the total process of education cannot be curtailed. We can vary the components of the task, just as we can vary the force and the length of the lever. However, we cannot save work in the lever situation, and I think we cannot save social cost, care, and attention in education, if we merely automate, speed up, cheapen, or truncate the obvious learning component. The cost, time, and pedagogical outlay of the non-obvious learning component must also be met.

Now, I want to take a moment to illustrate this point with an example that struck me when I first came to Canada as a post-doctoral fellow. At that time I was not familiar with ski lifts. Among those working in the lab I noticed that there were many able-bodied young men running around on crutches because of skiing accidents. It took me a while to understand why this was the case. Though I wasn't a great skier, I was reasonably competent, and knew that if you could manage to reach the top of a hill or slope—without a ski lift, of course—you could ski well enough to get down reasonably safely. You learned enough about falling and picking oneself up and about the look and feel of fresh snow over an icy surface, and you could spot problems created by such occurrences. The skills needed to get up the slope would do much to prevent problems on going down. If, on the other hand, there are ski lifts, the situation changes. The quick tow may give an illusion of competence, but the assessment of ground conditions no longer comes "by the way" of ascent. There is a new configuration that, if not recognized and attended to, can pose real dangers to the skier.

Please do not think that I am presenting an argument against ski lifts. I am instead trying to raise your awareness of problems that can arise when an activity changes through the use of a new technology. If adequate attention is not paid to the non-obvious component of the practice, harm can come to the practitioners. Do keep my ski lift illustration in mind as the discussions on education proceed. We need to enumerate and understand the skills and attitudes that are—often invisibly—cultivated in the classroom as part of the acquisition of knowledge. We and all those in our care cannot afford to lose them through a lack of attention to the implication of changes in educational practices.

You may well say, "Point made, but where do we go from here? Having understood that schools are social institutions with a specific mission, how, in practical terms, can we utilize the distinction between obvious and non-obvious learning, between the explicit and the implicit activities in the classroom? In plain language, what can we do differently next week?" As I see it, there are two necessary tasks ahead of us. The first task is to develop a thorough understanding of the ecology of our society and the role of public education in the well-being of the community. The second task relates to the content and method of education, the question of curriculum in its broad meaning.

I happen to have a strong commitment to public education, because I respect and admire the contribution of public schools to the richness of Canada. Canadian public schools in general, and the public schools of the greater Toronto area in particular, have made significant contributions to learning, as well as to social peace and understanding, contributions that cannot be overemphasized. Think for a moment of the non-obvious learning that involves not only students and teachers but also parents and guardians. Canada is a country of immigrants, and the strongest bond among all newcomers (remember that all of us, or our forebears, were at one time newcomers) is the wish for a better future for their children. This better life begins with access to good public education. When Mr. Chang and Mrs. Fitzgibbon meet over plans for the school picnic or the hockey team, they advance a common cause and begin to value the contributions each makes. When kids and parents taste each other's foods, meet each other's families, share in that normal process of living in a community, they learn from and about each other in ways that would be difficult to construct without the common interest in the school.

I am convinced that it is to a large extent on account of the public school system and the library system that the Greater Toronto Area has been able to absorb the very large number of diverse immigrants in a spirit of respect and without significant social upsets. Such an achievement has not come overnight, and it did not come without concerted and informed efforts. It has come from dedicated teachers, librarians, and officials and through an enlightened system of local governance that sees public expenses—such as the cost of translating notices into the language of the students' homes—as investment in the public good. It is a collective achievement of people, many of them very fine professionals. We have before us, I am sure, the clear evidence that good public schools—and I stress both "good" and "public"—are the price of peace in the community. To bring this evidence to all political discussions is our first task.

Our second task is embedded in the debates on curriculum, in the discussions of what should be taught in schools and how to teach it. Many aspects of these questions will be addressed in your sessions. But I would like to ask you not to become too concerned with the technical details, however novel and fascinating they may be. Below the surface of these presentations lies something much more interesting: look more closely and you will see two models of education, two very different ways of picturing the process and method of education.

First there is, as I've described elsewhere, the traditional, old-fashioned model of education that came from the collective wisdom of an agricultural society. Think of a garden, of planting and growing. In this image, young people are seen as young plants; those responsible for their care are expected to provide a nurturing environment. The young seedlings may need wind breaks, sun or shade, and just sufficient water so that growth may occur. Yet even with good care, growth can neither be forced nor engineered. Also, as a practising gardener, you do not pull out the carrots every three months to see how they are doing. The growth model, with its roots in nature, assumes that people, like plants, have different needs and patterns of response, but that all have the ability to grow, to bear fruit, to ripen. Though each may need a particular environment and individual pruning, different plants usually grow well together.

As the predominantly agricultural societies became industrial and technological nations, a different model of education began to appear. The new model reflected the increasing preoccupation of society with production. Since the Industrial Revolution more and more people have lived in an environment of production, making things (including money) rather than growing crops. At the end of the twentieth century the whole world seems to be one giant production site governed by considerations of raw materials, investment, production, and marketing. It is not surprising that in this type of society education is often regarded as a production activity: the school as a sausage factory, if you want a crude production model. Students starting their education are empty sausage skins that you, the teacher—one part of the production line—are to stuff according to the basic recipe. If the market needs Italian sausages, you may add a bit more garlic. If consumer reports indicate a latent interest in Chinese sausages, out comes the soy sauce. Since it is a production setting, testing and quality control become imperative. You don't want customers to say there was too little salt or too much pepper in the sausages. Once the production model of education is accepted, frequent testing, recycling, and rejection become obligatory. Within the framework of production, input and output, success and failure, have precise and definable meaning. But ask yourself: How far are these notions applicable to your classroom?

In the sausage factory, there is a distinct product for which the production line has been designed. There are measures of success, such as producing umpteen sausages per minute or becoming sausage-maker to the Queen. There are also clear indications of failure: costs that are too high, production runs that are too small, or slow sales. If nobody really wants these sausages, there may have to be a half-price sale. Now it's time to think again about this production model of education. Do you actually intend to discount those students whose reply to the question "What language have you studied?" is "Latin," and not "Pascal" or another programming language? Yet, in spite of its inappropriateness, the production model of education is currently much in vogue. Indeed it is so prevalent that you may be stuck with it for the moment. Nevertheless, I urge you to resist.

I can see two levels of opposition to the production model and its implications. One is on the basis of the assumptions underlying this model and their consequences. Your own human and professional experience will give you all the necessary arguments in favour of a sound process rather than the production model.

The second level of opposition should address the larger social context in which the production model of education is promoted and justified. The current political and social mindset is dominated by a market mentality that puts economic values above all others. A good way of resisting this mentality—and at the same time informing others of your opposition—is not to use the language and slang of the marketers.

I urge you to be careful in your use of language when you discuss matters of education and public policy. Personally, I am fussy about language, because our language conveys the images of our minds. You may find that, in many cases, structures are so firmly in place, that there are no great heroic deeds you can perform in favour of true education. But one thing that each and every one of us can do is to watch our language and refuse to use the production and market verbiage.

I have a great aversion to the use of both military and production images, and the two often intertwine in their daily metaphors. I do not find it helpful to speak about "target audiences," since I do not want to shoot the people who come to my lectures, I actually want to talk to them. Target audiences, strategic plans, and all that goes with them have, I think, no place in an education discourse, nor does the language of production and marketing. I've always thought, in spite of what people write about output-centred education, that output is something that cows drop and you try not to step into. Students have projects to do, they achieve, and they and we can rejoice in their achievements. Much as I like to see and assess student work, "output" or even "outcome" does not describe for me the fruits of learning.

I also object to the notions of service-providers and consumers of education. Though I am a pretty good cook and I like to prepare a meal and serve it to family and friends, I am not a meal-provider and my guests are not consumers of my supper. We are friends sharing a meal. In the same light, teachers are not servers of food for thought, and students are not consumers of the knowledge and the insights of their instructors. Teachers, students, and parents are potential friends. I urge you not to use the market vocabulary of service-providers, customers, clients, or consumers of education. (If we were to "consume" knowledge, there wouldn't be any knowledge left. Knowledge is shared and grows on sharing. You don't consume knowledge the way you consume chocolate bars.) I also dislike the concept of stakeholders in discussions about schools and feel its use gives a distorted image of society. In a real community, all members are part of the enterprise of the growth of knowledge and understanding, and no sector has privileged claims. But in the end, all discussions about schools must return to two focal points: one is our social ecology, the other is kids.

Let us never forget that social and human diversity is essential; that as a society, we are viable not in spite of being different but because of it. There is no future in monoculture. Some of your students will have very different gifts than others, but all are equally precious and all can make their contributions to society if educated in an environment of co-operation and respect for learning. They greatly depend on you to gain self-respect and high standards. Finally, when all is said and done, education is about young people. Education is about their future and how to equip them for it. We do not know their future. The only thing I do know is that it is essential for them to meet people of integrity, adults they can trust and who are honest and truthful with them. School should be a place where this happens every day.

May I leave with you, as my present, a phrase that I learned from Pauline Laing, who was director of education at the Durham Board of Education: "When parents send their children to school, they hope that, in the end, the young people will be personally happy and publicly useful." This to me is the essential task description that links education and society. Education can help to develop the resourcefulness on which personal happiness depends, while society needs to provide the work that can turn individual knowledge and understanding into public usefulness. It is a joint task in more ways than one, since, I am convinced, in the long run people cannot be happy without being publicly useful, nor can a person be publicly useful while unhappy in personal life.

I hope that these thoughts will be of assistance in your deliberations.

TEACHING AS ACTIVISM: EQUITY MEETS ENVIRONMENTALISM

Published as "Prologue," in Teaching as Activism: Equity Meets Environment, *ed. Peggy Tripp and Lina Muzzin (Montreal and Kingston: McGill-Queen's University Press, 2005).*

ACCEPTING THE TERM "Prologue" in its theatrical meaning—as opening reflections offered before the play begins—I am conscious of the generation gap between myself and most of the authors of this volume. They are not just of the generation of my students: some of them are my students' students. Thus, if this prologue is to be more than a ceremonial nod towards the past, it should concern itself with roots and with the soil in which the authors' works have grown. Over and above all personal encounters and influences, there exists a common soil, a collective pool of feminist experience and achievement that has nourished my young sisters to the point where they teach in established institutions and are able to reflect on the content, method, and thrust of their activities.

It is good to remember that today, *equity* is not merely a dream or a social construct, but a legal concept, containing expectation and entitlement. This has not always been so. By the same token, *environmentalism*, that is, "advocacy for or work toward protecting the natural environment," has only relatively recently become a curriculum subject. The seeds of these concerns, however, have long been present in our common soil, sown, more often than not, by women.

As part of my prologue, let me then highlight two components of this soil: women's struggle for peace and, contained in it, their struggle against nuclear war, nuclear weapons, and nuclear energy. The long and creative work of women for peace and against war and violence is part of our common feminist experience. It is work that reminds us how women have transcended boundaries of nationalism, class, and "race" in their advocacy for a just and peaceful world. Their understanding of how an equitable world could be structured is well documented.[1]

In Canada, women's struggle for equity and women's activism for peace have been intimately linked.[2] Within this development, the anti-nuclear movement has provided a particularly important practicum of feminist teaching and activism. During the 1960s, organizations such as Voice of Women made submissions to parliamentary committees on systemic barriers to equity for women, and at the same time they researched and presented briefs on radioactive fallout monitoring and on the health effects of strontium-90 and radioactive iodine on children—all children, all over the world—thus making ignored or uncomfortable research findings publicly available.[3]

Discussions of this new evidence, such as Rosalie Bertell's documentation of the effects of low-level ionizing radiation[4] or the Helen Caldicott film *If You Love This Planet*,[5] in innumerable church basements and classrooms, brought this new scientific knowledge and political activism to Canadian women. These women, in turn, became teachers of their communities, teachers who understood the essential links between all living beings, and who made this insight the centre of their personal and political understanding, as well as part of the common soil.

Today, it is interesting to recall the debates on the safety, cost, and reliability of nuclear power that took place over the past four decades because the argumentation is so similar to the current discourse on genetically modified seeds or food. When scientists such as Dr. Bertell or I argued the importance of long-term effects of radiation, the intrinsic difficulties of nuclear waste storage, and the miscalculation of the costs of nuclear power, there was usually a standard set of responses. What we presented was "shoddy science," "an unrepresentative situation," or "a lack of confidence in future scientific problem-solving." And, of course, there was the ever-present rhetorical question: "Do you want to deprive the Third World of this cheap and reliable source of energy?" Forty years later, nuclear reactors are expensive and dangerous burdens, and the same arguments of shoddy science and disregard for the needs of the hungry are levelled against those who question the promotion of genetically modified plants.

To me, this morphological correspondence indicates that present teaching and activism could benefit from remembering and re-evaluating past feminist teachings in the public sphere. It may not be particularly cheerful to realize how often feminists have been right. They were not only right on social and political grounds. They were also correct in terms of facts and predictions. Yet it may be necessary to stress such evidence, because the changes needed for the world to survive are *systemic* changes. The specific issues of our teaching and activism must be seen as illustrations of more basic problems, problems that can be resolved only through a fundamentally different ordering of social and political powers and priorities. Such essentially feminist ordering is built on the fundamental tenet of equality: *all in the biosphere are entitled to equal care and concern.*

It is the practical execution of this principle that will assure respect, survival, and peace. The wide spectrum of women's attempts to develop appropriate practices and to decline participation in inappropriate and destructive ones constitutes the core of feminist teaching and activism—past, present, and, likely, future. This is where our roots are, and where the source of our strength is found.

Notes

1   Gertrude Bussey and Margaret Tims, *Women's International League for Peace and Freedom 1916–1965: A Record of Fifty Years' Work* (London: Allen and Unwin, 1965).

2   Marion Douglas Kerans, *Muriel Duckworth: A Very Active Pacifist* (Halifax: Fernwood, 1996).

3   Kay Macpherson, *When in Doubt, Do Both: The Times of My Life* (Toronto: University of Toronto Press, 1994).

4   Rosalie Bertell, *No Immediate Danger: Prognosis for a Radioactive Earth* (Toronto: Women's Educational Press, 1985).

5   Helen Caldicott, *Nuclear Madness: What You Can Do* (Brookline, Mass.: Autumn Press, 1978).

FROM URSULA'S BOOKSHELF

A S WE PREPARED the *Reader* we wondered whether it should include a reading list, over and above the references within specific papers. Clearly, I am indebted to the work of many others and have incorporated their thoughts into mine. It would be impossible to acknowledge all of them. However, standing in front of my books I realized suddenly that there is a special group among them: the books with all the marks and slips sticking out— the works much consulted and checked. Like good and trusted friends they have stood by me, and it is with profound thankfulness that I list them below.

— U.F.

Berg, Maxine. *The Machinery Question and the Making of Political Economy, 1815–1848*. Cambridge: Cambridge University Press, 1980.

Bereano, Philip L. *Technology as a Social and Political Phenomenon*. New York: John Wiley, 1976.

Boulding, Elise. *The Underside of History: A View of Women through Time*. 2nd ed. Boulder, Col.: Westview Press, 1992.

Boulding, Kenneth E. *Conflict and Defense: A General Theory*. New York: Harper & Row, 1962.

—. *The Image: Knowledge in Life and Society*. Ann Arbor: University of Michigan Press, 1956.

Brock, Peter and Nigel Young. *Pacifism in the Twentieth Century*. Toronto: University of Toronto Press, 1999.

Brock, Peter and Nigel Young. *Pacifism in the Twentieth Century.* Toronto: University of Toronto Press, 1999.

Christian Faith and Practice in the Experience of the Society of Friends. London: London Yearly Meeting of the Religious Society of Friends, 1960.

Dunn, Ted, ed. *Alternatives to War and Violence: A Search.* London: James Clarke, 1963.

Ellul, Jacques. *Perspectives on Our Age: Jacques Ellul Speaks on His Life and Work,* ed. William H. Vanderburg. Rev. ed. Toronto: House of Anansi Press, 2004.

French, Marilyn. *Beyond Power: On Women, Men, and Morals.* New York: Ballantine, 1986.

Graham, Angus C. *Disputers of the Tao: Philosophical Argument in Ancient China.* La Salle, Il: Open Court, 1989.

Hill, Christopher. *The World Turned Upside Down: Radical Ideas during the English Revolution.* Harmondsworth: Penguin, 1975.

Hubbard, Ruth. *The Politics of Women's Biology.* New Brunswick, N.J.: Rutgers University Press, 1990.

Kass-Simon, Gabriele and Patricia Farnes, eds. *Women of Science: Righting the Record.* Bloomington: Indiana University Press, 1990.

Macpherson, C.B. *Democratic Theory: Essays in Retrieval.* Oxford: Clarendon Press, 1973.

Macpherson, Kay. *When in Doubt, Do Both: The Times of My Life.* Toronto: University of Toronto Press, 1994.

McAllister, Pat, ed. *Reweaving the Web of Life: Feminism and Nonviolence.* Philadelphia: New Society, 1982.

Mayer, Peter, ed. *The Pacifist Conscience.* Chicago: Henry Regnery, 1967.

Merchant, Carolyn. *The Death of Nature: Women, Ecology and the Scientific Revolution.* New York: Harper & Row, 1980.

Miles, Angela R. and G. Finn, eds. *Feminism: From Pressure to Politics.* 2nd rev. ed. Montreal: Black Rose, 1989.

Mumford, Lewis. *The Myth of the Machine: Technics and Human Development.* New York: Harcourt Brace Jovanovich, 1967.

Noble, David F. *Progress Without People: New Technology, Unemployment, and the Message of Resistance.* Toronto: Between the Lines, 1995.

Polanyi, Karl. *The Great Transformation.* New York: Holt Reinhart, 1944.

Schumacher, E.F. *A Guide for the Perplexed.* London: Jonathan Cape, 1977.

Shiva, Vandana. *Monocultures of the Mind: Perspectives on Biodiversity and Biotechnology.* London and Atlantic Highland, N.J.: Zed Books, 1993.

Sibley, Mulford Q., ed. *The Quiet Battle: Writings on the Theory and Practice of Non-Violent Resistance.* Garden City, N.Y.: Doubleday, 1963.

Trigger, Bruce G. *Understanding Early Civilizations: A Comparative Study.* Cambridge: Cambridge University Press, 2003.

Weil, Simone. *The Need for Roots: Prelude to a Declaration of Duties towards Mankind.* English translation of *L'enracinement.* London: Routledge and Kegan Paul, 1952.

Wilson, H.T. *Retreat from Governance: Canada and the Continental-International Challenge.* Hull, P.Q.: Voyageur, 1989.

URSULA M. FRANKLIN

D R. URSULA M. FRANKLIN received her Ph.D. in experimental physics at the Technical University of Berlin in 1948. She came to Canada the following year and began a distinguished scientific career. In 1967 she joined the University of Toronto's Department of Metallurgy and Materials Science, becoming a full professor in 1973. She has published more than a hundred papers and major contributions to books on the structure and properties of metals and alloys, and the history and social impact of technology. Her contributions to CBC-Radio's *Ideas* series include: "Democracy, Technology, and Terrorism" (1979), "Nuclear Peace" (1982), and "Complexity and Management" (1987). Her 1989 Massey Lectures, published as *The Real World of Technology* (1990), have influenced a generation of citizens and decision-makers.

Dr. Franklin is a Companion of the Order of Canada and a Fellow of the Royal Society of Canada, and has been a board member of the National Research Council and the Science Council of Canada, where she headed the Conserver Society Study.

She has received honorary degrees from many Canadian universities. In 1984 she became the first woman to be honoured with the title of University Professor by the University of Toronto.

In addition to her significant contributions as a scientist, Dr. Franklin is known for her achievements as a humanitarian. She received the award of merit for the City of Toronto in 1982, mainly for her contribution to neighbourhood planning. As a Quaker, she has been actively involved in work for peace and justice, international understanding, and issues related to women. She sits on the national council of the Voice of Women.

In 1987 Dr. Franklin was awarded the Elsie Gregory McGill Memorial Award, and in 1989 the Wiegand Award. In 1995 the Toronto Board of Education named a new public school, the Ursula Franklin Academy, in her honour. Dr. Franklin takes an active interest in the work of the school, which attempts to integrate its math, science, and liberal arts curricula by means of innovative technologies.

Ursula Franklin's 1990 award of the Order of Ontario followed her nomination by the Ontario Confederation of University Faculty Associations, which read:

> Dr. Franklin has made significant contributions to the life of Ontario as a scientist, educator, citizen, and humanitarian. She has enriched the lives of the colleagues, students, and staff who have been privileged to work with her. Her concerns about the quality of all our lives, particularly as they are affected by science and technology, have always been accompanied by action on behalf of those beliefs to help solve problems. She serves as an inspiration to women in society, in the university in general, and especially in the scientific, technological, and engineering fields, where she has been a role model in an environment populated by very few female faculty members. Dr. Franklin is truly an example of someone who lives her convictions, who is not afraid to act on the basis of her beliefs, and whose presence among us helps to make this world a better place to live.